Lecture Notes in Economics and Mathematical Systems

435

Springer

Berlin
Heidelberg
New York
Barcelona
Budapest
Hong Kong
London
Milan
Paris
Santa Clara
Singapore
Tokyo

Lin Chen

Interest Rate Dynamics, Derivatives Pricing, and Risk Management

 Springer

Author

Dr. Lin Chen
Federal Research Board
20th and Constitution Avenue
Washington, DC 20551, USA

332.6
C51u

Cataloging-in-Publication Data applied for

Die Deutsche Bibliothek - CIP-Einheitsaufnahme

Chen, Lin:
Interest rate dynamics, derivatives pricing, and risk
management / Lin Chen. - Berlin ; Heidelberg ; New York ;
London ; Paris ; Tokyo ; Hong Kong ; Barcelona ; Budapest :
Springer, 1996
  (Lecture notes in economics and mathematical systems ; 435)
  ISBN 3-540-60814-1
NE: GT

ISBN 3-540-60814-1 Springer-Verlag Berlin Heidelberg New York

© Springer-Verlag Berlin Heidelberg 1996
Printed in Germany

Typesetting: Camera ready by author
SPIN: 10516223   42/3142-543210 - Printed on acid-free paper

Preface

There are two types of term structure models in the literature: the equilibrium models and the no-arbitrage models. And there are, correspondingly, two types of interest rate derivatives pricing formulas based on each type of model of the term structure.

The no-arbitrage models are characterized by the work of Ho and Lee (1986), Heath, Jarrow, and Morton (1992), Hull and White (1990 and 1993), and Black, Derman and Toy (1990). Ho and Lee (1986) invent the no-arbitrage approach to the term structure modeling in the sense that the model term structure can fit the initial (observed) term structure of interest rates. There are a number of disadvantages with their model. First, the model describes the whole volatility structure by a single parameter, implying a number of unrealistic features. Furthermore, the model does not incorporate mean reversion. Black-Derman-Toy (1990) develop a model along the lines of Ho and Lee. They eliminate some of the problems of Ho and Lee (1986) but create a new one: for a certain specification of the volatility function, the short rate can be mean-fleeting rather than mean-reverting. Heath, Jarrow and Morton (1992) (HJM) construct a family of continuous models of the term structure consistent with the initial term structure data. Unfortunately, the interest rate models that result from the HJM approach is usually non-Markov (the distribution of interest rates in the next period depends not only on the current rate but also on the rates in the earlier periods). There are only a small number of known forward rate volatility functions that give rise to Markov models. Moreover, except for a few simple cases, it is difficult to obtain closed form solutions for the values of bond and interest rate derivatives. The approach of Hull and White (1990 and 1993) to the no-arbitrage model is to extend the equilibrium models by letting parameters be time-varying. These generalized term structure models have more flexibility to fit a given yield curve and the term structure of volatility. However, except for the extended Vasicek model, their approach provides no closed form solution and has to rely on numerical methods.

Generally speaking, the main problem with the no-arbitrage approach to the term structure models is that at any date a function for the term structure of interest rates needs to be estimated and there is no guarantee that the estimated function will be consistent with the previously estimated function. Not surprisingly, despite the no-arbitrage approach's ability to fit the initial term structure, its empirical performance is quite disappointing. For example, Flesaker (1993) tests HJM's model using a Generalized Method of Moments with three years of daily data for Eurodollar futures and futures options and shows that HJM's approach is incompatible with the data for most sub-periods. Furthermore, Backus, Foresi and Zin (1994) discover that the pricing of derivatives based on no-arbitrage term structure models can actually lead to systematic arbitrage opportunities as a result of its mispricing of some assets. They demonstrate that the Black-Derman-Toy model is likely to overprice call options on long bonds when interest rates exhibit mean reversion and that this mispricing can be exploited even when no other traders offer the mispriced assets. They conclude that the time-dependent parameters cannot substitute for sound fundamentals.

The equilibrium models of the term structure of interest rates, such as Varsicek (1977) and Cox-Ingersoll-Ross (1985) (CIR), have the important advantage that all interest rate derivatives are valued on a common basis. Nevertheless, these model term structures do not correctly price actual bonds. One primary reason is that there are too few model parameters to be adjusted. The other problem with their models is that they have not incorporated sufficient empirical realism. Their models either allow negative interest rates (Varsicek (1977)), assume a constant volatility of interest rates (Varsicek (1977)), or assume perfect correlation between volatility and the short rate (CIR 1985). Although one-factor models offer tractability, there is compelling reason to believe that a single state variable, such as the short rate, is not sufficient to capture reasonably well the direction of future yield curve changes. Stambaugh (1988) and Pearson and Sun (1993), among others, have documented more econometric evidence in favor of multi-factor models of interest rates. Brennan and Schwartz (1979) and Schaefer and Schwartz (1984) have developed two-factor term structure models by taking both the short rate and the long rate as factors. Longstaff and Schwartz (1992) have recently developed another two-factor model of interest rates. The choice of the model's two factors, the short rate and the volatility of the short rate, allow interest rate derivatives prices to reflect the current levels of the short rate and volatility. However, as pointed out by some authors, the joint process of the two factors was chosen for its analytical tractability rather than its empirical realism. Also, it is argued that the interest rate volatility in their model is not really stochastic, as it is related to the short rate in a way similar to how the volatility is related to the short rate in CIR's model.

It is generally believed that equilibrium derivatives pricing formulas will be useful for practical purposes only until substantial improvements have been made. This paper attempts to make such an improvement by bringing more empirical realism to the equilibrium models of derivatives valuation while maintaining the model's tractability. Although our model, along with other equilibrium models, has the merit that all interest rate derivatives are valued within a unified and consistent framework, it has the disadvantage that it may not fit perfectly a given initial term structure. However, this problem is less severe in our model; there are ten adjustable parameters which can be estimated to give the correct (i.e. market-priced) valuations for a handful of actively traded bonds by calibrating the model. Then the model can price other less actively traded bonds relative to these benchmark bonds. The appealing attributes of the model presented are not only its ability to fit data better but also its ability to explicitly relate the dynamics of the short mean and volatility to the movements of the term structure and the values of interest rate derivatives. It is this very property that makes the model useful in dealing with the practical day-to-day problems of pricing derivatives and managing risks of fixed income securities. Another major desirable feature of our method is that, with the Green's function, our approach has turned the valuation of derivative securities into a numerical integration. This feature has certain advantages over the currently available methods of derivatives valuation which normally deal with the solving of the valuation partial differential equation directly. Given the general issues of sensitivity and stability of numerical solutions to partial differential equation, our approach of valuing derivatives by evaluating integrals instead of solving partial differential equation is more reliable and efficient.

Acknowledgments

This book is based on my dissertation submitted to Harvard University. I would like to thank the following individuals whose helps had made possible my graduate studies at Harvard and Stanford: Li Guo-Guang, Li Yu-Chang, Chen Yi-Sheng, John Y. Campbell, James Coleman, Sanjiv R. Das, Joseph Kalt, Glenn Loury, Robert C. Merton, F. M. Scherer, James H. Stock, Daniel W. Stroock, Nancy B. Tuma, and Louisa van Baalen. I would also like to thank Christian Gilles, Gary Anderson, Mark Fisher, Pamela Gerbino, Noah Williams and many other supportive colleagues at the Federal Reserve Board for helps.

Lin Chen
Washington, D.C. USA
November 1, 1995

Contents

Chapter 1

A Three-Factor Model of the Term Structure of Interest Rates

1.1   Introduction

In this chapter a three-factor model of the term structure of interest rates is presented. In our model the future short rate depends on 1) the current short rate, 2) the short-term mean of the short rate, and 3) the current volatility of the short rate. Furthermore, it is assumed in the model that both the short term mean of the short rate and the volatility of the short rate are stochastic. These assumptions are based on extensive empirical studies in interest rate behavior, which are explained in the following.

Interest rates have a tendency to be pulled back to some long-run level. This phenomenon is known as mean reversion. Although there are economic arguments in favor of mean reversion, a number of studies (e.g., Chan, Karolyi, Longstaff, and Sanders (1992)) have shown that there appears to be only weak evidence of mean reversion in short rates. The weak evidence suggests that short rates should be better modeled as reverting to a short-run mean, rather than to a long-run constant mean. Therefore, in our model, the short rate is assumed to be reverting to a short-term mean and the short-term mean itself is time-varying and reverting to a constant long-term mean.

Empirical evidence that supports the assumption of stochastic means has been documented in a few papers such as those of Hamilton (1988), Driffill (1992), and Pearson and Sun (1993). Hamilton and Driffill's empirical studies of US Treasury bill rates over the period from 1953 to 1989 show that yields on three-month Treasury bills show significant changes in regimes, interpreted as occasional and discrete shifts in parameters. Pearson and Sun (1993) demonstrate that the mean parameters before and after the change in Fed policy in 1979 are significantly different.

In addition to the short term mean, the short rate volatility is another factor in our model to determine the term structure. It is well known that interest rate volatility is not constant, but changes over time. Empirical evidence of fat tails in the distribution of changes in short rates has also indicated the stochastic feature of the short rate volatility.

Stochastic volatility is explicitly modeled in this paper because it plays a central role in two of the most important applications of term structure modeling: valuing interest rate contingent claims and hedging interest rate risks. The volatility of interest rates is a fundamental determinant of the values of interest rate derivatives such as option or callable bonds. The ability of a term structure model to capture the stochastic feature of interest rate volatility is a direct measure of its hedging usefulness.

Besides being stochastic, the volatility of short rates appears to be mean reverting as well, as argued by a number of authors (Litterman and Scheinkman (1991)). Unlike other models of stochastic volatility in which volatility is modeled as either an Ornstein-Uhlembeck (O-U) process or a log-normal process (Stein and Stein (1991) and Heston (1992)) volatility is modeled in this paper as a square root process. In an O-U model, volatility can take undesirable negative values; in a lognormal model, volatility does not have mean reversion. As a square root process, our model of volatility has the advantage that it excludes negative values and allows for mean reversion.

Empirical works closely related to our model are that of Litterman, Scheinkman, and Weiss (1991) and Litterman and Scheinkman (1991). They estimate a model where future short rates depend on 1) today's short rate, 2) the level toward which the short rate is expected, as of today, to converge–which they call the "long" rate– and 3) the volatility of this "long" rate. Their studies confirm that, historically, variations in these three variables satisfactorily explain the past movements in the yield curves. It is interesting to note that the three factors they considered are similar to the three factors modeled in this paper. As will be clear later, our theoretical model is able to reproduce the stylized facts of interest rate behavior they found in their studies.

Many models of the term structure of interest rates in the literature are special cases of our model, as can be seen from Table 1 which lists in chronological order the developments in term structure modeling to date. [1]

This paper does not intend to construct explicitly a general equilibrium economy that supports the proposed dynamics of interest rates, like Cox-Ingersoll-Ross (1985). As pointed out by Duffie and Kan (1993), in any case, given any candidate for the short rate process satisfying mild regularity, it is easy to support the short rate process in a general equilibrium model based on a representative agent with an appropriate utility and a consumption process constructed on the interest rate process. The available equilibrium models provide useful theoretical relationships among the term structure, preference, technology, and macro-variables, but have

---

[1] Both equilibrium models and no-arbitrage models are listed in the table as these two kinds of models are essentially equivalent (see Rogers (1994)).

yet to add much to the practical day-to day problem of pricing and managing risks of fixed income instruments. This paper follows the lead of others by beginning with assumptions, deriving their implications, and subjecting these implications to empirical tests.

Table 1: Developments in Term Structure Modeling

Author(s)	Model Specifications	
Merton (1970)	$dr = \theta dt + \sigma dz$	θ, σ are constant
Vasicek (1977)	$dr = k(\theta - r)dt + \sigma dz$	k, θ, σ are constant
Dothan (1978)	$dr = \sigma r dz$	σ is constant
Brennan-Schwartz (1979)	$dr = \theta_r dt + \sigma_{r1} dz_1 + \sigma_{r2} dz_2$ $dl = \theta_l dt + \sigma_{l1} dz_1 + \sigma_{l2} dz_2$	$\theta_r, \theta_l, \sigma_{r1}, \sigma_{r2}, \sigma_{l1},$ σ_{l2} are constant
Constantinides-Ingersoll(1984)	$dr = \sigma r^{3/2} dz$	σ is constant
Schaefer-Schwartz (1984)	$ds = m(\mu - s)dt + \eta dz_1$ $dl = (\sigma^2 - ls)dt + \sigma\sqrt{l}dz_2$	m, μ, η, σ are constant
Cox-Ingersoll-Ross (1985)	$dr = k(\theta - r)dt + \sigma\sqrt{r}dz$	k, θ, σ are constant
Ho-Lee (1986)	$dr = \theta(t)dt + \sigma dz$	σ is constant
Black-Derman-Toy (1990)	$d\ln r = [\theta - \frac{\sigma'(t)}{\sigma(t)}\ln r]dt + \sigma(t)dz$	θ is time-varying
Hull-White (1990)	$dr = k(\theta - r)dt + \sigma\sqrt{r}dz$	θ, σ are time-varying
Heath-Jarrow-Morton (1992)	$df = \alpha(t)dt + \sigma(t)dz$	f is the forward rate
Longstaff-Schwartz (1992)	$dx = (\gamma - \delta x)dt + \sqrt{x}dz_1$ $dy = (\eta - \nu y)dt + \sqrt{y}dz_2$	$\gamma, \delta, \eta, \nu$ are constant
Our model (1994)	$dr = k(\theta - r)dt + \sqrt{\sigma}\sqrt{r}dz_1$ $d\theta = \nu(\overline{\theta} - \theta)dt + \zeta\sqrt{\theta}dz_2$ $d\sigma = \mu(\overline{\sigma} - \sigma)dt + \eta\sqrt{\sigma}dz_3$	$k, \nu, \overline{\theta}, \zeta, \mu, \overline{\sigma}, \eta$ are constant

The rest of the chapter is organized as follows. In the second section the assumptions on the dynamics of interest rates are presented and a proposition on the fundamental valuation equation for interest rate derivative securities is stated. A closed form solution for the discount bond price for a benchmark case is derived in section three. The Green's function for the fundamental valuation PDE is given in section four. A general formula for valuing interest rate derivatives is derived in section five. In section six, the effects of the three factors and model parameters on the term structure of interest rates are discussed. The computation of the expected future short rate is discussed in section seven. A brief discussion of forward interest rate behavior under the three-factor model is given in the final section.

1.2   The Model

The continuous time uncertainty will be specified by the filtered probability space $(\Omega, \mathcal{F}, F, P)$, where $F = \{\mathcal{F}_t : t \geq 0\}$ is the filtration of Standard Brownian Motion $B = (B_1, B_2, B_3)$ satisfying the usual conditions. Investors have only to agree on the null sets of the probability measure instead of an actual assessment of probabilities of certain events, which means that the probability measure P can be replaced by any equivalent measure P^*.

The dynamics of the short rate $r(t)$, its short term mean $\theta(t)$, and its volatility $v(t)$, are assumed in the following.

Assumption 1.*The dynamics of the short rate is given by the following stochastic differential equation:*

$$dr(t) = k(\theta(t) - r(t))dt + \sqrt{v(t)}\sqrt{r(t)}dB_1(t), \ t \geq 0, \ k > 0, \qquad (1.1)$$

where $\theta(t)$ is the short-term mean of the short rate and $\sqrt{v(t)}$ is the instantaneous variance (volatility) of the short rate.

Assumption 2.*The development of the short-term mean is given by the following stochastic differential equation:*

$$d\theta(t) = \nu(\bar{\theta} - \theta(t))dt + \zeta\sqrt{\theta(t)}dB_2(t), \ t \geq 0, \ \bar{\theta} > 0, \ \nu > 0, \qquad (1.2)$$

where $\bar{\theta}$ is the constant long-term mean of the short-term mean and ζ is the volatility of the short-term mean.

Assumption 3.*The development of the volatility of the short rate is given by the following stochastic differential equation:*

$$dv(t) = \mu(\bar{v} - v(t))dt + \eta\sqrt{v(t)}dB_3(t), \ t \geq 0, \ \mu > 0, \ \bar{v} > 0, \qquad (1.3)$$

where $\bar{v}$ is the long-term mean of the volatility and η is the volatility of the volatility.

In addition, the three Standard Brownian Motions are assumed to be correlated as follows:

$$dB_1(t)dB_2(t) \quad = \quad \rho_{12}dt,$$

$$dB_1(t)dB_3(t) = \rho_{13}dt, \qquad (1.4)$$
$$dB_2(t)dB_3(t) = \rho_{23}dt.$$

To derive the value of an interest rate derivative security, a unique equivalent probability measure, which is equivalent to P, must first be defined.

To derive such an equivalent measure in this particular interest rate economy, start with the specification of the familiar Radon-Nikodym derivative, $\rho = \{\rho(\lambda_r, r, \lambda_\theta, \theta, \lambda_v, v, t), t \geq 0\}$, as

$$
\begin{aligned}
\rho(\lambda_r, r, \lambda_\theta, \theta, \lambda_v, v, t) = \; & \exp\Big[\int_0^t \lambda_r \sqrt{v(t)r(t)}dB_1(s) - \int_0^t \lambda_\theta \sqrt{\theta(t)}dB_2(s) \\
& - \int_0^t \lambda_v \sqrt{v(t)}dB_3(s) - \frac{1}{2}\lambda_r^2 \int_0^t v(s)r(s)ds \\
& - \frac{1}{2}\lambda_\theta^2 \int_0^t \theta(s)ds - \frac{1}{2}\lambda_v^2 \int_0^t v(s)ds \Big],
\end{aligned}
$$

where λ_r, λ_θ, and λ_v are fixed real-valued constants and can be interpreted as the market prices of risks corresponding to stochastic factors r, θ, and v respectively.

The characteristic of the stochastic differential equations (1.1), (1.2), and (1.3) allow for application of Girsanov's Theorem[2] which states that the process $\{\tilde{B}(t) = (\tilde{B}_1(t), \tilde{B}_2(t), \tilde{B}_3(t), 0 \leq t \leq T\}$ defined by

$$\tilde{B}_1(t) = B_1(t) - \int_0^t \lambda_r \sqrt{v(s)r(s)}ds,$$

$$\tilde{B}_2(t) = B_2(t) - \int_0^t \lambda_\theta \sqrt{\theta(s)}ds, \text{ and}$$

$$\tilde{B}_3(t) = B_3(t) - \int_0^t \lambda_v \sqrt{v(s)}ds$$

is a 3-dimensional Standard Brownian Motion for the filtered probability space $(\Omega, \mathcal{F}, F, Q)$ restricted to the time set $[0, T]$. The unique equivalent probability measure Q given by

$$dQ = \rho(\lambda_r, r, \lambda_\theta, \theta, \lambda_v, v, t)dP$$

is an equivalent martingale measure. Aside from technical conditions, the existence of the martingale measure Q is equivalent to the absence of arbitrage.

An interest rate derivative, (C_t, G_T), is a financial instrument consisting of a payoff rate,

$$C = \{C_t, \mathcal{F}_t; 0 \leq t \leq T\},$$

---

[2] See, for example, Ikeda and Watanabe (1981).

and the payoff at maturity, G_T. Here C is a non-negative, measurable, and adapted process and G_T is a non-negative, $\mathcal{F}_T$-measurable random variable.

The unique arbitrage-free price at time t, $F(r, \theta, v, t)$, of the interest derivative security can be obtained as the discounted expected value. By the definition of an equivalent martingale measure, this expectation has to be taken with respect to Q, (Harrison and Kreps (1979) and Duffie (1988, 1992)), that is

$$F(r, \theta, v, t) = E_Q \left[\int_t^T e^{-\int_t^s r(l)dl} C_t ds + e^{-\int_t^T r(l)dl} G_T \mid \mathcal{F}_t \right], \ 0 \le t \le T. (1.5)$$

Under mild regularity conditions (for example, Friedman (1975)) and by virtue of the Feynman-Kac Formula (Duffie (1992)), $F(r, \theta, v, t)$ satisfies the partial differential equation,

$$\mathcal{D}F(r, \theta, v, t) - rF(r, \theta, v, t) + C_t = 0, \ (r, \theta, v, t) \in \mathcal{R}_+ \times \mathcal{R}_+ \times \mathcal{R}_+ \times [0, T),$$

with boundary condition

$$F(r, \theta, v, T) = G_T, (r, \theta, v) \in \mathcal{R}_+ \times \mathcal{R}_+ \times \mathcal{R}_+,$$

where

$$
\begin{aligned}
\mathcal{D}F &= \frac{1}{2} vr F_{rr} + \frac{1}{2} \eta^2 v F_{vv} + \frac{1}{2} \zeta^2 \theta F_{\theta\theta} + \rho_{12} \zeta \sqrt{v\theta r} F_{r\theta} \\
&\quad + \rho_{13} \eta v \sqrt{r} F_{rv} + \rho_{23} \zeta \eta \sqrt{\theta v} F_{\theta v} + [k(\theta - r) + \lambda_r vr] F_r \\
&\quad + [\nu\bar{\theta} - \acute{\nu}\theta] F_\theta + [\mu\bar{v} - \acute{\mu}v] F_v + F_t
\end{aligned} \tag{1.6}
$$

and

$$\acute{\nu} = \nu - \lambda_\theta \zeta, \quad \acute{\mu} = \mu - \lambda_v \eta.$$

The following lemma summarizes the above result[3].

Lemma 1: *Assuming the interest rate dynamics specified by equations (1.1), (1.2), and (1.3), the value at time t, $F(r, \theta, v, t)$, of the interest rate derivative which has a payoff rate $C_t, t \in (0, T]$, and a terminal payoff G_T at maturity T, is the solution to the partial differential equation,*

$$
\begin{aligned}
&\frac{1}{2} vr F_{rr} + \frac{1}{2} \eta^2 v F_{vv} + \frac{1}{2} \zeta^2 \theta F_{\theta\theta} + \rho_{12} \zeta \sqrt{v\theta r} F_{r\theta} + \rho_{13} \eta v \sqrt{r} F_{rv} \\
&+ \rho_{23} \zeta \eta \sqrt{\theta v} F_{\theta v} + [k(\theta - r) + \lambda_r vr] F_r + [\nu\bar{\theta} - \acute{\nu}\theta] F_\theta + \\
&[\mu\bar{v} - \acute{\mu}v] F_v + F_t - rF + C_t = 0,
\end{aligned} \tag{1.7}
$$

with boundary condition

$$F(r, \theta, v, T) = G_T.$$

The partial differential equation (1.7) will be often referred to as the fundamental valuation partial differential equation (PDE) in the remainder of this paper.

---

[3] An alternative proof of Lemma 1 is given in Appendix A.

1.3 Benchmark Case

It is usually difficult to solve the fundamental PDE (1.7) directly to obtain closed form solutions for prices of bonds and other interest rate derivative securities. However, the problem can be attacked by a perturbation method called the method of functional iteration. In order to do that, a benchmark case will first be solved as follows.

In the benchmark case the short rate $r(t)$ is assumed to follow the process,

$$dr(t) = k(\theta(t) - r(t))dt + \sqrt{v(t)}dz_1(t).$$

Therefore the system of stochastic differential equations that determines the interest rate dynamics is given by:

$$
\begin{align}
dr(t) &= k(\theta(t) - r(t))dt + \sqrt{v(t)}dz_1(t), & (1.8) \\
d\theta(t) &= \nu(\bar{\theta} - \theta(t))dt + \zeta\sqrt{\theta(t)}dz_2(t), & (1.9) \\
dv(t) &= \mu(\bar{v} - v(t))dt + \eta\sqrt{v(t)}dz_3(t). & (1.10)
\end{align}
$$

The benchmark case does not only serve as a basis to attack the problem under the general interest rate dynamics but also has an independent value as it is a substantial extension of Vasicek's (1977) model and others. Relative to the general interest rate dynamics specified by equations (1.1), (1.2), and (1.3), the interest rate dynamics specified by equations (1.8), (1.9), and (1.10) are sometimes called "special interest rate dynamics".

Let us consider the problem of valuing a default-free discount bond promising to pay one unit at time T. Let $P(r, \theta, v, t; T)$ be the price of the bond at time t which is given by

$$P(r, \theta, v, t; T) = E_Q[e^{-\int_t^T r(s)ds} \mid \mathcal{F}_t].$$

Following the same reasoning used for deriving the fundamental PDE (1.7) for derivative security prices, and assuming that all three Brownian processes $B_1(t)$, $B_2(t)$, and $B_3(t)$ are mutually independent,[4] the bond price in the benchmark case is the solution to the following PDE:

$$
\begin{align}
\frac{1}{2}vP_{rr} + \frac{1}{2}\eta^2 vP_{vv} + \frac{1}{2}\zeta^2\theta P_{\theta\theta} + [k(\theta - r) + \lambda_r v]P_r \\
+ [\nu\bar{\theta} - \nu'\theta]P_\theta + [\mu\bar{v} - \mu v]P_v + P_t - rP = 0, & (1.11)
\end{align}
$$

with the initial condition

$$P(r, \theta, v, T; T) = 1.$$

---

[4]Although $B_1(t)$, $B_2(t)$, and $B_3(t)$ are assumed independent, the short rate $r(t)$, its mean $\theta(t)$, and its volatility $v(t)$ are correlated through the stochastic differential equation for the short rate.

Solving PDE (1.11) by the method of the separation of variables leads to the following proposition[5].

Proposition 2: *The value at time t of a discount bond promising to pay one unit at time T, $P(r, \theta, v, t; T)$, is given by*

$$P(r, \theta, v; \tau) = A(\tau)e^{-B(\tau)r - C(\tau)\theta - D(\tau)v}, \qquad (1.12)$$

where $\tau = T - t$ and

$$A(\tau) = \left(\frac{X^{\frac{\nu'}{2k}}(\Gamma J_G(Z) + Y_G(Z))}{\Gamma J_G(\sqrt{2}\zeta/k) + Y_G(\sqrt{2}\zeta/k)} \right)^{-\frac{2\nu\bar{\theta}}{\zeta^2}} \times$$

$$\left(\frac{X^\rho e^{-\phi(X-1)}(\Lambda U(Q, S, 2\phi X) + M(Q, S, 2\phi X))}{\Lambda U(Q, S, 2\phi) + M(Q, S, 2\phi)} \right)^{-\frac{2\mu\bar{v}}{\eta^2}}, \qquad (1.13)$$

$$B(\tau) = \frac{1 - e^{-k\tau}}{k},$$

$$C(\tau) = -\frac{\nu'}{\zeta^2} - \frac{kZ\left[\Gamma(J_{G-1}(Z) - J_{G+1}(Z)) + Y_{G-1}(Z) - Y_{G+1}(Z)\right]}{2\zeta^2(\Gamma J_G(Z) + Y_G(Z))},$$

$$D(\tau) = \frac{2k}{\eta^2}\left[-\rho + \phi X + \frac{2X\Lambda Q\phi U(Q + 1, S + 1, 2\phi X)}{\Lambda U(Q, S, 2\phi X) + M(Q, S, 2\phi X)} \right.$$
$$\left. - \frac{2X\phi\frac{Q}{S}M(Q + 1, S + 1, 2\phi X)}{\Lambda U(Q, S, 2\phi X) + M(Q, S, 2\phi X)} \right],$$

with

$$X = e^{-k\tau},$$

$$Z = \frac{\sqrt{2}\zeta e^{-k\tau/2}}{k},$$

$$\Gamma = -\frac{\zeta\sqrt{2}Y_{G-1}(\sqrt{2}\zeta/k) + 2\nu'Y_G(\sqrt{2}\zeta/k) - \zeta\sqrt{2}Y_{G+1}(\sqrt{2}\zeta/k)}{\zeta\sqrt{2}J_{G-1}(\sqrt{2}\zeta/k) + 2\nu'J_G(\sqrt{2}\zeta/k) - \zeta\sqrt{2}J_{G+1}(\sqrt{2}\zeta/k)},$$

$$\Lambda = -\frac{(\rho - \phi)M(Q, S; 2\phi) - 2\phi\frac{Q}{S}M(Q + 1, S + 1; 2\phi)}{(\rho - \phi)U(Q, S; 2\phi) + 2\phi QU(Q + 1, S + 1; 2\phi)},$$

$$G = \frac{\sqrt{2\zeta^2 + \nu'^2}}{k},$$

$$Q = -\frac{\beta}{2\phi} + \frac{S}{2},$$

$$S = \frac{k + \sqrt{\mu'^2 - 4\alpha k^2}}{k},$$

$$\rho = \frac{\mu' + \sqrt{\mu'^2 - 4\alpha k^2}}{2k},$$

$$\alpha = (1 - 2k\lambda_r)\frac{\eta^2}{4k^4},$$

---

[5] See Appendix B for a proof.

$$\beta = (k\lambda_r - 1)\frac{\eta^2}{2k^4},$$

$$\phi = i\frac{\eta}{2k^2},$$

and $J_G(.)$ is the Bessel function of the first kind, $Y_G(.)$ is the Bessel function of the second kind, $M(a, b; z)$ is the Kummer function, and $U(a, b, z)$ is a confluent hypergeometric function [6].

As the system of the stochastic differential equations under study is a rather complex system involving ten parameters, there is no guarantee that for any set of parameters there are real solutions. The model poses certain restrictions on the parameters for the solutions to be real and meaningful.

Although transversality conditions are not imposed, the bond pricing formula (1.12) does show economically realistic features such as:

$$\lim_{\tau\uparrow\infty} P(r,\theta,v,\tau) = 0, \quad \lim_{r\uparrow\infty} P(r,\theta,v,\tau) = 0, \quad \lim_{\theta\uparrow\infty} P(r,\theta,v,\tau) = 0.$$

In addition, there are other economically desirable properties of bond price:

$$\frac{\partial P(r,\theta,v,\tau)}{\partial r} \leq 0, \quad \frac{\partial^2 P(r,\theta,v,\tau)}{\partial r^2} \geq 0, (0 \leq \tau \leq T).$$

Differentiating $P(r,\theta,v,\tau)$ with respect to v shows that the sign of this partial derivative is indeterminate as function $D(\tau)$ depends on model parameters in a complicated way. Specifically, depending on parameter values, this derivative can be positive or negative for all τ or take on opposite signs for different τ. This property will be discussed in more detail later in this chaper.

---

[6] $J_\nu(z), Y_\nu(z)$, and $M(a, b; z)$ are defined as the following respectively:

$$J_\nu(z) = (\frac{1}{2}z)^\nu \sum_{k=0}^{\infty} \frac{(-1/4z^2)^k}{k!\Gamma(\nu + k + 1)},$$

$$Y_\nu = \frac{\cos\nu\pi J_\nu(z) - J_{-\nu}(z)}{\sin\nu\pi},$$

$$M(a, b, z) = 1 + \frac{az}{b} + \frac{(a)_2 z^2}{(b)_2 2!} + .. + \frac{(a)_n z^n}{(b)_n n!} + ...$$

where

$$(a)_n = a(a + 1)(a + 2)...(a + n - 1), (a)_0 = 1,$$

and

$$U(a, b, z) = \frac{1}{\Gamma(a)} \int_0^\infty e^{-zt} t^{a-1}(1 + t)^{b-a-1} dt.$$

For a reference on special functions, see Abramowitz and Stegun (1972).

It is interesting to note here that as $D(\tau)$ can take both positive and negative values, an increase in volatility can increase the price of a bond with some maturities while decreasing the price of a bond with other maturities.

It can be also shown that:

$$\lim_{\tau \downarrow 0} \frac{\partial P(r, \theta, v; \tau)}{\partial v} = 0,$$

$$\lim_{\tau \downarrow 0} \frac{\partial P(r, \theta, v; \tau)}{\partial \theta} = 0.$$

Thus the prices of instantaneously maturing bonds are unaffected by changes in v and θ as the yields of these bonds are determined only by the instantaneous rate r.

Finally, from bond price formula (1.12) and Ito's lemma:

$$\begin{aligned}
\frac{dP}{P} &= (r + \lambda_r v B(\tau) + \lambda_v v D(\tau) + \lambda_\theta \theta C(\tau)) dt - B(\tau) \sqrt{v} dz_1 \\
&\quad - C(\tau) \zeta \sqrt{\theta} dz_2 - D(\tau) \eta \sqrt{v} dz_3.
\end{aligned}$$

Therefore, other things remaining equal, the volatility of return decreases as the bond approaches maturity since $B(0), C(0), D(0)$ are all zero. The above equation also shows that the assumptions regarding risk premium with three stochastic processes are internally consistent as they are exactly the same as the drift terms in the equation.

1.4 Green's Function

After rearranging terms, the fundamental partial differential equation (1.7) can be written as

$$\begin{aligned}
&\frac{1}{2} v F_{rr} + \frac{1}{2} \eta^2 v F_{vv} + \frac{1}{2} \zeta^2 \theta F_{\theta\theta} + [k(\theta - r) + \lambda_r v] F_r + [v\bar{\theta} - \acute{v}\theta] F_\theta \\
&+ [\mu\bar{v} - \acute{\mu}v] F_v + F_t - rF = \frac{1}{2} v(1 - r) F_{rr} + \lambda_r v(1 - r) F_r - \\
&\rho_{12} \zeta \sqrt{v\theta r} F_{r\theta} - \rho_{13} \eta v \sqrt{r} F_{rv} - \rho_{23} \zeta \eta \sqrt{\theta v} F_{\theta v} - C_t.
\end{aligned}$$

Changing the notations r, θ, v, to x_1, x_2, x_3, it can be written as

$$\begin{aligned}
\frac{\partial F}{\partial t} &+ \hat{H}(x_1, x_2, x_3, \partial_{x_1}, \partial_{x_2}, \partial_{x_3}) F = \\
&- \hat{V}(x_1, x_2, x_3, \partial_{x_1}, \partial_{x_2}, \partial_{x_3}) F - C_t
\end{aligned} \qquad (1.14)$$

with

$$F(x_1, x_2, x_3, T) = G_T,$$

where operators $\hat{H}$ and $\hat{V}$ are defined by

$$
\begin{aligned}
\hat{H}(x_1, x_2, x_3, \partial_{x_1}, \partial_{x_2}, \partial_{x_3}) &= \frac{1}{2}x_3\partial_{x_1x_1} + \frac{1}{2}\eta^2 x_3\partial_{x_3x_3} + \frac{1}{2}\zeta^2 x_2\partial_{x_2x_2} + \\
&\quad [k(x_2 - x_1) + \lambda_r x_3]\partial_{x_1} + [\nu\bar{\theta} - \acute{\nu}x_2]\partial_{x_2} \\
&\quad + [\mu\bar{\nu} - \acute{\mu}x_3]\partial_{x_3} - x_1, \qquad (1.15)
\end{aligned}
$$

$$
\begin{aligned}
-\hat{V}(x_1, x_2, x_3, \partial_{x_1}, \partial_{x_2}, \partial_{x_3}) &= \frac{1}{2}x_3(1 - x_1)\partial_{x_1x_1} + \lambda_r x_3(1 - x_1)\partial_{x_1} - \\
&\quad \rho_{12}\zeta\sqrt{x_1 x_2 x_3}\partial_{x_1x_2} - \rho_{13}\eta x_3\sqrt{x_1}\partial_{x_1x_3} \\
&\quad - \rho_{23}\eta\zeta\sqrt{x_2 x_3}\partial_{x_2x_3}. \qquad (1.16)
\end{aligned}
$$

In order to solve PDE (1.14), the Green's function for the PDE is needed. The Green's function, $G(y_1, y_2, y_3, s, x_1, x_2, x_3, t)$, is the solution to the following PDE:

$$
\frac{\partial G(y_1, y_2, y_3, s, x_1, x_2, x_3, t)}{\partial t} + \hat{H}G(y_1, y_2, y_3, s, x_1, x_2, x_3, t) = 0, \quad (1.17)
$$

with

$$
G(y_1, y_2, y_3, s, x_1, x_2, x_3, s) = \delta(x_1 - y_1)\delta(x_2 - y_2)\delta(x_3 - y_3),
$$

where $\delta(.)$ is the Dirac function.

With Fourier transformation and the method of characteristics, the problem (1.17) can be solved and the result is presented in the following lemma.

Lemma 3: *The Green's function to the fundamental PDE (1.17), $G(y_1, y_2, y_3, s, x_1, x_2, x_3, t)$, is given by*

$$
\begin{aligned}
G(y_1, y_2, y_3, s, x_1, x_2, x_3, t) &= \\
\frac{1}{(2\pi)^{3/2}} \int \int \int & e^{-iy_1\phi - iy_2\psi - iy_3\varphi} \tilde{G}(\phi, \psi, \varphi, \tau, x_1, x_2, x_3) d\phi d\psi d\varphi,
\end{aligned}
$$

(1.18)

where $\tau = s - t$ and

$$
\tilde{G}(\phi, \psi, \varphi, \tau, x_1, x_2, x_3) = A(\tau, \phi, \psi, \varphi)e^{-B(\tau, \phi, \psi, \varphi)x_1 - C(\tau, \phi, \psi, \varphi)x_2 - D(\tau, \phi, \psi, \varphi)x_3}
$$

and

$$
\begin{aligned}
A(\tau, \phi, \psi, \varphi) &= \left(\frac{X^{\frac{\nu'}{2k}}(\Omega J_\rho(Z) + Y_\rho(Z))}{\Omega J_\rho(\sqrt{2(1 - i\phi k)}\zeta/k) + Y_\rho(\sqrt{2(1 - i\phi k)}\zeta/k)} \right)^{-\frac{2\nu\bar{\theta}}{\zeta^2}} \\
&\quad \times \left(\frac{e^{\lambda(X-1)}X^\delta \left[\Lambda M(Q, S, Y) + (\frac{-Y}{2\lambda})^{1-S}M(1 + Q - S, 2 - S; Y) \right]}{\Lambda M(Q, S; -2\lambda) + M(1 + Q - S, 2 - S; -2\lambda)} \right)^{-\frac{2\mu\bar{\nu}}{\eta^2}},
\end{aligned}
$$

$$
B(\tau, \phi, \psi, \varphi) = i\phi e^{-k\tau} + \frac{1}{k}(1 - e^{-k\tau}),
$$

$$C(\tau, \phi, \psi, \varphi) = \frac{-\nu'}{\zeta^2} - kZ\left\{\frac{\Omega(J_{\rho-1}(Z) - J_{\rho+1}(Z)) + Y_{\rho-1}(Z) - Y_{\rho+1}(Z)}{2\zeta^2(\Omega J_\rho(Z) + Y_\rho(Z))}\right\},$$

$$D(\tau, \phi, \psi, \varphi) = \frac{k}{\eta^2}\left\{Y - 2\delta - 2Y\left[\frac{\Lambda QS^{-1}M(Q+1, S+1; Y)}{\Lambda M(Q, S; Y) + X^{1-S}M(1+Q-S, 2-S; Y)}\right.\right.$$
$$+ \frac{(S-1)(2\lambda)^{-1}X^{-S}M(1+Q-S, 2-S; Y)}{\Lambda M(Q, S; Y) + X^{1-S}M(1+Q-S, 2-S; Y)}$$
$$+ \left.\left.\frac{(1+Q-S)(2-S)^{-1}X^{1-S}M(2+Q-S, 3-S; Y)}{\Lambda M(Q, S; Y) + X^{1-S}M(1+Q-S, 2-S; Y)}\right]\right\},$$

$$X = e^{-k\tau},$$

$$Y = -2\lambda e^{-k\tau},$$

$$Z = \frac{\sqrt{2(1-i\phi k)}\zeta e^{-k\tau/2}}{k},$$

$$\Omega = -\frac{Y_{\rho-1}(\iota) - Y_{\rho+1}(\iota) - Y_\rho(\iota)\omega}{J_{\rho-1}(\iota) - J_{\rho+1}(\iota) - J_\rho(\iota)\omega},$$

$$\Lambda = \frac{(1-S)(-2\lambda)^{-1}M_2 + (1+Q-S)(2-S)^{-1}M_4 - \sigma M_2}{QS^{-1}M_3 - \sigma M_1},$$

$$M_1 = M(Q, S; -2\lambda),$$

$$M_2 = M(1+Q-S, 2-S, -2\lambda),$$

$$M_3 = M(Q+1, S+1; -2\lambda),$$

$$M_4 = M(2+Q-S, 3-S; -2\lambda),$$

$$Q = \frac{S}{2} + \frac{\beta}{2\lambda},$$

$$S = 2\delta + (1 - \frac{\mu'}{k}),$$

$$\rho = \frac{\sqrt{2\zeta^2 + \nu'^2}}{k},$$

$$\omega = -\frac{\sqrt{2}(i\psi\zeta^2 + \nu')}{\sqrt{1-i\phi k\zeta}},$$

$$\sigma = \frac{i\varphi\eta^2}{4k\lambda} + \frac{1}{2} + \frac{\delta}{2\lambda},$$

$$\alpha = (1 - 2k\lambda_r)\frac{\eta^2}{4k^4},$$

$$\beta = -\frac{\eta^2}{2k^4}(1 - k\lambda_r)(1 - i\phi k),$$

$$\lambda = -\frac{i\eta}{2k^2}(1 - i\phi k),$$

$$\delta = \frac{1}{2k}[\mu' + \sqrt{\mu'^2 - 4\alpha k^2}],$$

$$\iota = \frac{\sqrt{2(1-i\phi k)}\zeta}{k,}$$

where $M(a, b, z)$ is the Kummer function and $J_\nu(\cdot)$ and $Y_\nu(\cdot)$ are Bessel functions of the first and second kinds.

Essentially, the Green's function is the Arrow-Debreu state prices: $G(y_1, y_2, y_3, s, x_1, x_2, x_3, t)$ is the value at time t in a state (x_1, x_2, x_3) of a unit payoff at time s in a state (y_1, y_2, y_3).

Remark I. Let us use the Green's function obtained to prove the following relation which must be true based on economic considerations:

$$P(x, t, T) = \int G(y, T, x, t) dy.$$

In our case,[7]

$$
\begin{aligned}
\int G(y, T, x, t) dy &= \frac{1}{\sqrt{2\pi}} \int \int e^{-iy\phi} \tilde{G}(\phi, \tau, x) d\phi dy \\
&= \frac{1}{\sqrt{2\pi}} \int \int e^{-iy\phi} A(\tau, \phi) e^{-B(\tau, \phi)x} d\phi dy \\
&= \int \delta(\phi) A(\tau, \phi) e^{-B(\tau, \phi)x} d\phi \\
&= A(0, \tau) e^{-B(0, \tau)x} \\
&= A(\tau) e^{-B(\tau)x}.
\end{aligned}
$$

Here, the following relations,

$$\delta(\phi) = \frac{1}{\sqrt{2\pi}} \int_{-\infty}^{\infty} e^{-i\phi y} dy, \quad F(x) = \int_{-\infty}^{\infty} \delta(x - y) F(y) dy,$$

have been used.

Remark II. The Fourier transformation of the Green's function is closely related to the bond pricing formula by

$$P(r, \theta, v, t, T) = \tilde{G}(0, 0, 0, T - t, r, \theta, v).$$

Equivalently, the functions $A(\phi, \psi, \varphi, \tau), B(\phi, \psi, \varphi, \tau), C(\phi, \psi, \varphi, \tau),$ and $D(\phi, \psi, \varphi, \tau)$ in the Green's function are related to the functions $A(\tau), B(\tau), C(\tau),$ and $D(\tau)$ in the bond pricing formula by

$$A(0, 0, 0, \tau) = A(\tau), \quad B(0, 0, 0, \tau) = B(\tau),$$

$$C(0, 0, 0, \tau) = C(\tau), \quad D(0, 0, 0, \tau) = D(\tau).$$

These relations can be seen in the following. By definition,

$$\tilde{G}(\phi, \tau, x) = \int e^{iy\phi} G(y, s, x, t) dy$$

---

[7] For notational simplicity, the case of one dimensional state space is considered here.

letting $\phi = 0$ on both sides of the above equation yields

$$\tilde{G}(0, \tau, x) = \int G(y, s, x, t)dy = P(x, t, s).$$

Remark III. The Green's function is sometimes called the propagator, the meaning of which can be put into a neat equation:

$$F(x, t, T) = \int G(y, t', x, t)F(y, t', T)dy,$$

where $F(x, t, T)$ is the price of a security. It is easy to verify this relationship in the case of bond prices. In this case,

$$
\begin{aligned}
&\int G(y, t', x, t)P(y, t', T)dy \\
&= \frac{1}{\sqrt{2\pi}} \int\int e^{-iy\phi}\tilde{G}(\phi, t' - t, x)A(T - t')e^{-B(T-t')y}d\phi dy \\
&= \frac{1}{\sqrt{2\pi}} \int\int e^{-iy\phi}A(t' - t, \phi)e^{-B(t'-t,\phi)x}A(T - t')e^{-B(T-t')y}d\phi dy \\
&= \int \delta(\phi - iB(T - t'))A(t' - t, \phi)e^{-B(t'-t,\phi)x}A(T - t')d\phi \\
&= A(T - t)e^{-B(T-t)x} \\
&= P(x, t, T).
\end{aligned}
$$

A discrete time version of this relationship will be used in Chapter 3 to fit a discrete version of our model to a given initial yield curve.

Remark IV. The Green's function as the price of an Arrow-Debreu security also satisfies the relation in Remark III, so

$$G(z, T, x, t) = \int G(y, t', x, t)G(z, T, y, t')dy, \quad t < t' < T.$$

1.5 Derivatives Pricing

The Green's function for the fundamental valuation PDE derived in section 1.4 can be applied to evaluate interest rate derivatives under general interest rate dynamics. Given the general interest rate dynamics, the value at time t, $F(r, \theta, v, t; T) \equiv F(x_1, x_2, x_3, t; T)$, of an interest rate derivative with terminal payoff, $g(x_1, x_2, x_3, T)$, is the solution to the following PDE:

$$\frac{\partial F(x_1, x_2, x_3, t; T)}{\partial t} + \hat{H}(x_1, x_2, x_3, \partial_{x_1}, \partial_{x_2}, \partial_{x_3})F(x_1, x_2, x_3, t; T) =$$

$$-\hat{V}(x_1, x_2, x_3, \partial_{x_1}, \partial_{x_2}, \partial_{x_3})F(x_1, x_2, x_3, t; T) - C(x_1, x_2, x_3, t), \quad (1.19)$$

with

$$F(x_1, x_2, x_3, T; T) = g(x_1, x_2, x_3, T),$$

where operators $\hat{H}$ and $\hat{V}$ are given by (1.15) and (1.16). With the Green's function for (1.19), $G(y, s, x, t)$, the solution to the PDE can be written as[8]

$$
\begin{aligned}
F(x, t; T) &= \int G(y, T, x, t)g(y, T)dy \\
&\quad + \int\int_t^T G(y, s, x, t)[\hat{V}(y, \partial_y)F(y, s; T) + C(y, s)]dyds \\
&= F_0(x, t; T) + \int\int_t^T G(y, s, x, t)\hat{V}(y, \partial_y)F(y, s; T)dyds
\end{aligned}
$$
$$(1.20)$$

where

$$F_0(x, t; T) = \int G(y, T, x, t)g(y, T)dy + \int\int_t^T G(y, s, x, t)C(y, s)dyds$$

is the price of the derivative under the special interest rate dynamics.

If $F(x, t; T)$ as determined by the right-hand side of (1.20) is utilized in the integral, then

$$
\begin{aligned}
F(x, t; T) &= F_0(x, t; T) + \int\int\int\int G(y, s, x, t)\hat{V}(y)F_0(y, s; T)dsdy + \\
&\quad \int\int\int\int dyds_1 \int\int\int\int duds_2 G(y, s_1, x, t)\hat{V}(y) \\
&\quad \times G(u, s_2, y, s_1)\hat{V}(u)F_0(u, s_2; T) + \dots
\end{aligned}
$$

The following proposition is therefore obtained.[9]

---

[8] It is straightfoward to show that if $G(y, s, x, t)$ is the solution to the following problem:

$$
\begin{cases}
\frac{\partial G(y, s, x, t)}{\partial t} + \hat{H}(x, \partial x)G(y, s, x, t) = 0, \\
G(y, s, x, s) = \delta(x - y)
\end{cases}
$$

then the solution to the initial value problem,

$$
\begin{cases}
\frac{\partial F(x, t)}{\partial t} + \hat{H}(x, \partial x)F(x, t) = -h(x, t), \\
F(x, T) = g(x)
\end{cases}
$$

can be written as

$$F(x, t) = \int\int_t^T G(y, s, x, t)h(y, s)dyds + \int G(y, T, x, t)g(y)dy.$$

[9] In the rest of this chapter and the next chapter, x and $(x_1, x_2, x_3) \equiv (r, \theta, v)$, dy and $dy_1 dy_2 dy_3$, etc. will be used interchangeably.

Proposition 4: *Given the general interest rate dynamics specified by stochastic differential equations (1.1), (1.2), and (1.3), the value at time t, $F(x_1, x_2, x_3, t; T) \equiv F(x_1, x_2, x_3, \tau)$, of an interest rate derivative with the terminal payoff, $g(x_1, x_2, x_3, T)$, and dividend rate, $C(x_1, x_2, x_3, t)$, $0 \le t \le T, \tau = T - t$, is*

$$
\begin{aligned}
F(x_1, x_2, x_3, \tau) \;=\; & F_0(x_1, x_2, x_3, \tau) + F_1(x_1, x_2, x_3, \tau) \\
& + F_2(x_1, x_2, x_3, \tau) + ...,
\end{aligned} \tag{1.21}
$$

where

$$
\begin{aligned}
F_0(x_1, x_2, x_3, \tau) \;=\; & \int\int\int G(y, T, x, t) g(y, T) dy \\
& + \int\int\int\int G(y, s, x, t) C(y, s) dy ds
\end{aligned}
$$

is the price of the derivative under the benchmark interest rate dynamics [10] and

$$
\begin{aligned}
F_1(x_1, x_2, x_3, \tau) \;=\; & \int\int\int\int G(y, s, x, t)\hat{V}(y) F_0(y, s; T) ds dy, \\
F_2(x_1, x_2, x_3, \tau) \;=\; & \int\int\int\int dy ds_1 \int\int\int\int du ds_2 G(y, s_1, x, t) \\
& \times \hat{V}(y) G(u, s_2, y, s_1)\hat{V}(u) F_0(u, s_2; T).
\end{aligned}
$$

Other terms in (1.21) can be similarly determined by the following diagram:

$$
\begin{array}{ccccccccc}
F & = & F_0 & + & \downarrow\ y & + & \downarrow\ u & + & \downarrow\ v & + & \cdots \\
& & & & \downarrow\ x & & \downarrow\ y & & \downarrow\ u \\
& & & & & & \downarrow\ x & & \downarrow\ y \\
& & & & & & & & \downarrow\ x \\
\\
& & & & F_1 & & F_2 & & F_3
\end{array}
$$

For example, to write $F_3(x_1, x_2, x_3, \tau)$, note from the diagram that

$$
x \leftarrow y \leftarrow u \leftarrow v
$$

reads as

$$
G(y, x)\hat{V}(y) G(u, y)\hat{V}(u) G(v, u)\hat{V}(v) F_0(v).
$$

Writing out the time arguments and taking integrals yields

$$
F_3(x_1, x_2, x_3, \tau) \;=\; \int\int\int\int\int\int G(y, s_1, x, t)\hat{V}(y) G(u, s_2, y, s_1)\hat{V}(u)
$$

---

[10] Assume that the terminal payoffs have the same form in both special and general interest rate dynamics. It can be shown that the error caused by this assumption is a second-order term.

$$\times G(v, s_3, u, s_2)\hat{V}(v)F_0(v, s_3; T)dydudvds_1ds_2ds_3.$$

Remark I. Many interest rate derivatives can be evaluated by the same PDE (1.19) with similar initial conditions and therefore their values under the general interest rate dynamics can be obtained by the substituting appropriate dividend rate $C(x, t)$ and terminal payoff $g(x, T)$ into the formula (1.21). The following are a few examples.

a) An interest rate **swap** can be regarded as a contract paying the dividend rate $C(r, t) = r - r^*$, where r^* is a fixed rate with the terminal payoff $g(x, T)=0$.

b) A **cap** is a loan at a variable interest rate but with the proviso that the interest rate charged is guaranteed not to exceed the cap rate r^*. Per unit of the principle amount of the loan, the value of the cap can be obtained from formula (1.21) with $C(r, t) = \min[r - r^*]$ and $g(x, T)=1$[11].

c) A **floor** is defined symmetrically with a cap, that is, the interest rate charged does not fall below r^*. Therefore, for a floor, $C(r, t) = \max[r - r^*, 0]$ and $g(x, T)=1$.

d) The value at time t of a call **option** on a zero coupon bond maturing at time s with the strike price K and the expiration date $T < s$, is given by formula (1.21), with $C(x, t) = 0$ and $g(x, T) = \max[P(x, T, s) - K, 0]$ where $P(x, T, s)$ is the price at T of the bond.

e) A **swaption** is the right, not the obligation, to buy a swap for the strike price K at time $T < T_s$. Let $V_s(x, t)$ be the value at t of the swap which expires at T_s. The value of the swap can be obtained by letting $g(x, T) = \max[V_s(x, T) - K, 0]$ in formula (1.21).

f) For a call option of maturity T and the strike price K on a **basket** with the spot price $B(t) = \sum_i a_i P_i(t)$ made up of bonds i in specified quantities a_i, the value at expiry is given by $g(x, T) = \max[B(T) - K, 0] = \max[\sum_i a_i P_i(T)$-K, $0]$. The value at t of this basket call option can be obtained by substituting this terminal payoff into (1.21).

g) The value of a **yield curve call option** with the strike price K and expiration T is determined by formula (1.21), with $C(x, t) = 0$ and $g(x, T) = \max[R(x, T + s) - K, 0]$, where $R(x, T + s)$ is the yield at time T on a riskless bond maturing at $T + s$.

h) A **binary option** (cash-or-nothing call) can be valued by (1.21) with $C(x, t) = 0$ and the terminal payoff, $g(r, T) = B\mathcal{H}(r - r^*)$, where $\mathcal{H}(x)$ is the Heaviside

---

[11] In the following, x denotes the three factors (r, θ, v).

function defined by

$$\mathcal{H}(x) = \begin{cases} 0, \text{for } x < 0 \\ 1, \text{for } x \geq 0. \end{cases}$$

i) A **compound option** is an option on an option. Let us consider the vanilla call on a call option which is the right at time T_1 to buy the underlying vanilla option at the strike price K_1. The underlying option may be exercised at T_2 for the strike price K_2. Let $C(x, T_1)$ be the value at time T_1 of the underlying option. The terminal payoff at T_1 of the compound option is $\max[C(x, T_1) - K_1, 0]$.

j) A **chooser option** gives its owner the right to buy for the price K at time T either a call or a put with the strike price K_2 at time T_2. Let $C_c(x, t)$ and $C_p(x, t)$ be the call and put prices at time t respectively. Then the value of a chooser call option can be obtained from (1.21) with $g(x, t) = 0$ and $C(x, T) = \max[C_c(x, T) - K, C_p(x, T) - K, 0]$.

k) A **SYCURVE** option's payoff at the expiration T depends only on the yield spread between the two underlying securities, not on whether the general level of yield has increased or decreased during the term of the option. Formally, the SYCURVE has the final payoff

$$g(x, T) = \max[0, S_{m,n}(x, T) - K],$$

where $S_{m,n}(x, T)$ is the slope of the yield curve

$$S_{m,n}(x, T) = \frac{R(x, T + n) - R(x, T + m)}{n - m}.$$

l) The value at t of a call **option on volatility** v with maturity T can be evaluted by (1.21) with $g(x, T) = \max[0, v - K]$ and $C(x, t) = 0$.

More derivatives of European type can be included in this list. With our method, the value of these derivatives under the general interest rate dynamics can be determined in quasi-closed-form which normally needs to be computed numerically.

Remark II. Zero-Coupon Bond Pricing under General Interest Rate Dynamics.

The value at time t of a default-free zero-coupon bond under general interest rate dynamics, denoted $P_g(x_1, x_2, x_3, t; T)$, is given by (1.21), with $g(x_1, x_2, x_3, T) = 1$ and $C(x_1, x_2, x_3, t) = 0$:

$$P_g(x_1, x_2, x_3, \tau) = P_{g0}(x_1, x_2, x_3, \tau) + P_{g1}(x_1, x_2, x_3, \tau) + P_{g2}(\cdot) + ..., \quad (1.22)$$

where

$$P_{g0}(x_1, x_2, x_3, \tau) \equiv P(x_1, x_2, x_3, \tau) = \int G(y_1, y_2, y_2, T, x_1, x_2, x_3, t) dy_1 dy_2 dy_3$$

is the bond price formula under the benchmark case and

$$P_{g1}(x_1, x_2, x_3, \tau) = \int \int \int \int G(y, s, x, t)\hat{V}(y)P(y, s; T)dsdy,$$

$$P_{g2}(x_1, x_2, x_3, \tau) = \int dyds_1 \int duds_2 G(y, s_1, x, t)\hat{V}(y)G(u, s_2, y, s_1)$$
$$\times \hat{V}(u)P(u, s_2; T).$$

Formula (1.22) shows that the general bond price, $P_g(x_1, x_2, x_3, \tau)$, can be expanded around the benchmark bond price, $P(x_1, x_2, x_3, \tau)$, and $P_{g1}(x_1, x_2, x_3, \tau)$ can be considered the first order correction to the bond price, $P_{g2}(x_1, x_2, x_3, \tau)$ the second-order correction, etc. All the correction terms are in exact form, as they involve only known functions: $G(x_1, x_2, x_3, t, y_1, y_2, y_3, s)$ is given in equation (1.18); $\hat{V}(y_1, y_2, y_3, \partial_{y_1}, \partial_{y_2}, \partial_3)$ in equation (1.16); and $P(y_1, y_2, y_3, \tau)$ in (1.12). Under reasonable assumptions, it can be shown that the terms in the bond pricing formula (1.22) are descending in magnitude:

$$\| P(x_1, x_2, x_3, \tau) \| \quad >> \quad \| P_{g1}(x_1, x_2, x_3, \tau) \| >>$$
$$\| P_{g2}(x_1, x_2, x_3, \tau) \| >> \| P_{g3}(\cdot) \| >> \ldots$$

So it should be sufficient to retain only the first few order correction terms for most purposes.

Remark III. Coupon Bond Pricing under Special Interest Rate Dynamics.

Letting $\hat{V} = 0$ in formula (1.21) yields the derivatives pricing formula under special interest rate dynamics. Let $P_c(x_1, x_2, x_3, t; T)$ be the value at time t of a coupon bond with coupon rate $c(r, t)$ under the special interest rate dynamics. To obtain $P_c(x_1, x_2, x_3, t; T)$, set $g(x_1, x_2, x_3, T) = 1, C(x_1, x_2, x_3, t) = c(x_1, t)$, and $\hat{V} = 0$ in (1.21). In the case of discrete coupon payments occuring at dates $t_i, i = 1, ..., n$,

$$c(y_1, s) = \sum_{i=1}^{n} c_i \delta(s - t_i),$$

and

$$P_c(x_1, x_2, x_3, \tau) = P(x_1, x_2, x_3, \tau) + \int G(y, s, x_1, x_2, x_3, t) \sum_{i=1}^{n} c_i \delta(s - t_i)dyds$$

$$= P(x_1, x_2, x_3, \tau) + \sum_{i=1}^{n} \int c_i G(y, t_i, x_1, x_2, x_3, t)dy$$

$$= P(x_1, x_2, x_3, \tau) + \sum_{i=1}^{n} c_i P(x, x_2, x_3, t_i - t) \qquad (1.23)$$

as expected.

1.6   The Term Structure of Interest Rates

The yield to maturity on a discount bond under the general interest rate dynamics is given by:

$$R(r, \theta, v; \tau) \equiv -\frac{1}{\tau} \ln P_g(r, \theta, v; \tau) \simeq -\frac{1}{\tau}\left[\ln P_0(r, \theta, v; \tau) + \frac{P_{g1}(r, \theta, v; \tau)}{P_0(r, \theta, v; \tau)}\right] \text{(1.21)}$$

where $P_0(r, \theta, v; \tau)$ is the bond price under the special interest rate dynamics and $P_1(r, \theta, v; \tau)$ is the first order correction given by[13]:

$$
\begin{aligned}
P_{g1}(x, t, T) &= \int_t^T \int G(y, s, x, t)\hat{V}(y, \partial y)P_0(y, s, T)dyds \\
&= -\int_t^T \int G(y, s, x, t)y_3(1 - y_1)B(T - s)[\frac{1}{2}B(T - s) - \lambda_r] \\
&\quad \times A(T - s)e^{-B(T-s)y_1 - C(T-s)y_2 - C(T-s)y_3}dyds,
\end{aligned}
$$

which needs to be evaluated by some numerical integration algorithms.

Factor Loadings

To zero order approximation, the yield (1.24) is given by

$$R_0(r, \theta, v; \tau) = -\frac{1}{\tau} \ln P_0(r, \theta, v; \tau) = -\frac{1}{\tau}[\ln A(\tau) - B(\tau)r - C(\tau)\theta - D(\tau)v].$$

The functions $B(\tau), C(\tau)$, and $D(\tau)$ determine the sensitivity of a bond's yield to factors r, θ, and v and can therefore be called factor loadings for r, θ, and v respectively. Curves of these three loadings are shown in Figures 1.1 and 1.2 for their effects on changes in price and changes in yield respectively. These curves are similar in nature to the factor loadings empirically identified by Litterman and Scheinkman (1991).

An examination of both Figures 1.1 and 1.2 shows that the yield changes caused by the three factors are greater for short and intermediate maturities. All the changes die out as maturities approach infinity. This is consistent with the well-known flattening of yield curves for long-maturity bonds.

As can be seen from Figure 1.2, the loading for the short rate is more significant for short maturity yields, while the loading for the short mean has more effect on intermediate maturity yields. The impact of volatility on yields is more complex. As the loading for volatility $D(\tau)$, depending on model parameter values, can take positive values for some maturities and negative values for other maturities, or take negative or positive values for all maturities, an increase in volatility can either increase yields or decrease yields.

---

[13]Here again, without ambiguity, notations have been changed and correlation terms have been suppressed for simplicity.

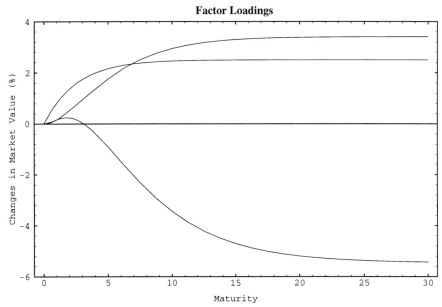

Figure 1.1: **Factor Loading: Effect on Price.** The three curves from the top down, viewing at the right end, correspond to loadings for r, θ, and v respectively. The values of the parameters are: $k = 0.40, \nu\bar{\theta} = 0.027, \mu\bar{v} = 0.001, \eta = 0.118, \zeta = 0.119, \nu' = 0.27, \mu' = 0.29$, and $\lambda_r = 0.70$.

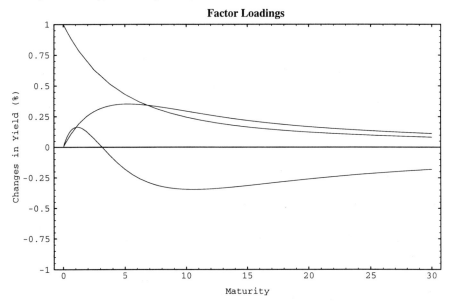

Figure 1.2: **Factor Loading: Effect on Yield.** The three curves from the top down, viewing at the right end, correspond to loading for θ, r and v respectively. The values of the parameters are: $k = 0.40, \nu\bar{\theta} = 0.027, \mu\bar{v} = 0.001, \eta = 0.118, \zeta = 0.119, \nu' = 0.27, \mu' = 0.29$, and $\lambda_r = 0.70$.

The Effect of Short Rate

Figure 1.3 shows yield curves for different values of the short rate. A change in the short rate results in a roughly parallel shift in the yield curve, which is more evident at the short end of the yield curves. The short rate can therefore be considered a level factor.

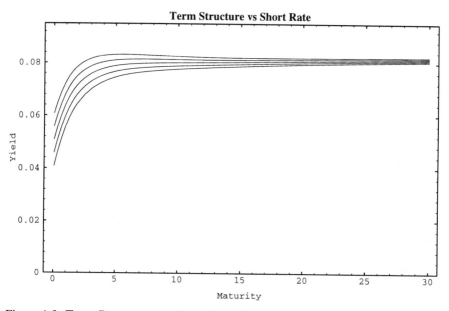

Figure 1.3: **Term Structure vs. Short Rate.** The values of the parameters are: $k = 0.40, \nu\bar{\theta} = 0.027, \mu\bar{v} = 0.001, \eta = 0.118, \zeta = 0.119, \nu' = 0.27, \mu' = 0.29$, and $\lambda_r = 0.70$. The values of the current short mean and volatility: $\theta = 0.13, v = 0.02$. The values of the current short rate corresponding to the curves from the top down are 0.06, 0.055, 0.05, 0.044, and 0.04 respectively.

The Effect of Volatility of Short Rate

Since the volatility $v(t)$ can vary even when the short rate $r(t)$ is held fixed, changes in the level of interest rate volatility can have a significant effect on the slope and the curvature of the yield curve. Figure 1.4 shows yield curves for several values of volatility.

The effect of the interest rate volatility on the term structure can be more complex than shown in Figure 1.4. As for some parameter values, the factor loading for volatility can take both positive and negative values, an increase in volatility can

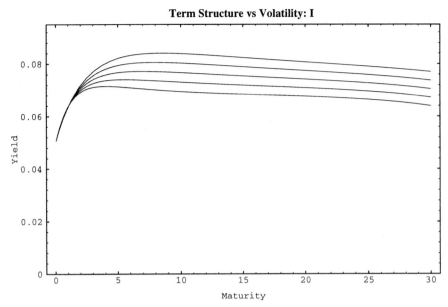

Figure 1.4: **Term Structure vs. Volatility I.** The values of the parameters are: $k = 0.40, \nu\bar{\theta} = 0.027, \mu\bar{v} = 0.002, \eta = 0.045, \zeta = 0.119, \nu' = 0.27, \mu' = 0.29,$ and $\lambda_r = 0.40.$ The current values of the short rate and mean: $r = 0.05, \theta = 0.13.$ The values of the volatility corresponding to the curves from the top down are 0.01, 0.02, 0.03, 0.04, and 0.05 respectively.

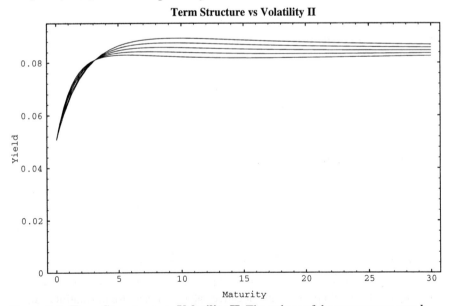

Figure 1.5: **Term Structure vs. Volatility II.** The values of the parameters are: $k = 0.40, \nu\bar{\theta} = 0.027, \mu\bar{v} = 0.001, \eta = 0.118, \zeta = 0.119, \nu' = 0.27, \mu' = 0.29,$ and $\lambda_r = 0.70.$ The current values of the short rate and mean: $r = 0.05, \theta = 0.13.$ The values of the volatility corresponding to the curves from the top down, viewing at the short end of the yield curves, are 0.03, 0.025, 0.02, 0.015, and 0.01 respectively.

increase yields on securities with some maturities and decrease yields on other maturities. To illustrate this feature, Figure 1.5 displays yield curves versus volatilities
for a different set of parameter values than that displayed in Figure 1.4. In the figure, an increase in volatility can increase yields for maturities up to four or five
years and decrease yields on securities with longer maturities. Figures 1.4 and 1.5
show that volatility is the major factor that changes the curvature of the yield curve,
so volatility can be considered the curvature factor in the conventional sense.

The Effect of Short Term Mean

Figure 1.6 depicts yield curves for several values of the short-term mean. It is evident from the figure that a change in the short mean results in a change in the slope
of the yield curve. The short mean is therefore the major factor determining the
slope of the yield curve, especially in the short run, and can be considered the steep-
ness factor in the conventional sense. Figure 6 is similar to the figure 3 in Campbell
(1995) showing observed yield curve shifts due to increases in target federal funds
rates.

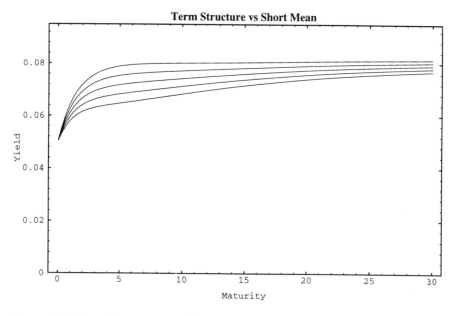

Figure 1.6: **Term Structure vs. Short Mean.** The values of the parameters are:
$k = 0.40, \nu\bar{\theta} = 0.027, \mu\bar{v} = 0.001, \eta = 0.1, \zeta = 0.119, \nu' = 0.27, \mu' = 0.29$, and
$\lambda_r = 0.40$. The current values of the short rate and volatility: $r = 0.05, v = 0.02$.
The values of the short mean corresponding to the curves from the top down are
$0.13, 0.12, 0.11, 0.10$, and 0.09 respectively.

The Effect of the Mean Reverting Tendency

Figure 1.7 shows the term structure of interest rates for several values of the mean reversion parameter k. The changes in k have less effect on the short end of the yield curve.

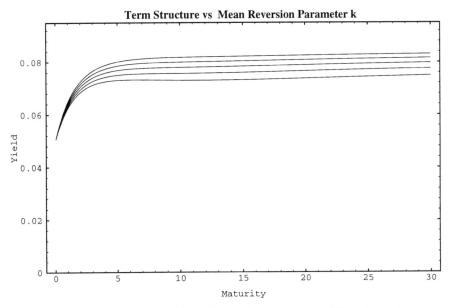

Figure 1.7: **Term Structure vs. Mean Reversion Parameter.** The values of the parameters are: $\nu\bar{\theta} = 0.027, \mu\bar{v} = 0.001, \eta = 0.1, \zeta = 0.119, \nu' = 0.27, \mu' = 0.29$, and $\lambda_r = 0.40$. The current values of the three factors: $r = 0.05, \theta = 0.13, v = 0.02$. The values of k corresponding to the curves from the top down are $0.36, 0.38, 0.40, 0.42$, and 0.44 respectively.

The Effect of the Volatility of Volatility

The volatility of volatility is considered an important factor in determining the movements of yield curves and in formulating risk management schemes. Within the framework of our model, one for the first time is able to analytically investigate the impact of volatility of volatility of the short rate on the yield curve. Figure 1.8 shows a set of yield curves for several values of the volatility of volatility of the short rate. As expected, changes in the volatility of volatility have a significant effect on the yield curve, especially on the long end of the yield curve. Unlike volatility, which has the most significant effect on short and intermediate maturity yields, the volatility of volatility affects long-maturity yields the most.

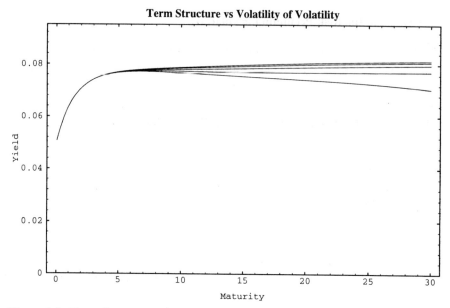

Figure 1.8: **Term Structure vs. Volatility of Volatility.** The values of the parameters are: $k = 0.4, \nu\bar{\theta} = 0.027, \mu\bar{v} = 0.001, \zeta = 0.119, \nu' = 0.27, \mu' = 0.29$, and $\lambda_r = 0.40$. The current values of the three factors: $r = 0.05, \theta = 0.13, v = 0.02$. The values of η corresponding to the curves from the top down are 0.04, 0.07, 0.1, 0.13, and 0.15 respectively.

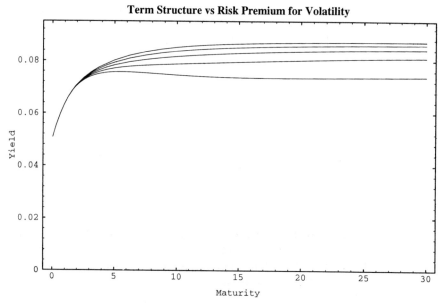

Figure 1.9: **Term Structure vs. Risk Premium for Volatility.** The values of the parameters are: $k = 0.4, \nu\bar{\theta} = 0.027, \mu\bar{v} = 0.001, \eta = 0.1, \zeta = 0.119, \nu' = 0.27$, and $\lambda_r = 0.40$. The current values of the three factors: $r = 0.05, \theta = 0.13, v = 0.02$. The values of the risk premium for volatility corresponding to the curves from the top down are 0.1, 0.2, 0.3, 0.4, and 0.5 respectively.

The Effect of the Risk Premium for Volatility

Figure 1.9 shows yield curves for different values of the risk premium for volatility. It is evident that the yields on bonds, especially long maturity bonds, are sensitively related to the risk premium for volatility.

The Effect of the Risk Premium for Volatility: A Closer Look

As bond yields are sensitively related to the risk premium for the short rate volatility, let us have a closer look at this relation.

Normally, a change in the risk premium affects bonds of different maturities differently. Figure 1.10 depicts how the yield on a bond with 4 years to maturity changes as the risk premium for volatility changes while holding all other parameters constant. It is interesting to note that this relation has a "smile" look; as the risk premium increases, it decreases the yield; however, once the risk premium exceeds a certain critical value, 0.38 in the diagram, an increase in the risk premium increases the yield.

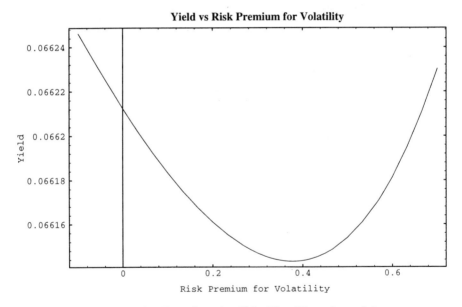

Figure 1.10: **Yield vs. Risk Premium for Volatility.** The values of the parameters are: $k = 0.40, \nu\bar\theta = 0.027, \mu\bar\upsilon = 0.002, \eta = 0.045, \zeta = 0.119, \nu' = 0.27,$ and $\lambda_r = 0.40$. The current values of the short rate, mean, and volatility: $r = 0.05, \theta = 0.13, \upsilon = 0.02$. The maturity of the bond is 4 years.

The Effect of the Risk Premium for Short Rate: A Closer Look

Figure 1.11 depicts how the bond yield changes as the risk premium for the short rate changes while holding all other parameters constant. It is no "smile" look. As the risk premium increases, the yield increases.

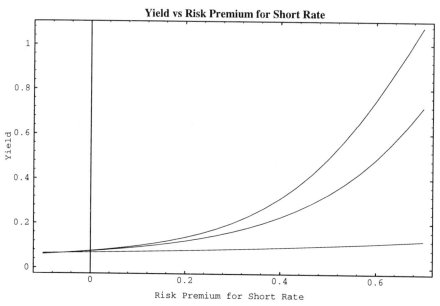

Figure 1.11: **Yield vs. Risk Premium for Short Rate.** The values of the parameters are: $k = 0.40, \nu\bar{\theta} = 0.027, \mu\bar{v} = 0.002, \eta = 0.045, \zeta = 0.119, \mu' = 0.29$. The current values of the short rate, mean and volatility: $r = 0.05, \theta = 0.13, v = 0.02$. The maturities corresponding to the curves from the top down, viewing at the short end, are 30, 20, and 3 years respectively.

1.7 Expected Future Short Rate

This section is devoted to the computing of the expected future short rate given the current values of the short rate, short mean, and volatility under both special and general interest rate dynamics.

Expected Future Short Rate under Special Interest Rate Dynamics

Under the special interest rate dynamics, the stochastic differential equation for r is equivalent to

$$d(e^{kt}r) = ke^{kt}\theta(t)dt + e^{kt}\sqrt{v(t)}dB_1.$$

It is easy to show that if $\theta(t)$ and $v(t)$ are not stochastic, but deterministic functions, then the distribution of re^{kt} is given by

$$L(re^{kt}, \Theta(t), V(t)) = \frac{1}{\sqrt{2\pi V(t)}} \exp\left\{ \frac{-(r(t)e^{kt} - r(t_0)e^{kt_0} - \Theta(t))^2}{2V(t)} \right\},$$

where

$$\Theta(t) = k \int_{t_0}^{t} e^{k\tau}\theta(\tau)d\tau$$

and

$$V(t) = \int_{t_0}^{t} e^{2k\tau}v(\tau)d\tau.$$

In our case, $\theta(t)$ and $v(t)$ are the stochastic process,

$$X_t = \{\theta(t), v(t)\}_{t\in[0,\infty)},$$

defined on a probability space, $(\Omega, \mathcal{F}, P)$, and assuming values in $\mathcal{R}^2$. For each fixed $t \in [0, \infty)$, there is a random variable,

$$\omega \rightarrow X_t(\omega), \omega \in \Omega.$$

On the other hand, fixing $\omega \in \Omega$, the function,

$$t \rightarrow X_t(\omega) = \{\theta_\omega(t), v_\omega(t)\}; t \in [0, \infty),$$

is called a path of X_t.

Let $\Theta_\omega(t)$ and $V_\omega(t)$ be

$$\begin{aligned} \Theta_\omega(t) &= k \int_{t_0}^{t} e^{k\tau}\theta_\omega(\tau)d\tau, \\ V_\omega(t) &= \int_{t_0}^{t} e^{2k\tau}v_\omega(\tau)d\tau. \end{aligned} \tag{1.22}$$

Each path ω implies a distribution for x:

$$L(x, \Theta_\omega(t), V_\omega(t)).$$

The desired transition probability density $f(x)$ is the expectation of

$$L(re^{kt}, \Theta_\omega(t), V_\omega(t))$$

over all the possible $\omega \in \Omega$:

$$f(x) = E_{\omega\in\Omega}L(x, \Theta_\omega(t), V_\omega(t)).$$

Let $m_t(\Theta, V)d\Theta dV$ [14] be the joint distribution function of Θ_ω and V_ω with t subscript on m_t to indicate that the distribution depends on the time horizon. For any function, $F(\Theta, V)$,

$$E_{\omega \in \Omega} F(\Theta(t), V(t)) = \int \int F(\Theta, V)m_t(\Theta, V)dV_\omega d\Theta_\omega.$$

Therefore, the desired transition probability density is

$$f(x) \equiv \int L(x, \Theta, V)m_t(\Theta, V)d\Theta_\omega dV_\omega$$

$$= \int \int \frac{1}{\sqrt{2\pi V}} \exp\left\{\frac{-(x - x_0 - \Theta)^2}{2V}\right\} m_t(\Theta, V)d\Theta_\omega dV_\omega. \quad (1.23)$$

Consider the characteristic function of $f(x)$, defined as:

$$g(\xi) = E\{e^{ix\xi}\} = \int_{-\infty}^{\infty} e^{ix\xi} f(x)dx$$

with $f(x)$ given in (1.26),

$$g(\xi) = \int \int m_t(\Theta, V) \int \frac{1}{\sqrt{2\pi V}} \exp\left(\frac{-(x - x_0 - \Theta)^2}{2V}\right) e^{ix\xi} dx \, d\Theta_\omega dV_\omega.$$

The term in braces can be computed to yield:

$$\exp\left\{-\frac{V}{2}\xi^2 + i\xi(x_0 + \Theta)\right\}.$$

Therefore,

$$g(\xi) = \int \int m_t(\Theta, V) \exp\left\{-\frac{V}{2}\xi^2 + i\xi(x_0 + \Theta)\right\} d\Theta_\omega dV_\omega.$$

Considering that under our specifications Θ and V are independent:

$$m_t(\Theta, V) = m_t(\Theta)m_t(V)$$

and thus

$$g(\xi) = e^{i\xi x_0} \int m_t(V) \exp(-\frac{V}{2}\xi^2)dV_\omega \int m_t(\Theta) \exp(i\xi\Theta)d\Theta_\omega.$$

The two integrals are denoted as

$$F(\xi) = \int m_t(V) \exp(-\frac{V}{2}\xi^2)dV_\omega, \quad (1.24)$$

$$G(\xi) = \int m_t(\Theta) \exp(i\xi\Theta)d\Theta_\omega. \quad (1.25)$$

[14]In the rest of this section, the subscript ω for Θ and V will be sometimes suppressed for simplicity.

Applying the inverse Fourier transformation to the characteristic function, $g(\xi)$, yields

$$f(x) = \frac{1}{2\pi} \int e^{-ix\xi} g(\xi) d\xi = \frac{1}{2\pi} \int e^{i\xi(x_0-x)} F(\xi) G(\xi) d\xi,$$

which is the transition probability density of $x = r(t)e^{kt}$ at time t conditional upon the current short rate $r(t_0)$, its mean $\theta(t_0)$, and its volatility $v(t_0)$. The transition probability density of r at time t, $f(r)$, conditional upon the current short rate $r(t_0)$, its mean $\theta(t_0)$, and its volatility $v(t_0)$ is given by

$$f(r) = e^{-kt} f(x) = e^{-kt} f(re^{kt}).$$

Two stochastic integrals (1.27) and (1.28) are expectations taken over all the possible $\omega \in \Omega$. For example, for $F(\xi)$,

$$F(\xi) = E_\omega(e^{-\frac{v}{2}\xi^2}) = E_\omega(e^{-\frac{\xi^2}{2} \int_{t_0}^{t} e^{2k\tau} v_\omega(\tau) d\tau}).$$

These expectations can be computed by solving the relevant PDE by virtue of the Feynman-Kac formula. Carrying out these computations yields the following proposition.

Proposition 5: *Given the value of three factors at time t_0, $r_0 = r(t_0), \theta_0 = \theta(t_0)$, and $v_0 = v(t_0)$, the future expected short rate at time t is*

$$E[r(t) \mid r_0, \theta_0, v_0] = \int r(t) f(r(t) \mid r_0, \theta_0, v_0) dr,$$

where $f(r(t) \mid r_0, \theta_0, v_0)$, the transition probability density, is given by

$$f(r(t)) \equiv f(r(t) \mid r_0, \theta_0, v_0) = \frac{e^{-kt}}{2\pi} \int_{-\infty}^{\infty} e^{i\xi(r_0 e^{kt_0} - r(t)e^{kt})} g(t, \xi) d\xi,$$

with

$$g(t, \xi) = e^{A(t,\xi)v_0 + B(t,\xi) + A'(t,\xi)\theta_0 + B'(t,\xi)}$$

and

$$A(t, \xi) = -\frac{\mu}{\eta^2} - 2k\lambda X$$
$$\times \frac{M[J_{h-1}(\lambda X) - J_{h+1}(\lambda X)] + Y_{h-1}(\lambda X) - Y_{h+1}(\lambda X)}{2\eta^2(M J_h(\lambda X) + Y_h(\lambda X))},$$

$$B(t, \xi) = \frac{2\mu\bar{v}}{\eta^2} \ln \frac{X^{-h}(M J_h(\lambda X) + Y_h(\lambda X))}{M J_h(\lambda e^{kt_0/2}) + Y_h(\lambda e^{kt_0/2})},$$

$$A'(t, \xi) = -\frac{v}{\zeta^2} - k\lambda' X^{1/2}$$

$$\times \frac{M[J_{h'-1}(\lambda' X^{1/2}) - J_{h'+1}(\lambda' X^{1/2})] + Y_{h'-1}(\lambda' X^{1/2}) - Y_{h'+1}(\lambda' X^{1/2})}{2\zeta^2 (M J_{h'}(\lambda' X^{1/2}) + Y_{h'}(\lambda' X^{1/2}))}$$

$$B'(t,\xi) = \frac{2\nu\bar{\theta}}{\zeta^2} \ln \frac{X^{\frac{-h'}{2}} (M J_{h'}(\lambda' X^{1/2}) + Y_{h'}(\lambda' X^{1/2}))}{M' J_{h'}(\lambda' e^{kt_0/2}) + Y_{h'}(\lambda' e^{kt_0/2})},$$

with

$$X = e^{kt},$$

$$M = -\frac{2\mu e^{-kt_0} Y_h(\lambda e^{kt_0}) + \eta\xi(Y_{h-1}(\lambda e^{kt_0}) - Y_{h+1}(\lambda e^{kt_0}))}{2\mu e^{-kt_0} J_h(\lambda e^{kt_0}) + \eta\xi(J_{h-1}(\lambda e^{kt_0}) - J_{h+1}(\lambda e^{kt_0}))},$$

$$h = \frac{\mu}{2k},$$

$$\lambda = \frac{\eta\xi}{2k},$$

$$M' = -\frac{2\nu e^{-kt_0/2} Y_{h'}(\lambda' e^{kt_0/2}) + \zeta\xi(Y_{h'-1}(\lambda' e^{kt_0/2}) - Y_{h'+1}(\lambda' e^{kt_0/2}))}{2\nu e^{-kt_0/2} J_{h'}(\lambda' e^{kt_0/2}) + \zeta\xi(J_{h'-1}(\lambda' e^{kt_0/2}) - J_{h'+1}(\lambda' e^{kt_0/2}))},$$

$$h' = \frac{\nu}{k},$$

$$\lambda' = \frac{\sqrt{2\zeta}(1+i)\xi}{k}.$$

For completeness, the following is the transition probability density function for the short mean and the expected short mean (Feller (1951)):

$$f(\theta(t) \mid r_0, \theta_0, v_0) = f(\theta \mid \theta_0) = ce^{-u-v} \left(\frac{v}{u}\right)^{q/2} I_q(2\sqrt{uv}),$$

$$E[\theta(t) \mid r_0, \theta_0, v_0] = \theta(t)e^{-\nu(t-t_0)+\bar{\theta}(1-e^{-\nu(t-t_0)})},$$

where

$$c = \frac{2\nu}{\zeta^2(1 - e^{-\nu(t-t_0)})},$$

$$u = c\theta_0 e^{-\nu(t-t_0)},$$

$$v = c\theta,$$

$$q = \frac{2\nu\bar{\theta}}{\zeta^2} - 1.$$

$f(v(t) \mid r_0, \theta_0, v_0)$ and $E[v(t) \mid r_0, \theta_0, v_0]$ have the same form.

Expected Future Short Rate under General Interest Rate Dynamics

Let $P(y_1, y_2, y_3, s; x_1, x_2, x_3, t)$ be the transition probability density function under the general interest rate dynamics. Under appropriate regularity conditions, $P(y_1, y_2, y_3, s; x_1, x_2, x_3, t)$ is the solution to the following Kolmogorov equation or backward equation (Gardiner (1983) and Duffie (1992)),

$$\left\{ \frac{1}{2}x_3\partial_{x_1x_1} + \frac{1}{2}\eta^2 x_3\partial_{x_3x_3} + \frac{1}{2}\zeta^2 x_2\partial_{x_2x_2} + [k(x_2 - x_1) + \lambda_r x_3]\partial_{x_1} \right.$$

$$[\nu\bar{\theta} - \acute{\nu}x_2]\partial_{x_2} + [\mu\bar{\nu} - \acute{\mu}x_3]\partial_{x_3} + \partial_t - \frac{1}{2}x_3(1 - x_1)\partial_{x_1 x_1}$$
$$-\lambda_r x_3(1 - x_1)\partial_{x_1}\Big\}P(y, s; x, t) = 0, \tag{1.27}$$

with the boundary condition

$$\lim_{t\uparrow s} P(y_1, y_2, y_3, s, x_1, x_2, x_3, s) = \delta(x_1 - y_1)\delta(x_2 - y_2)\delta(x_3 - y_3), \quad s \geq t.$$

This PDE is different from the valuation PDE in section 1.4 in that there is no term $-x_1 P$.

However, the same Green's function as in section 1.4 can be used to deal with the problem. To see this, rewrite the PDE (1.30) by adding the term $-x_1 P$ to both sides,

$$\Big\{\frac{1}{2}x_3\partial_{x_1 x_1} + \frac{1}{2}\eta^2 x_3\partial_{x_3 x_3} + \frac{1}{2}\varsigma^2 x_2\partial_{x_2 x_2} + [k(x_2 - x_1) + \lambda_r x_3]\partial_{x_1}$$
$$+[\nu\bar{\theta} - \acute{\nu}x_2]\partial_{x_2} + [\mu\bar{\nu} - \acute{\mu}x_3]\partial_{x_3} + \partial_t - x_1\Big\}P(y, s, x, t)$$
$$= \Big\{\frac{1}{2}x_3(1 - x_1)\partial_{x_1 x_1} + \lambda_r x_3(1 - x_1)\partial_{x_1} - x_1\Big\}P(y, s, x, t).$$

So the solution can be obtained from (1.21) with

$$\hat{V}(x_1, x_2, x_3, \partial_{x_1}, \partial_{x_2}, \partial_{x_3}) = \frac{1}{2}x_3(1 - x_1)\partial_{x_1 x_1} + \lambda_r x_3(1 - x_1)\partial_{x_1} - x_1,$$

$$g(y_1, y_2, y_3, s, x_1, x_2, x_3, s) = \delta(y_1 - x_1)\delta(y_2 - x_2)\delta(y_3 - x_3),$$

and

$$C(x_1, x_2, x_3, s) = 0.$$

The following proposition summarizes the results.

Proposition 6: *The expected future short rate under the general interest rate dynamics is given by*

$$E(y_1 \mid x) = \int y_1 P(y_1, y_2.y_3, s; x_1, x_2, x_3, t)dy_1 dy_2 dy_3$$

where the transition probability $P(y_1, y_2.y_3, s; x_1, x_2, x_3, t)$ is given by

$$P(y_1, y_2.y_3, s; x_1, x_2, x_3, t) \equiv P(y, s; x, t)$$
$$= P_0(y, s; x, t) + P_1(y, s; x, t) + P_2(y, s; x, t)$$
$$+P_3(\cdot) + ...,$$

with

$$P_0(y, s; x, t) = \int\int\int G(u, s, x, t)\delta(y - u)du = G(y, s, x, t),$$

$$P_1(y, s; x, t) = \int\int\int\int G(u, s', x, t)\hat{V}(u)P_0(y, s, u, s')ds'du,$$

$$P_2(y, s; x, t) = \int\int\int\int G(u, s', x, t)\hat{V}(u)P_1(y, s, u, s')ds'du,$$

etc.

1.8 Forward Rates

The forward rate $f(r, \theta, v, t; T)$ is defined by

$$f(r, \theta, v, t; T) \equiv -\frac{1}{P(r, \theta, v, \tau)}\frac{\partial P}{\partial T}.$$

Some calculus leads to the following proposition.

Proposition 7: *Under the special interest rate dynamics, the instantaneous forward rate of interest $f(r, \theta, v, t, T)$ at time t for the instantaneous future period at date T is given by:*

$$\begin{aligned}
f(r, \theta, v, t; T) = {} & r + (-kr + k\theta + \lambda_r v)B(t; T) + (v\bar{\theta} - v'\theta)C(t; T) \\
& + (\mu\bar{v} - \mu'v)D(t; T) - \frac{1}{2}vB^2(t; T) \\
& - \frac{1}{2}\varsigma^2\theta C^2(t; T) - \frac{1}{2}\eta^2 v D^2(t; T).
\end{aligned} \tag{1.28}$$

Figure 1.12 depicts an instantaneous forward rate curve. As the maturity approaches the long end, the forward rate starts declining. This is largely consistent with the empirical behavior of the forward rate.

The figure 1.13 and figure 1.14 depict the instantaneous forward rates versus volatility and short mean of the short rate respectively.

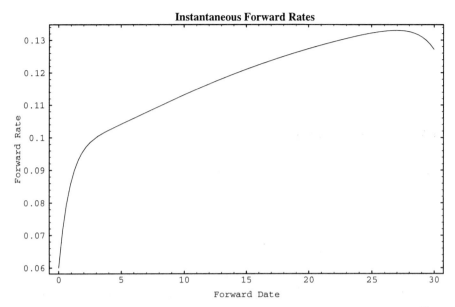

Figure 1.12: **Instantaneous Forward Rate.** The parameter values: $k = 0.4, \nu\bar{\theta} = 0.004, \mu\bar{v} = 0.004, \eta = 0.03, \zeta = 0.03, \nu' = 0.30, \mu' = 0.29, \lambda_r = 0.70$. Three factor values: $r = 0.06, \theta = 0.12, v = 0.02$.

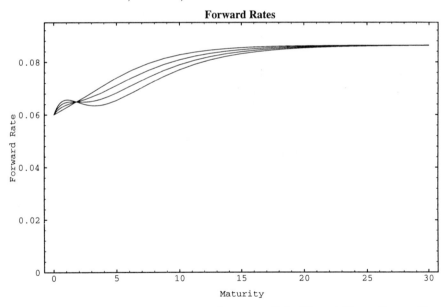

Figure 1.13: **Instantaneous Forward Rate vs. Volatility of Short Rate.** The parameter values: $k = 0.4, \nu\bar{\theta} = 0.027, \mu\bar{v} = 0.001, \eta = 0.118, \zeta = 0.119, \nu' = 0.27, \mu' = 0.29, \lambda_r = 0.70, r = 0.06, \theta = 0.08$. v are $0.02, 0.025, 0.03, 0.035$ corresponding to the curves from the top down viewing at the long end.

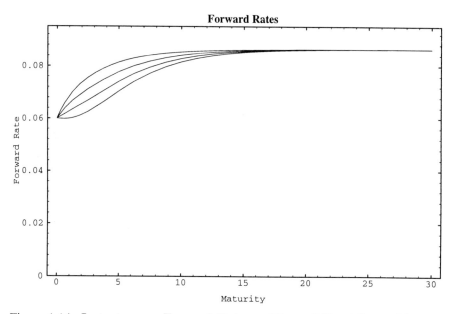

Figure 1.14: **Instantaneous Forward Rates vs Mean of Short Rate.** The parameter values: $k = 0.4, \nu\bar\theta = 0.027, \mu\bar v = 0.001, \eta = 0.118, \zeta = 0.119,$ $\nu' = 0.27, \mu' = 0.29, \lambda_r = 0.70, r = 0.06, v = 0.02.$ θ are 0.1, 0.09, 0.08, 0.07 corresponding to the curves from the top down.

Chapter 2

Pricing Interest Rate Derivatives

2.1 Introduction

In chapter 1, a three-factor model of interest rates was developed. In the model the three factors are 1) the current short rate, 2) the short-term mean of the short rate, and 3) the current volatility of the short rate. Furthermore, it was assumed that both the mean and the volatility of the short rate are stochastic and follow Feller processes.

Our model's specification is consistent with the main features of interest rate dynamics, and thus is able to reproduce empirical behavior of interest rates identified in a number of studies, such as those by Litterman and Scheinkman (1991) and Litterman, Scheinkman and Weiss (1991). Being more realistic, our model is useful for practical purposes such as pricing bonds, hedging bond portfolios, and formulating dynamic trading strategies. The model can also be used to perform other types of security analyses, such as the valuation of mortgage-backed securities, synthetic security construction, immunization, portfolio indexing, asset/liability management, etc.

This chapter will explore applications of our interest rate model in the pricing of interest rate derivatives. The growing demands for interest rate instruments have confronted researchers with the topics of derivatives research. An important part of derivatives research involves the pursuit of closed form solutions for the prices of various instruments. To this end, a set of closed form solutions for the values of bond options, default-free caps, floors, collars, futures and forwards, swaps and futures options are derived in a contingent claim framework under our three-factor model of the term structure of interest rates. One of the significant properties of these formulas is that the prices of derivatives explicitly depend on the current levels of the interest rate volatility and mean; the property that is long desired by professionals in the areas of derivatives trading and risk management.

The rest of this chapter presents pricing formulas for bond options, caps, floors, swaps, quality delivery options, futures options and other basic interest rate derivatives. The pricing of more complex exotic options will be discussed in the chapter that follows.

2.2 Bond Options

Let $C(r,\theta,v,t,T;s,K)$ denote the value at time t, with $r(t) = r$, $\theta(t) = \theta$, and $v(t) = v$, of a European call option on a zero-coupon bond maturing at date s, with the option exercise price K and expiration date T. At the expiration date $t = T$,

$$\begin{aligned}
C(r,\theta,v,T,T;s,K) &= [P(r,\theta,v,T;s) - K]^+ \\
&\equiv \max(0, P(r,\theta,v,T;s) - K), t \le T \le s, \quad (2.1)
\end{aligned}$$

where $P(r,\theta,v,T;s)$ is the bond price given by formula (1.12).

By (1.5), the bond option price $C(r,\theta,v,t,T;s,K)$ is given by

$$C(r,\theta,v,t,T;s,K) = E_Q\left[e^{-\int_0^T r(s)ds}[P(r,\theta,v,T;s) - K]^+ \mid \mathcal{F}_t\right],$$

which is the solution to the fundamental valuation PDE with the boundary condition (2.1). By the Green's function method, the solution can be written as

$$\begin{aligned}
C(r,\theta,v,t,T;s,K) = &\int\int^B\int [P(y_1,y_2,y_3,T;s) - K] \\
&\times G(y_1,y_2,y_3,T,r,\theta,v,t)dy_1dy_2dy_3, 0 \le t \le T \le s,
\end{aligned}$$

where y_1, y_2, and y_3 denote $r(T), \theta(T)$, and $v(T)$ respectively, $G(y_1,y_2,y_3,T,r,\theta, v,t)$ is the Green's function and B is the range of values of r,θ, and v over which the option is in the money at the expiration date T. B is defined by

$$B = \{(y_1,y_2,y_3) \in R^3 \mid P(y_1,y_2,y_3,T;s) - K \ge 0\}$$

or equivalently

$$B = \{(y_1,y_2,y_3) \in R^3 \mid B(T,s)y_1+C(T,s)y_2+D(T,s)y_3 \le K^* \equiv \ln\frac{A(T,s)}{K}\}.$$

Simplifying the integral yields the following proposition[1].

Proposition 8: *Let $C(r,\theta,v,t,T;s,K)$ denote the value at time t, (with $r(t) = r, \theta(t) = \theta$, and $v(t) = v$), of a European call option on a zero-coupon bond maturing at date s, with the option exercise price K and expiration date T, ($s \ge T \ge t$). The discount bond option price is given by*

$$\begin{aligned}
&C(r,\theta,v,t,T;s,K) = \\
&\quad P(r,\theta,v,t,s)\Psi\left(\frac{A(\tau,\phi,\psi,\varphi)}{A(s-t)}, B(\tau,\phi,\psi,\varphi) - B(s-t)\right),
\end{aligned}$$

---

[1] See Appendix D for a proof.

$$C(\tau,\phi,\psi,\varphi) - C(s-t), D(\tau,\phi,\psi,\varphi) - D(s-t);$$
$$A(s-T), \phi - iB(s-T), \psi - iC(s-T), \varphi - iD(s-T);$$
$$\ln\frac{A(T,s)}{K}, B(T,s), C(T,s), D(T,s)\Big)$$
$$-P(r,\theta,v,t,T)\Psi\Big(\frac{A(\tau,\phi,\psi,\varphi)}{A(\tau)}, B(\tau,\phi,\psi,\varphi) - B(\tau),$$
$$C(\tau,\phi,\psi,\varphi) - C(\tau), D(\tau,\phi,\psi,\varphi) - D(\tau); 1, \phi, \psi, \varphi;$$
$$\ln\frac{A(T,s)}{K}, B(T,s), C(T,s), D(T,s)\Big) \tag{2.2}$$

where $\tau = T - t$ and $\Psi(\cdot)$ is defined by

$$\Psi(\eta_0,\eta_1,\eta_2,\eta_3;\xi_0,\xi_1,\xi_2,\xi_3;\gamma_0,\gamma_1,\gamma_2,\gamma_3)$$
$$= \frac{1}{(2\pi)^{3/2}} \int_{-\infty}^{\infty} \int_{-\infty}^{\infty} \int_{-\infty}^{\infty} I(\xi_0,\xi_1,\xi_2,\xi_3;\gamma_0,\gamma_1,\gamma_2,\gamma_3)\eta_0(\phi,\psi,\varphi,\tau)$$
$$\times e^{-\eta_1(\phi,\psi,\varphi,\tau)r - \eta_2(\phi,\psi,\varphi,\tau)\theta - \eta_3(\phi,\psi,\varphi,\tau)v}\, d\phi d\psi d\varphi,$$

$I(\cdot)$ *is defined by*

$$I(\xi_0,\xi_1,\xi_2,\xi_3;\gamma_0,\gamma_1,\gamma_2,\gamma_3)$$
$$\equiv \int \xi_0 e^{-ix_1\xi_1 - ix_2\xi_2 - ix_3\xi_3} 1_{\{\gamma_1 x_1 + \gamma_2 x_2 + \gamma_3 x_3 \le \gamma_0\}}\, dx_1 dx_2 dx_3,$$

and is given in Appendix D.

Introducing the following notations,

$$\alpha_1 = A(s-T),$$
$$\alpha_2 = \phi - iB(s-T),$$
$$\alpha_3 = \psi - iC(s-T),$$
$$\alpha_4 = \varphi - iD(s-T),$$
$$\alpha_5 = 1,$$
$$\alpha_6 = \phi,$$
$$\alpha_7 = \psi,$$
$$\alpha_8 = \varphi,$$
$$\beta_1 = \frac{A(\tau,\phi,\psi,\varphi)}{A(s-t)},$$
$$\beta_2 = B(\tau,\phi,\psi,\varphi) - B(s-t),$$
$$\beta_3 = C(\tau,\phi,\psi,\varphi) - C(s-t),$$
$$\beta_4 = D(\tau,\phi,\psi,\varphi) - D(s-t),$$
$$\beta_5 = \frac{A(\tau,\phi,\psi,\varphi)}{A(\tau)},$$
$$\beta_6 = B(\tau,\phi,\psi,\varphi) - B(\tau),$$
$$\beta_7 = C(\tau,\phi,\psi,\varphi) - C(\tau),$$

$$
\begin{aligned}
\beta_8 &= D(\tau, \phi, \psi, \varphi) - D(\tau), \\
\gamma_1 &= \ln \frac{A(T, s)}{K}, \\
\gamma_2 &= B(T, s), \\
\gamma_3 &= C(T, s), \\
\gamma_4 &= D(T, s),
\end{aligned}
$$

(2.2) can be written as

$$
\begin{aligned}
&C(r, \theta, v, t, T; s, K) \\
&= P(r, \theta, v, t; s)\Psi(\beta_1, \beta_2, \beta_3, \beta_4; \alpha_1, \alpha_2, \alpha_3, \alpha_4; \gamma_1, \gamma_2, \gamma_3, \gamma_4) \\
&\quad - P(r, \theta, v, t; T)K\Psi(\beta_5, \beta_6, \beta_7, \beta_8; \alpha_5, \alpha_6, \alpha_7, \alpha_8; \gamma_1, \gamma_2, \gamma_3, \gamma_4). \quad (2.3)
\end{aligned}
$$

European put options can be priced according to put-call parity:

$$
C(r, \theta, v, t, T; s, K) - V(r, \theta, v, t, T; s, K) = P(r, \theta, v, t; s) - KP(r, \theta, v, t; T),
$$

$$
0 \leq t \leq T \leq s,
$$

where $V(r, \theta, v, t, T; s, K)$ denotes the European put option value. It thus has

$$
\begin{aligned}
V(r, \theta, v, t, T; s, K) &= P(r, \theta, v, t; s)[\Psi(\beta; \alpha; \gamma) - 1] \\
&\quad - P(r, \theta, v, t; T)K\left[\Psi(\beta'; \alpha'; \gamma) - 1\right], \quad (2.4)
\end{aligned}
$$

where

$$
\beta = (\beta_1, \beta_2, \beta_3, \beta_4), \beta' = (\beta_5, \beta_6, \beta_7, \beta_8), \gamma = (\gamma_1, \gamma_2, \gamma_3, \gamma_4),
$$

$$
\alpha = (\alpha_1, \alpha_2, \alpha_3, \alpha_4), \alpha' = (\alpha_5, \alpha_6, \alpha_7, \alpha_8).
$$

Similar to the bond option formulas of CIR (1985) for a one-factor model and Longstaff and Schwartz (1992) for a two-factor model, our three-factor bond option price formula also involves integrations. Since the volatility and mean of interest rates are stochastic in our model, the bond option pricing formula (2.2) provides an extension to the existing literature on option pricing.

The pricing formula of bond options under the general interest rate dynamics can be written down by the general derivative valuation formula (1.21). Let $C_g(r, \theta, v, t, T; s, K)$ be the option price, then up to the first order[2]:

$$
C_g(r, \theta, v, t, T; s, K) = C(r, \theta, v, t, T; s, K)
$$

---

[2]See footnote [11] in Chapter 1. More specifically,

$$
\begin{aligned}
C_g &= \int (P_g - K)G dy + \int \int G\hat{V}C_g dy dl \\
&= \int \left(P + \sum_{i=1}^{\infty} P_i - K\right)G dy + \int \int G\hat{V}C_g dy dl
\end{aligned}
$$

$$+ \int G(y_1, y_2, y_3, l, r, \theta, v, t) \hat{V}(y_1, y_2, y_3, \partial_{y_1}, \partial_{y_2}, \partial_{y_3})$$
$$\times C(y_1, y_2, y_3, l, T; s, K) dy_1 dy_2 dy_3 dl, \qquad t \leq T \leq s,$$

where $G(y_1, y_2, y_3, l, r, \theta, v, t)$ is given in (1.18) and $\hat{V}(y_1, y_2, y_3, \partial_{y_1}, \partial_{y_2}, \partial_{y_3})$ is (1.16).

2.3 Caps, Floors, and Collars

An interest rate cap is a financial instrument that effectively places a maximum amount on the interest payments made on floating-rate debt. Many businesses borrow funds through loans or bonds on which a period interest payment varies according to a widely quoted short-term interest rate. The most important such rate is LIBOR. Other short-term rates that are used in conjunction with the cap and floor include commercial bank certificate of deposit rates, the prime interest rate, Treasury bill rates, commercial paper rates, and even certain tax-exempt interest rates. Although these cap and floor agreements are mainly issued by commercial banks, the default risk is not considered in this chapter; caps and floors are treated as default-free.

A standard cap is a strip of sequentially maturing European call options on an interest rate index. Each such option is called a caplet. More specifically, if the cap rate is h, the principal is L, and interest payments are made at times $\tau, 2\tau, ..n\tau$ from the beginning of the life of the cap, the writer of the cap is required to make payment at time $(k+1)\tau$ given by

$$\tau L \max(I_k - h, 0), \tag{2.5}$$

where τ is the reset interval, I_k is the actual interest rate for the period from $k\tau$ to $(k+1)\tau$, and h is the cap rate. Both I_k and h are assumed to be compounded once during each reset interval.

The discount value of the caplet payoff (2.5) at time $(t+1)\tau$ is equivalent to

$$\frac{\tau L}{1 + \tau I_k} \max[I_k - h, 0]$$

$$= \int (P - K) G dy + \int \int G \hat{V} C dy dl + \int \sum_{i=1}^{\infty} P_i G dy$$
$$+ \int \int \int G \hat{V} \sum_{i=1}^{\infty} P_i G dy dy' dl \ , ..$$

where arguments have been suppressed for notational simplicity. The third term in the above equation is the major error due to the difference in terminal payoffs between special and general dynamics.

at time $k\tau$, and can be further written as

$$\max\left[L - \frac{L(1+h\tau)}{1+\tau I_k}, 0\right].\qquad(2.6)$$

If the caplet is on the annual LIBOR rate, then I_k is given by the money market convention:

$$\tau I_k = \frac{1}{P(k\tau;(k+1)\tau)} - 1,$$

where $P(k\tau;(k+1)\tau)$ is the price at time $k\tau$ of a zero-coupon bond maturing at $(k+1)\tau$. The payoff (2.6) therefore becomes

$$\max\left[0, L - L(1+h\tau)P(k\tau;(k+1)\tau)\right]$$
$$= L(1+h\tau)\max\left[0, \frac{1}{1+h\tau} - P(k\tau;(k+1)\tau)\right].\qquad(2.7)$$

This expression shows that a caplet can be regarded as $L(1+h\tau)$ European puts with the exercise price $1/(1+h\tau)$ and expiration date $k\tau$ on a \$1 face value zero-coupon bond maturing at time $(k+1)\tau$. As a cap agreement is a sequence of such caplets, it can be treated as a portfolio of European options on zero-coupon bonds. Being a portfolio of individual options, a cap possesses many attributes common to most familiar exchange-traded options. For example, the valuation of a cap relies heavily on option pricing theory, and a cap price is often expressed in terms of the volatility level implied for the underlying interest rate indexes.

From the European put pricing formula (2.4) the value of the caplet $K_k(t,\tau)$ is given by

$$K_k(t,\tau) = L(1+h\tau)\left\{P(t;(k+1)\tau)\left[\Psi(\beta;\alpha;\gamma) - 1\right]\right.$$
$$\left. - \frac{1}{1+h\tau}P(t;k\tau)\left[\Psi(\beta';\alpha';\gamma) - 1\right]\right\},$$

where $\alpha_j, \beta_j, j = 1, ..., 8; \gamma_i, i = 1, 2, 3, 4$ can be obtained from relevant equations in section 2.2 with appropriate transformations.

The value of the cap is simply the sum of the values of these caplets:

$$K(t;\tau) = \sum_{k=1}^{n} K_k(t,\tau)$$
$$= L(1+h\tau)\left\{\sum_{k=1}^{n} P(t;(k+1)\tau)[\Psi(\beta;\alpha;\gamma) - 1]\right.$$
$$\left. - \frac{1}{1+h\tau}\sum_{k=1}^{n} P(t;k\tau)\left[\Psi(\beta';\alpha';\gamma) - 1\right]\right\}.\qquad(2.8)$$

An interest rate floor agreement can be interpreted analogously; a floor is equivalent to a string of call options with the same underlying instruments and settlements dates as the corresponding cap. Each call option of the floor has the same strike price which corresponds to the value of a zero coupon bond with the time to maturity equal to the reset interval and the yield to maturity equal to the floor rate. The value of the floor can be written as

$$
\begin{aligned}
F(t;\tau) &= \sum_{k=1}^{n} F_k(t,\tau) \\
&= L(1+m\tau)\Big\{\sum_{k=1}^{n} P(t;(k+1)\tau)\Psi(\beta;\alpha;\gamma) \\
&\quad -\frac{1}{1+m\tau}\sum_{k=1}^{n} P(t;k\tau)\Psi(\beta';\alpha';\gamma)\Big\},
\end{aligned}
\tag{2.9}
$$

where m is the floor rate.

A default-free collar is just a long position on a default-free cap and a short position on a default-free floor with the same settlement dates and reset interval. The price of a collar is therefore equal to the difference between the price of a put portfolio and the price of a call portfolio.

2.4 Futures Price and Forward Price

A futures or forward contract is a commitment to purchase or deliver a specified quality of goods on a designated date in the future for a price determined competitively when the contract is transacted. The difference between forward contracts and futures contracts is that futures contracts are subject to marking to market every day while forward contracts are not. Marking to market refers to the daily settlement of the difference between the contract price and the market price. The effect of marking to market is to rewrite the futures contract each day at the new futures price. Hence, the value of the futures contract after the daily settlement will be zero since the value of a newly written futures contract is always zero. Due to the day-to-day settlement of futures contracts, a futures price should be lower than the forward price on the same underlying asset.

The most actively traded futures contracts in the world are interest rate futures such as Eurodollar contracts or US T-bond futures. The Eurodollar futures contract, introduced by the Chicago Merchandise Exchange, is currently the most actively traded interest rate futures in the United States. The Eurodollar futures contract sets offered rates on three-month Eurodollar time deposits.

There is a difference between Eurodollar futures and Treasury-bill futures in their terminal payoffs. For Eurodollar futures, the terminal payoff is a yield while for the Treasury bill futures the terminal payoff depends on the price of a bond. The

Eurodollar futures price is equal to an index formed by subtracting the annualized return from 100.

The formulas for futures price and forward price have been derived by Cox-Ingersoll-Ross (1981) for a general valuation model, by Sundaresan (1991) for Eurodollar futures and by Feldman (1993) for T-bond futures. All of them are within the framework of one-factor models of interest rates. In this section forward and futures prices will be given in closed form under our three-factor model of interest rates.

Eurodollar Forward Price

The following symbols will be used in this section:

$$
\begin{aligned}
I(s;\tau) &= \text{index yield at time } s \text{ with maturity } \tau, \\
P(t;s) &= \text{bond price at time } t \text{ maturing at } s, \\
F(t;T_F) &= \text{futures price at time } t \text{ for futures contract maturing at } T_F, \\
W(t;s) &= \text{forward price at time } t \text{ for forward contract maturing at } s.
\end{aligned}
$$

The Eurodollar forward contract is an agreement (established at $t \leq s$) to pay or receive on maturity date s an amount equal to

$$100[1 - I(s;90)]$$

at a currently agreed upon forward price $W(t;s)$. The contract is not marked to market and settles by cash on the maturity date s. The index yield $I(s;90)$, or more generally $I(s;\tau)$, may be expressed in terms of underlying state variables. The annualized LIBOR at time s on a Eurodollar time deposit with a maturity τ is defined by the money market convention,

$$I(s;\tau) = \frac{1}{\tau}\left(\frac{1}{P(s;s+\tau)} - 1\right), \tag{2.10}$$

where $P(s; s + \tau)$ is the price at time s of a discount bond paying \$1 at time $s + \tau$ in the interbank market.

The forward price at time t is to make the true price of a forward contract zero, so

$$E_Q\left[e^{-\int_t^s r(u)du}(100(1 - I(s;\tau)) - W(t;s))\right] = 0.$$

The forward price is therefore given by

$$W(t;s) = \frac{E_Q\left[e^{-\int_t^s r(u)du}(100(1 - I(s;\tau)) \mid \mathcal{F}_t\right]}{E_Q\left[e^{-\int_t^s r(u)du}\right]}. \tag{2.11}$$

By the Green's function method,

$$E_Q\left[e^{-\int_t^s r(u)du}\left(100(1-I(s;\tau))\right)\mid \mathcal{F}_t\right] = \int \left(100(1-I(s;\tau))\right)G(y,s,r,\theta,v,t)dy$$

Simplifying the integral yields the following proposition.

Proposition 9: *Let $W(t;s)$ be the forward price for a Eurodollar forward contract that matures at time s with a terminal value*

$$W(s;s) = 100[1-I(s;\tau)].$$

Under our three-factor model of interest rates, $W(t;s)$ is given by

$$W(t;s) = 100 - \frac{100}{\tau P(t;s)}\left\{A^*(t,s)e^{-B^*(t,s)r-C^*(t,s)\theta-D^*(t,s)v} - 1\right\} \quad (2.12)$$

where r,θ, and v are the values of three factors at time t, $P(t;s)$ is the bond price formula and

$$A^*(t,s) = \left(\frac{X^{\frac{\nu'}{2k}}(\Gamma J_\rho(Z) + Y_\rho(Z))}{\Gamma J_\rho(\sqrt{2(1+B(\tau)k)}\zeta/k) + Y_\rho(\sqrt{2(1+B(\tau)k)}\zeta/k)}\right)^{-\frac{2\nu\bar\theta}{\zeta^2}}$$

$$\times \left(\frac{e^{\lambda(X-1)}X^\delta(\Lambda M(T,S,Y) + (\frac{-Y}{2\lambda})^{1-S}M(1+T-S,2-S;Y))}{\Lambda M(T,S;-2\lambda) + M(1+T-S,2-S;-2\lambda)}\right)^{-\frac{2\mu\bar v}{\eta^2}},$$

$$B^*(t,s) = -B(\tau)e^{-k(s-t)} + \frac{1}{k}(1-e^{-k(s-t)}),$$

$$C^*(t,s) = -\frac{\nu'}{\zeta^2} - \frac{kZ\left[\Omega(J_{\rho-1}(Z)-J_{\rho+1}(Z))+Y_{\rho-1}(Z)-Y_{\rho+1}(Z)\right]}{2\zeta^2(\Omega J_\rho(Z) + Y_\rho(Z))},$$

$$D^*(t,s) = \frac{1}{\eta^2}(kY - 2k\delta - 2kY[\frac{\Lambda T}{S}M(T+1,S+1;Y)$$

$$+\frac{S-1}{2\lambda}X^{-S}M(1+T-S,2-S;Y)$$

$$+\frac{1+T-S}{2-S}X^{1-S}M(2+T-S,3-S;Y)]$$

$$(\Lambda M(T,S;Y) + X^{1-S}M(1+T-S,2-S;Y))^{-1}),$$

$$X = e^{-k(s-t)},$$

$$Y = -2\lambda e^{-k(s-t)},$$

$$Z = \frac{\sqrt{2(1+B(\tau)k)}\zeta e^{-k(s-t)/2}}{k},$$

$$\Gamma = -\frac{(Y_{\rho-1}(\iota) - Y_{\rho+1}(\iota)) - Y_\rho(\iota)\omega}{(J_{\rho-1}(\iota) - J_{\rho+1}(\iota)) - J_\rho(\iota)\omega},$$

$$\Lambda = \frac{(1-S)(-2\lambda)^{-1}M_2 + \frac{1+T-S}{2-S}M_4 - HM_2}{\frac{T}{S}M_3 - HM_1},$$

$$\omega = -\frac{-C(\tau)\zeta^2 + \nu'}{\sqrt{2(1+B(\tau)k)}\zeta},$$

$$H = \frac{-D(\tau)\eta^2}{4k\lambda} + \frac{1}{2} + \frac{\delta}{2\lambda},$$

$$M_1 = M(T,S;-2\lambda),$$

$$M_2 = M(1+T-S,2-S,-2\lambda),$$

$$M_3 = M(T+1,S+1;-2\lambda),$$

$$M_4 = M(2+T-S,3-S;-2\lambda),$$

$$\rho = \frac{\sqrt{2\zeta^2 + \nu'^2}}{k},$$

$$T = \delta + \frac{1}{2}(1-\frac{\mu'}{k}) + \frac{\beta}{2\lambda},$$

$$S = \frac{1}{k}[\mu' + \sqrt{\mu'^2 - 4\alpha k^2}] + (1-\frac{\mu'}{k}),$$

$$\alpha = (1-2k\lambda_r)\frac{\eta^2}{4k^4},$$

$$\beta = -\frac{\eta^2}{2k^4}(1-k\lambda_r)(1+B(\tau)k),$$

$$\delta = \frac{1}{2k}[\mu' + \sqrt{\mu'^2 - 4\alpha k^2}],$$

$$\lambda = \frac{\eta i}{2k^2}(1+B(\tau)k),$$

$$\iota = \frac{\sqrt{2(1+B(\tau)k)}\zeta}{k},$$

where $A(\tau), B(\tau), C(\tau)$, and $D(\tau)$ are given in the bond price formula.

The Eurodollar forward price under the general interest rate dynamics can be written down by the general derivative valuation formula (1.21). Let $W_g(t;s)$ be the price, then up to the first order correction[3]

$$W_g(r,\theta,v,t;s) = W(r,\theta,v,t;s) + \int\int\int\int G(y_1,y_2,y_3,l,r,\theta,v,t)$$
$$\times \hat{V}(y_1,y_2,y_3,\partial_{y_1},\partial_{y_2},\partial_{y_3})W(t;l)dy_1 dy_2 dy_3 dl, t \le s$$

where $W(r,\theta,v,l;t)$ and $W(r,\theta,v,l;s)$ are given in formula (2.12) and $\hat{V}(y_1,y_2,y_3,\partial_{y_1},\partial_{y_2},\partial_{y_3})$ is given by (1.16). Again the four dimensional integral in the pricing formula needs to be evaluated by numerical methods.

Bond Futures Price

The price at t of a futures contract, delivering at T_F a unit of a discount bond maturing at $T_F + \tau$, is given by the expected payoff with respect to Q:

$$F(t;T_F) = E_Q[P(T_F;\tau) \mid \mathcal{F}_t] \tag{2.13}$$

[3]See footnote [11] in Chapter 1 and footnote [2] in Chapter 2.

By the Feynman-Kac method, under some regularity conditions, $F(t; T_F)$ solves the following PDE (Cox-Ingersoll-Ross (1981), Sundaresan (1991), and Feldman (1993)) [4]:

$$\frac{1}{2}vF_{rr} + \frac{1}{2}\eta^2 vF_{vv} + \frac{1}{2}\zeta^2\theta F_{\theta\theta} + [k(\theta - r) + \lambda_r v]F_r +$$
$$[\nu\bar{\theta} - \nu'\theta]F_\theta + [\mu\bar{v} - \acute{\mu}v]F_v + F_t = 0, \qquad (2.14)$$

with the initial condition

$$F(T_F; T_F) = P(T_F; \tau). \qquad (2.15)$$

Solving PDE (2.14) with (2.15) yields the following proposition.

Proposition 10: *Let $P(T_F; \tau)$ be the bond price at time T_F maturing at τ. Let $F(t; T_F)$ be the futures price at time t for a futures contract that matures at time T_F with the terminal value*

$$F(T_F; T_F) = P(T_F; \tau). \qquad (2.16)$$

Under our three-factor model of interest rates, the futures price is given by

$$F(t; T_F) = A'(t, T_F, \tau)e^{-B'(t,T_F,\tau)r - C'(t,T_F,\tau)\theta - D'(t,T_F,\tau)v}, \qquad (2.17)$$

where r, θ, and v are the values of three factors at time t and

$$A'(t, T_F, \tau) = \left(\frac{X^{h/2}(\Gamma J_h(Z) + Y_h(Z))}{\Gamma J_h(\sqrt{2}\zeta/k) + Y_h(\sqrt{2}\zeta/k)}\right)^{-\frac{2\nu\bar{\theta}}{\zeta^2}}$$
$$\times \left(\frac{e^{\lambda(X-1)}X^{\frac{\nu'}{k}}(\Lambda M(T, S, Y) + Y^{1-T}M(1 + T - S, 2 - S; Y))}{\Lambda M(T, S; -2\lambda) + (2\lambda)^{1-T}M(1 + T - S, 2 - S; -2\lambda)}\right)^{-\frac{2\mu\bar{v}}{\eta^2}},$$

$$B'(t, T_F, \tau) = B(\tau)e^{-k(T_F - t)},$$
$$C'((t, T_F, \tau) = \frac{-\nu'}{\zeta^2} - kZ\left\{\frac{\Omega(J_{h-1}(Z) - J_{h+1}(Z)) + Y_{h-1}(Z) - Y_{h+1}(Z)}{2\zeta^2(\Omega J_h(Z) + Y_h(Z))}\right\},$$
$$D'(t, T_F, \tau) = \frac{1}{\eta^2}\left\{kY - 2\nu' - 2kY\left[\frac{\Lambda T}{S}M(T + 1, S + 1; Y) + \frac{S - 1}{2\lambda}X^{-S}M(1 + T - S, 2 - S; Y)\right.\right.$$
$$\left.+ \frac{1 + T - S}{2 - S}X^{1-S}M(2 + T - S, 3 - S; Y)\right]$$
$$\times(\Lambda M(T, S; Y) + X^{1-S}M(1 + T - S, 2 - S; Y))^{-1}\bigg\},$$

---

[4]The PDE is similar to the PDE for forward prices except that there is no term rF. This difference is due to the marking to market for the futures contract.

and

$$
\begin{aligned}
X &= e^{-k(T_F - t)}, \\
Y &= -2\lambda X, \\
Z &= \kappa X^{1/2}, \\
\Omega &= -\frac{2\nu' Y_h(\kappa) - k\kappa(Y_{h-1}(\kappa) - Y_{h+1}(\kappa)) + C(\tau)\zeta^2 Y_h}{2\nu' J_h(\kappa) - k\kappa(J_{h-1}(\kappa) - J_{h+1}(\kappa)) + C(\tau)\zeta^2 J_h}, \\
\Lambda &= \frac{(1-S)(-2\lambda)^{-1} M_2 + \frac{1+T-S}{2-S} M_4 - H M_2}{\frac{T}{S} M_3 - H M_1}, \\
M_1 &= M(T, S; -2\lambda), \\
M_2 &= M(1 + T - S, 2 - S, -2\lambda), \\
M_3 &= M(T + 1, S + 1; -2\lambda), \\
M_4 &= M(2 + T - S, 3 - S; -2\lambda), \\
H &= \frac{1}{2\lambda}(\lambda + h + \frac{D(\tau)\eta^2}{2k}), \\
S &= 1 + h, \\
T &= \frac{S}{2} + \frac{\eta^2 \lambda_r B(\tau)}{4k^2 \lambda}, \\
h &= \frac{\nu'}{k}, \\
\kappa &= \frac{i\zeta\sqrt{2B(\tau)}}{k}, \\
\lambda &= -i\frac{\eta B(\tau)}{2k},
\end{aligned}
$$

where $A(\tau), B(\tau), C(\tau),$ and $D(\tau)$ are given in the bond price formula.

The futures price under the general interest rate dynamics can be written down by formula (1.21). Let $F_g(t; T_F)$ be the price, then up to the first order correction:

$$
\begin{aligned}
F_g(r, \theta, v, t; T_F) &= F(r, \theta, v, t; T_F) + \int \int \int \int G(y_1, y_2, y_3, l, r, \theta, v, t) \\
&\quad \times \hat{V}(y_1, y_2, y_3, \partial_{y_1}, \partial_{y_2}, \partial_{y_3}) F(l; T_F) dy_1 dy_2 dy_3 dl. \quad (2.18)
\end{aligned}
$$

2.5 Swaps

An interest rate swap is an agreement between two institutions in which each commits to make periodic payments to the other based on a predetermined amount of notional principle for a predetermined maturity. The periodic payments may be either fixed or float with an agreed-upon floating index such as the six-month LIBOR.

The so-called generic interest rate swap refers to a floating to fixed swap in which the payment made by one counterparty is based on a floating interest rate while the payment made by the other counterparty is based on a fixed interest rate.

The typical swap mandates the fixed-rate payer to make a fixed payment every year. A second party, the floating-rate payer, makes several payments each year.

Interest rate swaps are often motivated by a desire to reduce the cost of financing. In this case, one party has access to comparatively cheap fixed-rate funding but desires floating-rate funding while the other party has access to comparatively cheap floating-rate funding but desires fixed-rate funding. By entering into a swap with a swap dealer, both parties can obtain the form of funding they desire and simultaneously exploit their relative borrowing advantages.

The groundwork for pricing swaps is the valuation of floating-rate instruments. A generic interest rate swap can be evaluated by finding the level of fixed payment that will have the same present value as the floating-rate payment (Ramaswamy and Sundaresan (1986)). In this section a valuation formula for generic interest rate swaps is derived under our three-factor model of interest rates.

The following symbols will be used in this section:

$$
\begin{aligned}
s_i, i = 1, 2.., n &= \text{a sequence of reset dates,} \\
t_p(s_i), i = 1, 2, .., n &= \text{a sequence of payment dates,} \\
I(s_i) &= \text{index yield,} \\
\tau &= \text{the time to maturity of the index,} \\
P(t; T) &= \text{bond prices at time } t \text{ maturing at } T.
\end{aligned}
$$

For the annualized LIBOR, by convention:

$$
I(s) = \frac{1}{\tau} \left(\frac{1}{P(s; s+\tau)} - 1 \right),
$$

where $P(s; s + \tau)$ is the bond price.

A generic swap is an exchange of a sequence of fixed payments $\{c\}$ with a sequence of floating payments $\{I(s_i)\}$ such that

$$
\sum_{i=1}^{n} PV_t[c; t_p(s_i)] = \sum_{i=1}^{n} PV_t[I(s_i); t_p(s_i)],
$$

where $PV_t[\alpha, t_s]$ denotes the present value at time t of a sequence of payments $\{\alpha\}$ made at t_s. If the reset dates s_i and payment dates $t_p(s_i)$ coincide, then the multi-period swap is a portfolio of single-period swaps, each of which is a forward contract on the floating index. If the two dates do not coincide, then the multi-period swap is a portfolio of a random number $P(s; t_p(s))$ of forward contracts with payments brought back to the reset dates (see Ramaswamy and Sundaresan (1986)).

Let us consider a basic element of a swap, a floating rate payment of $\tau I(s)$ at s:

$$
\tau I(s) \equiv \frac{1}{P(s; s+\tau)} - 1.
$$

Let the value at time t of this payment be $V(t; s)$. It is the value of a forward contract similar to the one derived in section 2.4 and is given by

$$V(t; s) = A^*(t, s)e^{-B^*(t,s)r - C^*(t,s)\theta - D^*(t,s)v} - P(t; s), \tag{2.19}$$

where $A^*(t, s), B^*(t, s), C^*(t, s)$, and $D^*(t, s)$ are given in section 2.4.

With this formula, the value of a sequence of payments $\{I(s_i)\}$ can be obtained by summing the present value for each payment

$$\sum_{i=1}^{n} V(t, s_i).$$

Equating it with the present value of a sequence of fixed rate payments,

$$\sum_{i=1}^{n} cP(t, s_i),$$

leads to

$$c = \frac{\sum_{i=1}^{n} \left[A^*(t, s_i)e^{-B^*(t,s_i)r - C^*(t,s_i)\theta - D^*(t,s_i)v} - P(t; s_i) \right]}{\sum_{i=1}^{n} P(t; s_i)}.$$

The pair, $\{c, I(s_i)\}$, constitutes a swap at equilibrium.

2.6 Quality Delivery Options

An investor who has an open short position in T-bond (T-note) futures contracts during the delivery month has the flexibility of delivering one or more T-bonds (T-notes) from a set of deliverable securities. This flexibility is called quality delivery option.

Gay and Manaster (1984), Boyle (1989), Boyle and Tse (1990), and Hemler (1990), among others, have analyzed quality delivery options. This section is to evaluate the quality option in T-bond futures given our three factor model of interest rates. Like most papers on the quality options, this paper assumes that all contracts are delivered on some predetermined day. Although this assumption is undesirable, studies of quality options typically have ignored timing options.

The T-bond futures contract requires the short position to deliver either $\frac{1}{a_1}$ bond of type 1, $\frac{1}{a_2}$ bond of type 2, ... or $\frac{1}{a_n}$ bond of type n. Since the short position will deliver the cheapest-to-deliver bond, the value of the underlying asset at the maturity T is

$$\min_{i=1,..,n} \left\{ \frac{P(T, T_i)}{a_i} \right\},$$

where $P(t, T_i)$ is the time t price of the ith bond characterized by its maturity T_i and conversion factor a_i.

Following a reasoning similar to that of several other papers (Cox-Ingersoll-Ross (1981), Sundaresan (1991)), it can be shown that given our three-factor model of interest rates, the futures price for a futures contract that provides the short position with the option to deliver at maturity T any one of n discount bonds in exchange for the futures price, denoted $F(t, T)$, satisfies the PDE

$$\frac{1}{2}vF_{rr} + \frac{1}{2}\eta^2vF_{vv} + \frac{1}{2}\zeta^2\theta F_{\theta\theta} + [k(\theta - r) + \lambda_r v]F_r + [\nu\bar{\theta} - \nu'\theta]F_\theta + [\mu\bar{v} - \acute{\mu}v]F_v + F_t = 0, \tag{2.20}$$

and the boundary condition:

$$F(T, T) = \min_{i=1,..,n} \left\{ \frac{P(T, T_i)}{a_i} \right\}.$$

To solve this problem, one needs to calculate the Green's function for PDE (2.20), which is slightly different from the fundamental evaluation PDE in Chapter 1. Let $G(r, \theta, v, t, x_1, x_2, x_3, T)$ be the Green's function, the solution to (2.20) is

$$\begin{aligned} F(t, T) &= \int \min\left\{ \frac{P(x_1, x_2, x_3, T, T_1)}{a_1}, ..., \frac{P(x_1, x_2, x_3, T, T_n)}{a_n} \right\} \\ &\qquad G(x_1, x_2, x_3, T, r, \theta, v, t)dx_1 dx_2 dx_3 \\ &= \sum_1^n \int_{\mathcal{B}_i} \left\{ \frac{P(x_1, x_2, x_3, T, T_i)}{a_i} \right\} G(x_1, x_2, x_3, T, r, \theta, v, t)dx_1 dx_2 dx_3, \end{aligned}$$

where $\mathcal{B}_i$ is defined by

$$\begin{aligned} \mathcal{B}_i &= \left\{ (x_1, x_2, x_3) \in R^3 | \frac{P(x_1, x_2, x_3, T, T_j)}{a_j} \le \frac{P(x_1, x_2, x_3, T, T_i)}{a_i}, \forall i \neq j \right\} \\ &= \left\{ (x_1, x_2, x_3) \in R^3 | (B_j - B_i)x_1 + (C_j - C_i)x_2 + (D_j - D_i)x_3 \ge K_{ji}, \right. \\ &\qquad \left. \forall j > i; (B_j - B_i)x_1 + (C_j - C_i)x_2 + (D_j - D_i)x_3 \le K_{ji}, \forall j < i \right\}, \end{aligned}$$

where

$$K_{ji} \equiv \ln \frac{A_j a_i}{A_i a_j},$$

$$B_j \equiv B(\tau_j) \equiv B(T_j - T), C_j \equiv C(T_j - T), j = 1, 2, .., n,$$

etc. So,

$$\mathcal{B}_1 \cup \mathcal{B}_2 \cup ... \cup \mathcal{B}_n = (-\infty, \infty) \times [0, \infty) \times [0, \infty).$$

Defining

$$\underline{K}_j = \max_{i<j} \ln \frac{A_j a_i}{A_i a_j}, \quad \overline{K}_j = \min_{i>j} \ln \frac{A_j a_i}{A_i a_j},$$

$\mathcal{B}_j$ can be rewritten as

$$
\mathcal{B}_j = \begin{cases} (x_1, x_2, , x_3) \in R^3 \mid \underline{K}_j \le (B_j - B_i)x_1 + (C_j - C_i)x_2 + (D_j - D_i)x_3 \\ \qquad\qquad \le \overline{K}_j, \ \ \text{if } \underline{K}_j < \overline{K}_j \\ \varnothing, \text{otherwise} \end{cases}
$$

and

$$
\int_{\mathcal{B}_j} \left\{ \frac{P(x_1, x_2, x_3, T, T_j)}{a_j} \right\} G(x_1, x_2, x_3, T, r, \theta, v, t) dx_1 dx_2 dx_3
$$

$$
= \int \frac{P(T, T_j)}{a_j} 1_{\{(B_j - B_i)x_1 + (C_j - C_i)x_2 + (D_j - D_i)x_3 \le \overline{K}_j\}}
$$
$$
\times G(x_1, x_2, x_3, T, r, \theta, v, t) dx_1 dx_2 dx_3
$$
$$
- \int \frac{P(T, T_i)}{a_i} 1_{\{(B_j - B_i)x_1 + (C_j - C_i)x_2 + (D_j - D_i)x_3 \le \underline{K}_j\}}
$$
$$
\times G(x_1, x_2, x_3, T, r, \theta, v, t) dx_1 dx_2 dx_3
$$

$$
= \begin{cases} \Psi(\beta_1, \beta_2, \beta_3, \beta_4; \alpha_{1j}, \alpha_{2j}, \alpha_{3j}, \alpha_{4j}; \gamma_{1j}, \gamma_{2j}, \gamma_{3j}, \gamma_{4j}) \\ \qquad - \Psi(\beta_1, \beta_2, \beta_3, \beta_4; \alpha_{1j}, \alpha_{2j}, \alpha_{3j}, \alpha_{4j}; \gamma'_{1j}, \gamma_{2j}, \gamma_{3j}, \gamma_{4j}), \ (2.21) \\ \text{if } \underline{K}_j < \overline{K}_j \\ 0, \qquad \text{otherwise} \end{cases}
$$

where $\Psi(\cdot)$ is defined in section 2.2. The following proposition summarizes the results.

Proposition 11: *Let $F(r, \theta, v, t; T)$ be the futures price at time t for a futures contract that provides the short position with the option to deliver one of n discount bonds in exchange for the futures price. Given our three-factor model of interest rates, the futures price is*

$$
F(t, T) \equiv F(r, \theta, v, t; T)
$$
$$
= \sum_{j=1}^{n} \Big(\Psi(\beta_1, \beta_2, \beta_3, \beta_4; \alpha_{1j}, \alpha_{2j}, \alpha_{3j}, \alpha_{4j}; \gamma_{1j}, \gamma_{2j}, \gamma_{3j}, \gamma_{4j})
$$
$$
- \Psi(\beta_1, \beta_2, \beta_3, \beta_4; \alpha_{1j}, \alpha_{2j}, \alpha_{3j}, \alpha_{4j}; \gamma'_{1j}, \gamma_{2j}, \gamma_{3j}, \gamma_{4j}) \Big),
$$

$$(2.22)$$

with

$$
\begin{aligned}
\alpha_{1j} &= A(T_j - T), \\
\alpha_{2j} &= \phi - iB(T_j - T), \\
\alpha_{3j} &= \psi - iC(T_j - T), \\
\alpha_{4j} &= \varphi - iD(T_j - T), \\
\beta_1 &= \frac{A(\phi, \psi, \varphi, T - s)}{a_j},
\end{aligned}
$$

$$
\begin{aligned}
\beta_2 &= B(\phi, \psi, \varphi, T - s), \\
\beta_3 &= C(\phi, \psi, \varphi, T - s), \\
\beta_4 &= D(\phi, \psi, \varphi, T - s), \\
\gamma_{1j} &= \min_{i>j} \left(\ln(A(T_j - T)a_i) - \ln(A(T_i - T)a_j) \right), \\
\gamma'_{1j} &= \max_{i<j} \left(\ln(A(T_j - T)a_i) - \ln(A(T_i - T)a_j) \right), \\
\gamma_{2j} &= B(T_j - T) - B(T_i - T), \\
\gamma_{3j} &= C(T_j - T) - C(T_i - T), \\
\gamma_{2j} &= D(T_j - T) - D(T_i - T),
\end{aligned}
$$

with $A(T_j - T), B(T_j - T), C(T_j - T), D(T_j - T)$ given in the bond price formula and $A(\phi, \psi, \varphi, T - s), B(\phi, \psi, \varphi, T - s), C(\phi, \psi, \varphi, T - s), D(\phi, \psi, \varphi, T - s)$ given in the Green's function formula.

2.7 Futures Options

Futures options are written on commodities as well as financial futures and are now traded on many different exchanges. A futures option requires the delivery of an underlying futures contract when exercised. If a call futures option is exercised, the holder acquires a long position in the underlying futures contract plus a cash amount equal to the current futures price minus the exercise price. If a put futures option is exercised, the holder acquires a short position in the underlying futures contract plus a cash amount equal to the exercise price minus the current futures price. The most popular interest rate futures options are the T-bond futures options traded on CBOT and the Eurodollar futures options traded on the IMM.

Ramaswamy and Sundaresan (1986), Barone-Adesi and Whaley (1987), and Feldman (1993), among others, have studied the pricing of both financial and commodity futures options under one-factor models of interest rates with constant volatility. This section is devoted to the pricing of T-bond futures options under our three-factor model of interest rates.

Let $F(r, \theta, v, t; T_F, T)$ be the futures price at time t for a T-bond futures contract that matures at T_F. The contract is written on a T-bond that matures at time T; the prevailing short rate, short mean, and short rate volatility at time t are r, θ, and v, respectively, and $t \leq T_F \leq T$. Let $C_F(r, \theta, v, t; T_C, T_F, T, K)$ be the price at time t of a European call option that expires at time T_C. The option is written on the aforementioned futures contract. The exercise price of the option is K and $t < T_C < T_F < T$.

At the expiration date T_C,

$$
C_F(r, \theta, v, T_C; T_C, T_F, T, K) = [F(r, \theta, v, T_C; T_F, T) - K]^+
$$

$$\equiv \quad \max(0, F(r, \theta, v, T_C; T_F, T) - K) \tag{2.23}$$

where $F(r, \theta, v, t; T_F, T) \equiv F(t; T_F, T) \equiv F(t; T_F, \tau)$, the futures price, is given by

$$F(t; T_F, \tau) \quad = \quad A'(t, T_F, \tau) e^{-B'(t, T_F, \tau)r - C'(t, T_F, \tau)\theta - D'(t, T_F, \tau)v},$$
$$t \le T_F \le T_F + \tau \equiv T, \tag{2.24}$$

where functions $A'(t, T_F, \tau), B'(t, T_F, \tau), C'(t, T_F, \tau)$, and $D'(t, T_F, \tau)$ are given in section 2.4. Using the Green's function method, the price of the futures option is given by

$$C_F(r, \theta, v, t; T_C, T_F, T, K) =$$
$$\int^B [F(y, T_C; T_F, \tau) - K]G(y, T_C, r, \theta, v, t)dy, \tag{2.25}$$

where $y = (y_1, y_2, y_3) = (r(T_C), \theta(T_C), v(T_C))$ and $G(r, \theta, v, t, y_1, y_2, y_3, T_C)$ is the Green's function for the fundamental valuation PDE for interest rate derivatives and B is the range of values of r, θ, and v over which the futures option is in the money at the expiration date T_C and is defined by the following inequality:

$$B'(T_C, T_F, \tau)r(T_C) + C'(T_C, T_F, \tau)\theta(T_C)$$
$$+D'(T_C, T_F, \tau)v(T_C) \le K^* \equiv \ln \frac{A'(T_C, T_F, \tau)}{K}.$$

Some calculations lead to in the following proposition.

Proposition 12: *Let $F(r, \theta, v, t; T_F, T)$ be the futures price at time t for a futures contract that matures at time T_F. The contract is written on a default-free unit discount bond that matures at time T and the prevailing spot rate, short mean, and short rate volatility at time t are r, θ, and v respectively. Let $C_F(r, \theta, v, t; T_C, T_F, T, K)$ be the price at time t of a European call option which is written on the futures contract. The exercise price of the option is K and its maturity is T_C, with $t < T_C < T_F < T$. Given the special interest rate dynamics, $C_F(r, \theta, v, t; T_C, T_F, T, K)$ is given by*

$$C_F(r, \theta, v, t, T_C, T_F; T, K)$$
$$= F(r, \theta, v, t; T_F, T)\Psi(\beta_1, \beta_2, \beta_3, \beta_4; \alpha_1, \alpha_2, \alpha_3, \alpha_4; \gamma_1, \gamma_2, \gamma_3, \gamma_4)$$
$$-P(r, \theta, v, t; T)K\Psi(\beta_5, \beta_6, \beta_7, \beta_8; \alpha_5, \alpha_6, \alpha_7, \alpha_8; \gamma_1, \gamma_2, \gamma_3, \gamma_4), \tag{2.26}$$

where $F(r, \theta, v, t; T_F, T)$ is the futures price and $P(r, \theta, v, t; T)$ is the bond price. Function $\Psi(\cdot)$ and parametrs are defined in the following:

$$\Psi(\eta_0, \eta_1, \eta_2, \eta_3; \xi_0, \xi_1, \xi_2, \xi_3; \gamma_0, \gamma_1, \gamma_2, \gamma_3) = \frac{1}{(2\pi)^{3/2}} \int_{-\infty}^{\infty} \int_{-\infty}^{\infty} \int_{-\infty}^{\infty} \eta_0(\Phi, \tau)$$

$$e^{-\eta_1(\Phi,\tau)r-\eta_2(\Phi,\tau)\theta-\eta_3(\Phi,\tau)v}I(\xi_0,\xi_1,\xi_2,\xi_3;\gamma_0,\gamma_1,\gamma_2,\gamma_3)d\phi d\psi d\varphi$$

$$I(\xi_0,\xi_1,\xi_2,\xi_3;\gamma_0,\gamma_1,\gamma_2,\gamma_3) \equiv \int \alpha_0 e^{-ix_1\xi_1-ix_2\xi_2-ix_3\xi_3}$$
$$\times 1_{\{x_1\gamma_1+x_2\gamma_2+x_3\gamma_3\le\gamma_0\}}dx_1\,dx_2\,dx_3,$$

$$\alpha_1 = A'(T_C,T_F,T),$$
$$\alpha_2 = \phi - iB'(T_C,T_F,T),$$
$$\alpha_3 = \psi - iC'(T_C,T_F,T),$$
$$\alpha_4 = \varphi - iD'(T_C,T_F,T),$$
$$\alpha_5 = 1,$$
$$\alpha_6 = \phi,$$
$$\alpha_7 = \psi,$$
$$\alpha_8 = \varphi,$$
$$\beta_1 = \frac{A(\tau,\phi,\psi,\varphi)}{A'(t,T_F,T)},$$
$$\beta_2 = B(\tau,\phi,\psi,\varphi) - B'(t,T_F,T),$$
$$\beta_3 = C(\tau,\phi,\psi,\varphi) - C(t,T_F,T),$$
$$\beta_4 = D(\tau,\phi,\psi,\varphi) - D(t,T_F,T),$$
$$\beta_5 = \frac{A(\tau,\phi,\psi,\varphi)}{A(\tau)},$$
$$\beta_6 = B(\tau,\phi,\psi,\varphi) - B(\tau),$$
$$\beta_7 = C(\tau,\phi,\psi,\varphi) - C(\tau),$$
$$\beta_8 = D(\tau,\phi,\psi,\varphi) - D(\tau),$$
$$\gamma_1 = \ln\frac{A'(T_C,T_F,T)}{K},$$
$$\gamma_2 = B'(T_C,T_F,T),$$
$$\gamma_3 = C'(T_C,T_F,T),$$
$$\gamma_4 = D'(T_C,T_F,T),$$

where $A(\tau), B(\tau), C(\tau)$, and $D(\tau)$ are known functions given in the bond price formula; $A'(T_C,T_F,T)$, $B'(T_C,T_F,T), C'(T_C,T_F,T)$, and $D'(T_C,T_F,T)$ are given in the futures price formula; and $A(\tau,\phi,\psi,\varphi), B(\tau,\phi,\psi,\varphi), C(\tau,\phi,\psi,\varphi)$, and $\hspace{6cm} D(\tau,\phi,\psi,$ $\varphi)$ are in the Green's function formula.

Since the underlying bond makes no payment through the life of the option, a bond option is never exercised early. By contrast, the bond futures option may be exercised early. For a bond futures option, the underlying futures price is the value of a contract that pays a continuous cash flow equal to the prevailing interest rate times the prevailing futures price, plus a single payment at the maturity of the value of the bond on which it is written. The continuous cash flow associated with the bond futures price may induce the early exercise of a bond futures option.

The value, $V(x, t, T_C, T_F, T)$, of the futures put can be valuated as the following

$$
\begin{aligned}
V(x, t, T_C, T_F, T) &= \int_{\mathcal{R}^3 - B} (K - F(y, T_C, T_F, T)) G(y, T_C, x, t) dy \\
&= \int_{\mathcal{R}^3} (K - F(y, T_C, T_F, T)) G(y, T_C, x, t) dy \\
&\quad + \int_B (F(y, T_C, T_F, T) - K) G(y, T_C, x, t) dy \\
&= K P(x, t, T_C) - F(x, t, T_F, T) + C(x, t, T_C, T_F, T),
\end{aligned}
$$

where $C(x, t, T_C, T_F, T)$ is given in (2.26) and $F(x, t, T_F, T)$ is given in (2.17).

2.8　American Options

The valuation of American options on equity are given in Barone-Adesi and Waley (1987), Kim (1990), Carr, Jarrow and Myneni (1992), among others. The valuation of American options on bonds under one-factor model of interest rates are given in Chesney, Elliott and Gibson (1993) and Yu (1993). This section will present a quasi-closed-form solution to American bond option pricing under our model of interest rates in which the volatility of interest rates is stochastic.

Consider an American call that has an exercise price of K and expires at time T. Assume that the option is written on a coupon bond paying a continuous dividend at a rate of $\alpha(t)$ and maturing at time τ, $\tau \geq T$. Also assume a perfect market, continuous trading and no arbitrage opportunities. Let $V(r, \theta, v, t, T, \tau), V : \mathcal{R}^3 \times [0, T] \to \mathcal{R}$ be the value at time t of the American option. Let $P(r, \theta, v, t, \tau) \equiv P(t, \tau), \tau \geq T$ be the value at time t of the bond.

The value of the American call option is the solution to the fundamental valuation PDE,

$$
\begin{aligned}
L[V(r, \theta, v, t, T, \tau)] &= \frac{1}{2} v V_{rr} + \frac{1}{2} \eta^2 v V_{vv} + \frac{1}{2} \zeta^2 \theta V_{\theta\theta} + [k(\theta - r) + \lambda_r v] V_r \\
&\quad + [\nu\bar\theta - \nu'\theta] V_\theta + [\mu\bar v - \mu v] V_v + V_t - r V = 0,
\end{aligned}
$$

subject to the following boundary conditions:

$$
\begin{aligned}
V(r, \theta, v, T, T, \tau) &= \max[0, P(r, \theta, v, T, \tau) - K], &\quad (2.27) \\
\lim_{(r,\theta,v) \to B} V(r, \theta, v, t, T, \tau) &= P(r, \theta, v, t, \tau) - K, &\quad (2.28) \\
\lim_{(r,\theta,v) \to B} \frac{\partial V(r, \theta, v, t, T, \tau)}{\partial P(r, \theta, v, t, \tau)} &= -1, &\quad (2.29)
\end{aligned}
$$

where $\mathcal{B}$ denotes the exercise region, which represents the bond price above which the America call is exercised optimally:

$$\mathcal{B} = \{(r^*, \theta^*, v^*) \in \mathcal{R} \times \mathcal{R}_+^2 \mid P(r^*, \theta^*, v^*, \tau) \geq B^*\}.$$

It is assumed that the exercise region for this American option is well defined, unique, and has a continuous sample path.

Condition (2.28) is called the "value matching" condition and condition (2.29) is called the "supper contact" condition. They are jointly referred to as the "smooth pasting" condition.

Standard arbitrage arguments lead to the following relation which explicitly determines the exercise region:

$$
\begin{aligned}
P(r^*, & \theta^*, v^*, t^*, T, \tau) - K \\
&= \int_{P(y_1, y_2, y_3, T, \tau) > K} G(y_1, y_2, y_3, T, r^*, \theta^*, v^*, t^*)[P(y_1, y_2, y_3, T, \tau) - K] dy \\
&+ \int_{\{(y_1, y_2, y_3) \in \mathcal{B}\}} \int_{t^*}^T G(y_1, y_2, y_3, s, r^*, \theta^*, v^*, t^*) \times [\alpha(s) - y_1 K] dy ds \\
&= C(r^*, \theta^*, v^*, t^*, T, \tau) \\
&+ \int_{\{(y_1, y_2, y_3) \in \mathcal{B}\}} \int_{t^*}^T G(y_1, y_2, y_3, s, r^*, \theta^*, v^*, t^*) \times [\alpha(s) - y_1 K] dy ds \quad (2.30)
\end{aligned}
$$

The left-hand-side of (2.30) is the payoff of early exercised. The first term of the right-hand-side of (2.30), $C(r^*, \theta^*, v^*, t^*, T, \tau)$ is the value at t^* of the otherwise identical European call option. The second term of the right-hand-side of (2.30) represents the gain due to dividend earned and the loss due to interest rate forgone through early exercise which are reflected in the increased value of the American option over an otherwise identical European option.

If $(r, \theta, v) \in \mathcal{B}$ or $P(r, \theta, v, t, \tau) \geq B^*$, then the option will be exercised, and thus $V(r, \theta, v, t, T, \tau) = P(r, \theta, v, t, \tau) - K$. Therefore,

$$L[V(r, \theta, v, t, T, \tau)] = L[P(r, \theta, v, t, \tau) - K] = \alpha(t) - rK, \quad (2.31)$$

$$\forall (r, \theta, v, t) \in \mathcal{B}.$$

In (2.31), the fundamental valuation PDE for bond price has been made use of. If $(r, \theta, v) \notin \mathcal{B}$, the option will not be exercised, so by arbitrage arguments,

$$L[V(r, \theta, v, t, T, \tau)] = 0. \quad (2.32)$$

Combining (2.31) and (2.32), the option price $V(r, \theta, v, t, T, \tau)$ satisfies the following PDE:

$$L[V(r, \theta, v, t, T, \tau)] - [\alpha(t) - rK(t)]1_{\{(r, \theta, v) \in \mathcal{B}\}} = 0, \quad (2.33)$$

with the boundary condition

$$V(r, \theta, v, T, T, \tau) = \max[P(r, \theta, v, T, \tau) - K, 0],$$

where $1_{\{(r,\theta,v)\in B\}}$ is the indicator function.

The initial-boundary-value problem (2.33) has the form posed in section 1.5 and can be solved by the Green's function method. The solution is given by

$$
\begin{aligned}
V&(r, \theta, v, t, T, \tau) \\
&= \int_{P(T,\tau)>K} G(y_1, y_2, y_3, T, r, \theta, v, t)[P(y_1, y_2, y_3, T, \tau) - K]dy_1 dy_2 dy_3 \\
&+ \int_{\{(y_1,y_2,y_3)\in B\}} \int_t^T G(y_1, y_2, y_3, s, r, \theta, v, t)[\alpha(s) - y_1 K]dy_1 dy_2 dy_3 ds.
\end{aligned}
$$

The following proposition summaries the results.

Proposition 13: *Let $V(r, \theta, v, t, T, \tau)$ be the value at time t of an American call option on a coupon bond with the coupon rate $\alpha(t)$ and maturity $\tau, \tau \geq T$. Let $P(r, \theta, v, t, \tau)$ denote the bond price at time t. Let T be the option's maturity and K be its strike price. $V(r, \theta, v, t, T, \tau)$ is given by*

$$
\begin{aligned}
V(r, \theta, v, t, T, \tau) &= C(r, \theta, v, t; T, \tau) \\
&+ \int_{\{(y_1,y_2,y_3)\in B\}} \int_t^T G(y_1, y_2, y_3, s, r, \theta, v, t)[\alpha(s) - y_1 K]dy_1 dy_2 dy_3 ds,
\end{aligned}
$$

$$(2.34)$$

where

$$
\begin{aligned}
C(r, \theta, v, t; T, \tau) &= \\
\int_{P(T,\tau)>K} & G(y_1, y_2, y_3, T, r, \theta, v, t)[P(y_1, y_2, y_3, T, \tau) - K]dy_1 dy_2 dy_3
\end{aligned}
$$

$$(2.35)$$

is the price of the European call option with the same terms as the American option under consideration. In addition, the exercise region $B = \{r^*, \theta^*, v^*\}$ is defined by the following equation:

$$
\begin{aligned}
P(r^*, \theta^*, v^*, t^*, T, \tau) &- K = C(r^*, \theta^*, v^*, t^*)+ \\
\int_{\{(y_1,y_2,y_3)\in B\}} & \int_{t^*}^T G(y_1, y_2, y_3, s, r^*, \theta^*, v^*, t^*) \times [\alpha(s) - y_1 K]dyds.
\end{aligned}
$$

$$(2.36)$$

Therefore, the value function of the American call has been decomposed as the sum of two parts; the European call value function and the early exercise premium.

A dynamic trading strategy equivalent to that suggested by Car, Jarrow and Meyneni (1992) for American stock options can be used to explain the terms in the decomposition.

Following an analogous arguments the American put price $V(r, \theta, v, t, T, \tau)$ is given by

$$V(r, \theta, v, t, T, \tau) = p(r, \theta, v, t; T, \tau)$$
$$+ \int_{\{(y_1, y_2, y_3) \in B^*\}} \int_t^T G(y_1, y_2, y_3, s, r, \theta, v, t)[-\alpha(s) + y_1 K] dy_1 dy_2 dy_3 ds,$$
$$(2.37)$$

where $p(r, \theta, v, t; T, \tau)$ is the price of an otherwise identical European put option.

The option values can be numerically computed using equation (2.34) by first estimating the exercise boundary B^* from solving the integral equation (2.36) recursively. The advantage of the Green's function approach to the valuation of American bond options is again that the option price can be more easily treated by numerical integration than from a direct numerical attack on the relevant partial differential equation by finite-difference methods or Monte Carlo methods.

The expressions (2.34) and (2.37) can be further simplified when the option is written on discount bonds. For example, consider an American put on a discount bond. In this case, the American put value is

$$V(r, \theta, v, t, T, \tau) = p(r, \theta, v, t; T, \tau)$$
$$+ \int_{\{(y_1, y_2, y_3) \in B^*\}} \int_t^T G(y_1, y_2, y_3, s, r, \theta, v, t) y_1 K dy_1 dy_2 dy_3 ds,$$
$$(2.38)$$

where $p(r, \theta, v, t; T, \tau)$, the European put value on the discount bond, is given in section 2.2:

$$p(r, \theta, v, t, T; s, K) = P(r, \theta, v, t; s)[\Psi(\beta; \alpha; \gamma) - 1]$$
$$- P(r, \theta, v, t; T) K [\Psi(\beta'; \alpha'; \gamma) - 1]$$

and

$$\int_{\{(y_1, y_2, y_3) \in B^*\}} \int_t^T G(y_1, y_2, y_3, s, r, \theta, v, t) y_1 K dy_1 dy_2 dy_3 ds$$
$$= \int_t^T K \Psi_1(\eta_0, \eta_1, \eta_2, \eta_3, \xi_0, \xi_1, \xi_2, \xi_3; \gamma_0, \gamma_1, \gamma_2, \gamma_3), ds$$

where

$$\Psi_1(\eta_0, \eta_1, \eta_2, \eta_3, \xi_0, \xi_1, \xi_2, \xi_3; \gamma_0, \gamma_1, \gamma_2, \gamma_3)$$

$$= \frac{1}{(2\pi)^{3/2}} \int_{-\infty}^{\infty} \int_{-\infty}^{\infty} \int_{-\infty}^{\infty} I_1(\xi_0, \xi_1, \xi_2, \xi_3; \gamma_0, \gamma_1, \gamma_2, \gamma_3) \eta_0(\phi, \psi, \varphi, \tau)$$
$$\times e^{-\eta_1(\phi,\psi,\varphi,\tau)r - \eta_2(\phi,\psi,\varphi,\tau)\theta - \eta_3(\phi,\psi,\varphi,\tau)v} d\phi d\psi d\varphi \qquad (2.39)$$

and $I_1(\cdot)$ is defined by

$$I_1(\xi_0, \xi_1, \xi_2, \xi_3; \gamma_0, \gamma_1, \gamma_2, \gamma_3) \equiv$$
$$\int \xi_0 x_1 e^{-ix_1\xi_1 - ix_2\xi_2 - ix_3\xi_3} 1_{\{\gamma_1 x_1 + \gamma_2 x_2 + \gamma_3 x_3 \leq \gamma_0\}} dx_1 dx_2 dx_3,$$

which can be computed analytically, see Appendix D. All the parameters in (2.39) can be obtained easily from section 2.2.

Chapter 3

Pricing Exotic Options

3.1 Introduction

Vanilla derivatives, such as the plain put or call options discussed in the last chpater, are only part of the financial derivative instruments being traded in financial markets. A great deal of financial derivative instruments are exotic. They are out of the ordinary, tailored to special needs and traded on the over-the-counter markets. Usually, exotic derivatives brokers bring together both sides of a contract and construct a product which does not exist as an exchanged-traded option. As such, exotic options are given a variety of unconventional features which make their valuation a challenging topic.

An enormous amount of literature on the valuation of exotic derivatives mainly focuses on equity exotic derivatives. The valuation of interest rate exotic derivatives are more complex and have largely been undertaken within one-factor models of the term structure of interest rates.

This chapter discusses the pricing of interest rate exotic derivatives under our three-factor model of interest rates including both the special and general interest rate dynamics. Although the pricing formulas to be presented may look formidable at first glance, the actual programming and computation is rather straightforward.

3.2 Green's Function in the Presence of Boundaries

The Green's function of an equation is a particular solution of that equation for a point source. Solutions for more general source terms, including initial conditions, can then be represented as a linear combination of the Green's function in the form of an integral. The initial-value problem encountered in the context of derivatives valuation so far is without boundaries. Many derivatives, especially exotic derivatives, impose boundaries and involve payments at random times. To be able to evaluate such derivatives by the Green's function method, one needs first to derive the Green's function in the presence of boundaries. This section will present a general discussion of the Green's function with boundaries. It will be shown that the Green's function in the presence of boundaries can also be obtained as a linear combination of the Green's function given in Chapter 1.

Let $D \in R^3$ be an open set and ∂D be its boundary. Let $\hat{\partial} D$ be the closed subset of ∂D such that $x(\tau) \in \hat{\partial} D$ for all $x(t)$ where τ is the time of first passage from D. Under technical conditions, there is a Green's function $G : R^3 \times [0, T] \times R^3 \times [0, T] \to R$ having the following properties.

For any $(x, t) \in R^3 \times [0, T)$, $(y, t') \in R^3 \times [0, T)$, the function $G(y, t', x, t)$ solves the following problem:

$$
\begin{align}
L_{x,t}[G(y, t', x, t)] &= 0; \text{ for } x \in D, &(3.1)\\
G(y, t', x, t) &= \delta(x - y), \text{ for } x \in D, &(3.2)\\
G(y, t', x, t) &= 0, \text{ for } x_b \in \partial D, &(3.3)
\end{align}
$$

where

$$
L_{x,t} = \frac{1}{2} x_3 \partial^2_{x_1 x_1} + \frac{1}{2} \eta^2 x_3 \partial^2_{x_3 x_3} + \frac{1}{2} \zeta^2 x_2 \partial^2_{x_2 x_2} + [k(x_2 - x_1) + \lambda_r x_3] \partial_{x_1} + [\nu \bar{\theta} - \nu' x_2] \partial_{x_2} + [\mu \bar{\upsilon} - \dot{\mu} x_3] \partial_{x_3} + \partial_t - x_1.
$$

Generally for an arbitrarily given D, it is difficult to find the Green's function in closed form. However, if D is given by

$$
x \in D \equiv [a_1, a_2] \times [b_1, b_2] \times [c_1, c_2],
$$

an explicit expression for the Green's function can be derived by the method of images (see, for example, Wilmott, Dewynne, and Howison (1993)).

Lemma 14: *If D is defined by*

$$
D \equiv [a_1, a_2] \times [b_1, b_2] \times [c_1, c_2],
$$

then the Green's function $G(y, t', x, t)$, the solution to the problem (3.1)-(3.3), is

$$
\begin{align}
G(y, t', x, t) = \sum_{n_1,n_2,n_3=-\infty}^{\infty} \Big[&G_0 \Big(y_1 + 2n_1(a_2 - a_1), y_2 + 2n_2(b_2 - b_1), \\
& y_3 + 2n_3(c_2 - c_1), t', x, t \Big) - G_0 \Big(2a_1 - y_1 + 2n_2(a_2 - a_1), \\
& 2b_1 - y_2 + 2n_2(b_2 - b_1), 2c_1 - y_3 + 2n_3(c_2 - c_1), t', x, t \Big) \Big]
\end{align}
$$
$$(3.4)$$

where $G_0(y_1, y_2, y_3, t', x, t)$ is the Green's function given in section 1.6

3.3 Derivatives with Payoffs at Random Times

Consider the boundary-initial-value problem raised in the pricing of derivatives with payoffs at random times. For a given $T > t > 0$, find a $u(x, t)$ solving the following problem:

$$L_{x,t}[u] = -f(x, t), \text{ for } x \in D, \tag{3.5}$$

$$u(x_b, t) = g(x_b, t), \text{ for } x_b \in \partial D, \tag{3.6}$$

$$u(x, T) = h(x), \text{ for } x \in D, \tag{3.7}$$

where $h : R^3 \to R$, is the contractually specified value of the derivatives at the maturity of the contract; $g : R^3 \times [0, T] \to R$ is also contractually specified payments received if and when x reaches ∂D.

The unique arbitrage free price at time t, $u(x, t)$, of the interest rate derivative security can be obtained as the discounted expected value. By the definition of an equivalent martingale measure, this expectation has to be taken with respect to Q. The following lemma summarizes this result.

Lemma 15: *(Cox-Ingersoll-Ross (1985)). The unique solution* [1] *to (3.5) with boundary conditions (3.6) and (3.7) is given by*

$$u(x, t) = E_Q\left[\int_t^{\tau \wedge T} e^{-\int_t^u r(s)ds} f(y, u)du + g(y, \tau)e^{-\int_t^\tau r(s)ds} 1_{\{\tau < T\}} \right.$$
$$\left. + h(y, T)e^{-\int_t^T r(s)ds} 1_{\{\tau \geq T\}} \right], \tag{3.8}$$

where E_Q denotes expectation with respect to equivalent martingale Q as defined in Chapter 1, $1(.)$ is an indicator function, and τ is the time of first passage to $\hat{\partial}D$.

The solution as given in (3.8) is not useful for computational purposes. To actually be able to compute the solution, the Green's function method needs to be employed. Given $G(y, t', x, t)$ as the solution to (3.1)-(3.3), the solution to (3.5)-(3.7) is given in the following Lemma.

Lemma 16: *Under technical conditions on $f(x, t), g(x_b, t), h(x)$, the solution to (3.5)-(3.7) is given by*

$$u(x, t) = \int_t^T dt' \int_D dy G(y, t', x, t)f(y, t') + \int_D h(y, T)G(y, T, x, t)dy$$

---

[1] The existence and uniqueness of a solution to the problem (3.4)-(3.5) can be established under some appropriate regularity conditions but will not presented here. Interested readers should refer to Friedman (1975).

$$+ \int_t^T dt' \int_{\partial D} dag(y_b, t') \frac{\partial G(y_b, t', x, t)}{\partial n_y}, \tag{3.9}$$

where $G(y, t', x, t)$ is the solution to the problem (3.1)-(3.3) and $da \in \partial D$, $\partial/\partial n_y$ in the last integral means normal differentiation with respect to the first argument of the Green's function.

Remark. $G(x, t; y; t')$ is analog to the defective density for the three factors with absorbing barrier, ∂D, imposed and conditional on the current values of three factors. $\partial G(x, t; y_b, t')/\partial n_y$ is analog to the first passage time density of x through the absorbing barrier ∂D. The solution in Chapter 17 of Ingersoll (1987) and the formulas (7.37) and (E.10) in Duffie (1992) are particular cases of the formula (3.9).

3.4 Barrier Options

There are a set of options involving known payments at unknown times. An example is barrier options, the basic form of which are "down-and-out", "down-and-in", "up-and-out", and "up-and-in". These options have the common feature that the right to exercise either appears or disappears on some pre-specified boundary, above or below the current underlying asset price or other index. More specifically, a "down-and-out" (knock-out) option differs from a standard option in that a knockout rate must be selected in addition to the regular strike price. The knockout rate represents the level at which the option will cease to exist if it is reached or crossed by the underlying spot price or other index at any time during the life of the option. The knock-out option performs exactly as a standard option unless the knockout rate is hit. Features of other barrier options can be understood similarly.

The valuation of barrier options on equity are given in Ingersoll (1987) and Wilmott, Dewynne and Howison (1993). This section will present the pricing of a down-and-out option on interest rates by the Green's function method discussed in the previous section.

Let r^* be the knockout rate and $R(t)$ be the rebate at time t. The value at t, $C(r, \theta, v, t, T)$ of the down-and-out option maturing at T with strike price K satisfies the following PDE:

$$\frac{1}{2}vC_{rr} + \frac{1}{2}\eta^2 vC_{vv} + \frac{1}{2}\zeta^2\theta C_{\theta\theta} + [k(\theta - r) + \lambda_r v]C_r +$$
$$[v\bar{\theta} - v'\theta]C_\theta + [\mu\bar{v} - \acute{\mu}v]C_v + C_t - rC = 0, \quad r > r^* \tag{3.10}$$

with the boundary and initial conditions,

$$C(r^*, \theta, v, t, T) \quad = \quad R(t), \quad r(u) > r^*, \quad u < t,$$

$$C(r, \theta, v, T, T) \quad = \quad \max[r - K, 0], \text{for } r > r^*, \quad k > r^*. \qquad (3.11)$$

Utilizing the general solution formula in section 3.3 yields the following proposition.

Proposition 17: *Let $C(r, \theta, v, t, T, r^*)$ be the price at time t of a standard down-and-out European call which pays $\max[r - K, 0]$ at the expiration date T if $r(t) > r^*, \forall t \in [0, T]$, and pays $R(t)$ if $r(t) = r^*$ at time t. $C(r, \theta, v, t, T, r^*)$ is given by*

$$\begin{aligned}
C(r, \theta, v, t, T, r^*) \quad = \quad & \int \int \int^{\mathcal{B}} (y_1 - K) G_1(y_1, y_2, y_3, T; r, \theta, v, t) dy_1 dy_2 dy_3 \\
& + \int_t^T \int \int R(s) G_2(y_1, y_2, y_3, s; r, \theta, v, t)_{|y_1 = r^*} dy_2 dy_3 ds,
\end{aligned}$$

$$(3.12)$$

where $\mathcal{B} \equiv [K, +\infty) \times [0, +\infty) \times [0, +\infty)$ and

$$\begin{aligned}
G_1(y_1, y_2, y_3, T; r, \theta, v, t) \quad = \quad & G(y_1, y_2, y_3, T; r, \theta, v, t) \\
& - G(2r^* - y_1, y_2, y_3, T; r, \theta, v, t), \\
G_2(y_1, y_2, y_3, T; r, \theta, v, t) \quad = \quad & \frac{\partial G_1(y_1, y_2, y_3, T; r, \theta, v, t)}{\partial y_1}, \qquad (3.13)
\end{aligned}$$

and $G(y_1, y_2, y_3, t'; r, \theta, v, t)$ is given in section 1.6.

The integrals in (3.12) can be further simplified by the method used in deriving vanilla option pricing formulas given in Appendix D.

3.5 Lookback Options

A lookback option is a derivative product whose payoff depends on the maximum or minimum realized asset price or index over a pre-specified period. Lookback options might be of interest to traders who wish to bet on rate volatility or hedging portfolios which are sensitive to rate volatility. The valuation of lookback options on equity is discussed in Goldman, Sosin, and Gatto (1979), Conze and Viswanathan (1991), He, Keirstead and Rebholz (1994), among others. In this section an analytical solution for an interest rate lookback option will be presented under our three-factor model of the term structure of interest rates.

Consider the value of a lookback option at time 0. The option expires at time T, and the lookback period runs from t^* to T. Note that t^* may be either positive or negative. Let the running minimum and maximum of the short rate be defined by

$$\underline{r}(t) \quad = \quad \min_{t^* \le s \le t} r(s),$$

$$\bar{r}(t) \;=\; \max_{t^* \le s \le t} r(s).$$

Assume that a lookback call is written on the spread between the maximum and minimum of the short rate with the terminal payoff at maturity T:

$$\max\left[(\bar{r}(T) - \underline{r}(T)) - K\right].$$

The value of the lookback option satisfies the following PDE:

$$\frac{1}{2}vC_{rr} + \frac{1}{2}\eta^2 vC_{vv} + \frac{1}{2}\zeta^2\theta C_{\theta\theta} + [k(\theta - r) + \lambda_r v]C_r +$$
$$[\nu\bar{\theta} - \nu'\theta]C_\theta + [\mu\bar{v} - \acute{\mu}v]C_v + C_t - rC = 0, \quad r > r^*(t)$$

with the boundary condition

$$\max\left[(\bar{r}(T) - \underline{r}(T)) - K\right].$$

Utilizing the general solution formula in section 3.2 yields the following proposition.

Proposition 18: *Let $C(r, \theta, v, T)$ be the price at time 0 of a standard lookback call which pays $r_1(T) - \underline{r}_1(T)$ at the expiration date T. Then,*

$$C(r, \theta, v, t, T) = \int \max[(y_2 - y_1 - K), 0]G_{+-}(y_1, y_2, t, r, \theta, v, T)dy_1 dy_2,$$

$$(3.14)$$

where

$$G_{+-}(y_1, y_2, t, r, \theta, v, T) \;=\; \int_{y_1}^{y_2} G_1(y, y_1, y_2, t, r, \theta, v, T)dx,$$

$$G_1(y, y_1, y_2, t, r, \theta, v, T) \;=\; \sum_{n=-\infty}^{n=+\infty} [G_2(y + 2n(y_2 - y_1), t; r, \theta, v, T)$$
$$-G_2(2y_1 - y + 2ny_2, t; r, \theta, v, T),$$

$$G_2(y_1, t, r, \theta, v, t') \;=\; \int\int G(y_1, y_2, y_3, t; r, \theta, v, t')dy_2 dy_3, \quad (3.15)$$

and $G(y_1, y_2, y_3, t; r, \theta, v, T)$ is given in section 1.6.

3.6 Yield Options

The yield curve changes every day, and uncertainty as to its future course has left many market participants looking for efficient ways to either take positions with respect to the future shape of the yield curve or reduce the risk to their portfolio associated with yield curve movements. Yield options, such as SYCURVE, are derivative securities that allow one to speculate or hedge based on the levels of the yield in question. Besides, many fixed and floating debt instruments and financial contingent claims have incorporated yield options. For example, interest rate caps, locks, floors, options on interest rate swaps, options on actively traded Eurodollar contracts, and extendable corporate bonds all contain features that can be modeled as yield options.

A closed-form expression for the value of European yield options with the CIR (1985) framework is given in Longstaff (1990) and the pricing of American yield options within the CIR framework is in Chesney, Elliott and Gibson (1993). This section derives a closed form solution to the value of European yield options within our three-factor model of the term structure of interest rates.

Let $C(r, \theta, v, t; T_C, T, K)$ be the price at time t of a European call yield option that expires at time T_C. The exercise price of the option is K and the maturity of the option is T_C. At the expiration date T_C,

$$
\begin{aligned}
C(r, \theta, v, T_C; T_C, T, K) &= [R(r, \theta, v, T_C; T) - K]^+ \\
&\equiv \max(0, Y(r, \theta, v, T_C; T) - K). \quad (3.16)
\end{aligned}
$$

By the interest rate derivatives valuation formula (1.5), the yield option price at t is given by

$$
C(r, \theta, v, t, T_C; T, K) = E_Q\left[e^{-\int_0^T r(s)ds} [R(r, \theta, v, T_C; T) - K]^+ \mid \mathcal{F}_t \right]
$$

which is the solution to the fundamental valuation PDE with the boundary condition (3.14). By the Green's function method, the price at time t of the yield option is

$$
\begin{aligned}
&C(r, \theta, v, t; T_C, T, K) \\
&= \int^B (R(y_1, y_2, y_3, T_C; T) - K)G(y_1, y_2, y_3, T_C, r, \theta, v, t)dy_1 dy_2 dy_3,
\end{aligned}
$$
$$(3.17)$$

where $y = (y_1, y_2, y_3) = (r(T_C), \theta(T_C), v(T_C))$; $G(r, \theta, v, t, y_1, y_2, y_3, T_C)$ is the Green's function for the fundamental valuation PDE for interest rate derivatives; $\mathcal{B}$ is the range of values of y_1, y_2, and y_3 over which the yield option is in the money at the expiration date T_C and is defined by the following inequality:

$$
\begin{aligned}
B(T_C, T)y_1 + C(T_C, T)y_2 + D(T_C, T)y_3 &\geq K^* \\
&\equiv \ln A(T_C, T) + K(T - T_C).
\end{aligned}
$$

(3.16) can be written as

$$
C(r, \theta, v, t; T_C, T, K)
$$

$$
= \int^{B} \left[\frac{1}{\tau} (-\ln A(\tau) + B(\tau)y_1 + C(\tau)y_2 + D(\tau)y_3) - K \right]
$$
$$
\times G(y_1, y_2, y_3, T_C, r, \theta, v, t) dy_1 dy_2 dy_3
$$
$$
= \frac{1}{(2\pi)^{3/2}} \int^{B} \int \int \left[\frac{1}{\tau} (-\ln A(\tau) + B(\tau)y_1 + C(\tau)y_2 + D(\tau)y_3) - K \right]
$$
$$
\times e^{-iy_1\xi_1 - iy_2\xi_2 - iy_3\xi_3} A(\xi, \tau') e^{-B(\xi,\tau')r - C(\xi,\tau')\theta - D(\xi,\tau')v}
$$
$$
dy_1 dy_2 dy_3 d\xi_1 d\xi_2 d\xi_3, \tag{3.18}
$$

where $\tau = T - T_C$, $\tau' = T_C - t$, and $\xi = (\xi_1, \xi_2, \xi_3)$. Let $I_j(\xi_1, \xi_2, \xi_3; \gamma_0, \gamma_1, \gamma_{2,3}), j = 0, 1, 2, 3$ be defined as

$$
I_0(\xi_1, \xi_2, \xi_3; \gamma_0, \gamma_1, \gamma_2, \gamma_3)
$$
$$
= \int_{\gamma_1 y_1 + \gamma_2 y_2 + \gamma_3 y_3 \geq \gamma_0} e^{-iy_1\xi_1 - iy_2\xi_2 - iy_3\xi_3} dy_1 dy_2 dy_3
$$
$$
I_j(\xi_1, \xi_2, \xi_3; \gamma_0, \gamma_1, \gamma_2, \gamma_3)
$$
$$
= \int_{\gamma_1 y_1 + \gamma_2 y_2 + \gamma_3 y_3 \geq \gamma_0} y_j e^{-iy_1\xi_1 - iy_2\xi_2 - iy_3\xi_3} dy_1 dy_2 dy_3
$$
$$
\equiv i \frac{\partial I_0(\xi_1, \xi_2, \xi_3; \gamma_0, \gamma_1, \gamma_{2,3})}{\partial \xi_j}.
$$

With $I_j(\xi_1, \xi_2, \xi_3; \gamma_0, \gamma_1, \gamma_{2,3}), j = 0, 1, 2, 3$, the yield option price (3.16) can be written as

$$
C(r, \theta, v, t; T_C, T, K)
$$
$$
= \int_{-\infty}^{\infty} \int_{-\infty}^{\infty} \int_{-\infty}^{\infty} \left[\frac{1}{\tau} (-\ln A(\tau) I_0(\xi, \gamma) + B(\tau) I_1(\xi, \gamma) + C(\tau) I_2(\xi, \gamma) + \right.
$$
$$
\left. D(\tau) I_3(\xi, \gamma)) - K I_0(\xi, \gamma) \right] A(\xi, \tau') e^{-B(\xi,\tau')r - C(\xi,\tau')\theta - D(\xi,\tau')v} d\xi_1 d\xi_2 d\xi_3
$$
$$
= P(r, \theta, v, t, T) \int_{-\infty}^{\infty} \left[\frac{1}{\tau} (-\ln A(\tau) I_0(\xi, \gamma) + B(\tau) I_1(\xi, \gamma) \right.
$$
$$
+ C(\tau) I_2(\xi, \gamma) + D(\tau) I_3(\xi, \gamma)) - K I_0(\xi, \gamma) \left] \frac{A(\xi, \tau')}{A(t, T)} \right.
$$
$$
\times e^{-(B(\xi,\tau') - B(t,T))r - (C(\xi,\tau') - C(t,T))\theta - (D(\xi,\tau') - D(t,T))v} d\xi_1 d\xi_2 d\xi_3
$$
$$
= P(r, \theta, v, t, T) \left[\left((-\frac{1}{\tau} \ln A(\tau) - K) \int I_0(\xi, \gamma) \right. \right.
$$
$$
+ \frac{B(\tau)}{\tau} \int i \frac{\partial I_0(\xi, \gamma)}{\partial \xi_1} + \frac{C(\tau)}{\tau} \int i \frac{\partial I_0(\xi, \gamma)}{\partial \xi_2} + \frac{D(\tau)}{\tau} \int i \frac{\partial I_0(\xi, \gamma)}{\partial \xi_3} \right) \frac{A(\xi, \tau')}{A(t, T)}
$$
$$
\times e^{-(B(\xi,\tau') - B(t,T))r - (C(\xi,\tau') - C(t,T))\theta - (D(\xi,\tau') - D(t,T))v} d\xi_1 d\xi_2 d\xi_3 \Big]
$$
$$
= P(r, \theta, v, t, T) \left[\Psi \left(\frac{1}{\tau} (-\ln A(\tau) - K) \right) \frac{A(\xi, \tau')}{A(t, T)}, B(\xi, \tau') - B(t, T), \right.
$$
$$
(C(\xi, \tau') - C(t, T), D(\xi, \tau') - D(t, T); \xi, \gamma)
$$
$$
+ \Psi_1 \left(\frac{A(\xi, \tau') B(\tau)}{\tau A(t, T)}, B(\xi, \tau') - B(t, T), C(\xi, \tau') - C(t, T), \right.
$$
$$
D(\xi, \tau') - D(t, T); \xi, \gamma)
$$

$$+\Psi_2\Big(\frac{A(\xi,\tau')C(\tau)}{\tau A(t,T)}, B(\xi,\tau') - B(t,T), C(\xi,\tau') - C(t,T),$$
$$D(\xi,\tau') - D(t,T); \xi, \gamma\Big)$$
$$+\Psi_3\Big(\frac{A(\xi,\tau')D(\tau)}{\tau A(t,T)}, B(\xi,\tau') - B(t,T), C(\xi,\tau') - C(t,T),$$
$$D(\xi,\tau') - D(t,T); \xi, \gamma\Big)\Big], \tag{3.19}$$

where $\gamma = (\gamma_0, \gamma_1, \gamma_3, \gamma_3)$.

Therefore the following proposition is obtained.

Proposition 19: *Let $R(r,\theta,v,t;,T)$ be the yield at time t for a bond that matures at time T. At time T, the prevailing spot rate, short mean, and short rate volatility at time t are r, θ, and v respectively. Let $C(r,\theta,v,t;T_C,T,K)$ be the price at time t of a European yield call option. The exercise price of the option is K and its maturity is T_C, with $t < T_C < T$. The payoff of the option at maturity is*

$$\begin{aligned}C(r,\theta,v,T_C;T_C,T,K) &= [R(r,\theta,v,T_C;T) - K]^+ \\ &\equiv \max(0, R(r,\theta,v,T_C;T) - K). \end{aligned} \tag{3.20}$$

Under the special interest rate dynamics, $C(r,\theta,v,t;T_C,T,K)$ is given by

$$\begin{aligned}C(r,&\theta,v,t,T_C,;T,K) \\ =~&P(r,\theta,v,t;T)\Big[\Psi(\omega_1,\alpha_2,\alpha_3,\alpha_4;\beta_1,\beta_2,\beta_3;\gamma_0,\gamma_1,\gamma_2,\gamma_3) \\ &+\Psi_1(\omega_2,\alpha_2,\alpha_3,\alpha_4;\beta_1,\beta_2,\beta_3;\gamma_0,\gamma_1,\gamma_2,\gamma_3) \\ &+\Psi_2(\omega_3,\alpha_2,\alpha_3,\alpha_4;\beta_1,\beta_2,\beta_3;\gamma_0,\gamma_1,\gamma_2,\gamma_3) \\ &+\Psi_3(\omega_4,\alpha_2,\alpha_3,\alpha_4;\beta_1,\beta_2,\beta_3;\gamma_0,\gamma_1,\gamma_2,\gamma_3)\Big], \end{aligned}\tag{3.21}$$

where $P(r,\theta,v,t;T)$ is the bond price; $\Psi(\alpha_1,\alpha_2,\alpha_3,\alpha_4;\beta_1,\beta_2,\beta_3;\gamma_0,\gamma_1,\gamma_2,\gamma_3)$ and $\Psi_j(\alpha_1,\alpha_2,\alpha_3,\alpha_4;\beta_1,\beta_2,\beta_3;\gamma_0,\gamma_1,\gamma_{2,3}), j = 1,2,3$ are defined as

$$\begin{aligned}\Psi(&\eta_0,\eta_1,\eta_2,\eta_3;\xi_0,\xi_1,\xi_2;\gamma_0,\gamma_1,\gamma_2,\gamma_3) \\ =~&\frac{1}{(2\pi)^{3/2}}\int_{-\infty}^{\infty}\int_{-\infty}^{\infty}\int_{-\infty}^{\infty}\eta_0(\xi,\tau)e^{-\eta_1(\xi,\tau)r-\eta_2(\xi,\tau)\theta-\eta_3(\xi,\tau)v} \\ &\times I(\xi_0,\xi_1,\xi_2;\gamma_0,\gamma_1,\gamma_2,\gamma_3)d\xi_1 d\xi_2 d\xi_3 \end{aligned}\tag{3.22}$$

$$\begin{aligned}\Psi_j(&\eta_0,\eta_1,\eta_2,\eta_3;\xi_0,\xi_1,\xi_2;\gamma_0,\gamma_1,\gamma_2,\gamma_3) \\ =~&\frac{1}{(2\pi)^{3/2}}\int_{-\infty}^{\infty}\int_{-\infty}^{\infty}\int_{-\infty}^{\infty}\eta_0(\xi,\tau)e^{-\eta_1(\xi,\tau)r-\eta_2(\xi,\tau)\theta-\eta_3(\xi,\tau)v} \\ &\times I_j(\xi_0,\xi_1,\xi_2;\gamma_0\gamma_1,\gamma_2,\gamma_3)d\xi_1 d\xi_2 d\xi_3 \end{aligned}\tag{3.23}$$

with

$$\omega_1 = \frac{1}{\tau}(-\ln A(\tau) - K))\frac{A(\xi,\tau')}{A(t,T)},$$

$$\omega_2 = \frac{A(\xi,\tau')B(\tau)}{\tau A(t,T)},$$

$$\omega_3 = \frac{A(\xi,\tau')C(\tau)}{\tau A(t,T)},$$

$$\omega_4 = \frac{A(\xi,\tau')D(\tau)}{\tau A(t,T)},$$

$$\alpha_2 = B(\xi,\tau') - B(t,T),$$

$$\alpha_3 = C(\xi,\tau') - C(t,T),$$

$$\alpha_4 = D(\xi,\tau') - D(t,T),$$

$$\beta_1 = \xi_1,$$

$$\beta_2 = \xi_2,$$

$$\beta_3 = \xi_3,$$

$$\gamma_1 = \ln A(T_C,T) + K(T - T_C),$$

$$\gamma_2 = B(T_C,T),$$

$$\gamma_3 = C(T_C,T),$$

$$\gamma_4 = D(T_C,T),$$

where $A(\tau), B(\tau), C(\tau)$, and $D(\tau)$ are known functions given in the bond price formula and $A(\xi,\tau) = A(\xi_1,\xi_2,\xi_3,\tau)$, etc. are in the Green's function formula.

The value of a yield put option can be obtained from the following call-put parity relation:

$$
\begin{aligned}
V(x,t,T_C,T) &= \int_{\mathcal{R}^3 - B} (K - R(y,T_C,T))G(y,T_C,x,t)dy \\
&= \int_{\mathcal{R}^3} (K - R(y,T_C,T))G(y,T_C,x,t)dy \\
&\quad + \int_B (R(y,T_C,T) - K)G(y,T_C,x,t)dy \\
&= KP(x,t,T_C) - C_0(x,t,T_C,T) + C(x,t,T_C,T),
\end{aligned}
$$

where $P(x,t,T_C)$ is the bond pricing formula, $C(x,t,T_C,T)$ is the call yield option given in (3.20), and

$$C_0(x,t,T_C,T) = \int_{\mathcal{R}^3} R(y,T_C,T)G(y,T_C,x,t)dy$$

is the value at t of the yield call option with a strike 0, which is the value at T_C of the security that pays $R(x,T_C,T)$ at T_C.

Chapter 4

Fitting to a Given Term Structure

4.1 Introduction

For practical purposes, it is sometimes desirable that the model term structure fit a given yield curve exactly. To accommodate such needs, this chapter outlines two procedures to fit our three-factor model of the term structure to any pre-specified yield curve. Section 4.2 shows how our model can be merged to the Health-Jarrow-Morton (HJM) framework. Second 4.3 shows a procedure to fit our model to a given yield curve using the method of Hull and White (1990). Both procedures are discussed in the continuous-time setting. Fitting a yield curve in discrete-time setting is given in chapter 6 where a discrete-time version of our three-factor model is presented.

4.2 Merging to the Heath-Jarrow-Morton Framework

The term structure of forward rates $f(0, t)$, $t \in [0, T]$ at the initial trade date 0 is a known function. The forward rate at time t maturing at time s, $t < s, t, s \in [0, T]$, is defined as

$$f(t, s) = \frac{\partial \ln P(t; s - t)}{\partial s}$$

and is assumed to obey the following stochastic integral equation:

$$f(t, s) = f(0, s) + \int_0^t \alpha(l, s, f(l, s))dl + \sum_{i=1}^3 \int_0^t \sigma_i(l, s, f(l, s))dz_i(l). \quad (4.1)$$

The functions $\alpha(\cdot)$ and $\sigma_i(\cdot)$, $i = 1, 2, 3$, are Lipschitz continuous, bounded and satisfy

$$\int_0^T \mid \alpha(t, s, f(t, s)) \mid ds < \infty, \quad \int_0^T \sigma_i(t, s, f(t, s))^2 ds < \infty$$

with probability one for fixed, but arbitrary $s \in [0, T]$. At this point, the volatility functions are left unspecified to preserve the general treatments of the arbitrage-free approach to the term structure modeling.

The stochastic differential equation of the forward rates has to ensure that at the initial trade date, values of discount bonds determined by means of discounted expectations be equal to their given values. The value of a discount bond $P(t, s-t)$ at some time $t \in [0, T]$ with the maturity $s-t$ is defined by

$$P(t; s-t) = e^{-\int_t^s f(t,l)dl}$$

and the value of the money market account $B(t), t \in [0, T]$, is given by

$$B(t) = e^{\int_0^t r(l)dl}.$$

The stochastic differential equation of which the relative bond price, defined by

$$Z(t, s-t) = \frac{P(t; s-t)}{B(t)},$$

is a strong solution, is now

$$\frac{dZ(t, s-t)}{Z(t, s-t)} = -\int_t^s \alpha(t, l, f(l, s))dl\, dt + \sum_{i=1}^3 \frac{1}{2} \left[\int_t^s \sigma_i(t, l, f(l, s))dl \right]^2 dt$$
$$- \sum_{i=1}^3 \int_t^s \sigma_i(t, l, f(l, s))dl\, dz_i(t). \tag{4.2}$$

It is easy to verify that, at the initial trade date, bond prices obeying these specifications are consistent with the given term structure of interest rates or forward rates.

HJM (1992) show that in the absence of arbitrage the drift term for the corresponding risk-adjusted process is a particular function of the volatility term. More specifically, to exclude arbitrage opportunities, the process $Z(t, s)$ has to be martingale with respect to the unique probability measure Q. To accomplish this, take the function $\alpha(t, s), t < s, t, s \in [0, T]$, as the solution to

$$\int_t^s \alpha(t, l, f(l, s))dl = \sum_{i=1}^3 \frac{1}{2} \left[\int_t^s \sigma_i(t, l, f(l, s))dl \right]^2$$

yielding, by taking the derivative with respect to s,

$$\alpha(t, l, f(l, s)) = \sum_{i=1}^3 \sigma_i(t, s) \int_t^s \sigma_i(t, l, f(l, s))dl.$$

At every time t, the values of all forward rates are known if the particular path of the standard Brownian motion up to this time is known also. The bond price is given by

$$P(t; s) = e^{-\int_t^{t+s} f(t,l)dl}$$

$$= \exp \left[\int_t^{t+s} f(0,l)dl \right.$$

$$+ \sum_{i=1}^3 \int_t^{t+s} \int_0^t \sigma_i(l,s) \int_t^s \sigma_i(l,s,f(l,s))dl ds$$

$$+ \left. \sum_{i=1}^3 \int_t^{t+s} \int_0^t \sigma_i(l,s,f(l,s))dz_i(l)ds \right] \tag{4.3}$$

and

$$\frac{dP(t;s-t)}{P(t;s-t)} = \mu(\cdot)dt + \sum_{i=1}^3 \int_t^s \sigma_i(t,l,f(l,s))dl dz_i(t). \tag{4.4}$$

Recall that in our model the bond pricing formula (1.12) satisfies

$$\frac{dP(t;s-t)}{P(t;s-t)} = (r + \lambda_r v B(s) + \lambda_v v D(s) + \lambda_\theta \theta C(s))dt - B(s)\sqrt{v}dz_1$$

$$-C(s)\zeta\sqrt{\theta}dz_2 - D(s)\eta\sqrt{v}dz_3. \tag{4.5}$$

To see how our model fits into the HJM framework, it is necessary to establish the particular assumption for the model with respect to the volatility of forward rates. This can be accomplished by computing the volatility of bond returns from equation (4.4) and comparing them with equation (4.5):

$$\int_t^s \sigma_1(t,l,f(l,s))dl = -B(s)\sqrt{v},$$

$$\int_t^s \sigma_2(t,l,f(l,s))dl = -C(s)\zeta\sqrt{\theta},$$

$$\int_t^s \sigma_3(t,l,f(l,s))dl = -D(s)\eta\sqrt{v}.$$

Substituting $\sigma_i, i = 1,2,3$ into equation (4.3) yields the closed form solution for the bond price under the HJM framework. This pricing formula is consistent with any given initial yield curve in addition to having the property that the short mean and volatility of interest rates are stochastic. However, its computation requires numerical methods and is rather tedious.

4.3   Whole-Yield Model

For completeness, in the following a procedure based on Hull and White (1990) for fitting a given yield curve under the continuous-time setting is outlined. To fit the initial yield curve exactly, let us assume that the long-term mean of volatility $\bar{v}$

is time-varying. It is easy to verify that under the special interest rate model, the differential equation that determines $A(t, T)$ is

$$\nu \bar{\theta} C(t) - \mu \bar{v}(t) D(t) + \frac{\dot{A}(t)}{A(t)} = 0. \tag{4.6}$$

The ODE (4.6) can be integrated to find that

$$\ln A(t) = -\nu \int_t^T \bar{\theta} C(T - s) ds - \int_t^T \mu \bar{v}(s) D(T - s) ds. \tag{4.7}$$

Given any time t, let $R(t, T)$ be the known yield curve to be fit and $r(t) = r$, $v(t) = v$, and $\theta(t) = \theta$ under the special interest rate dynamics. By definition,

$$R(t, T) = \frac{1}{T - t} \left[-\ln A(t, T) + r B(t, T) + \theta C(t, T) + v D(t, T) \right]. \tag{4.8}$$

From equations (4.7) and (4.8),

$$\int_t^T \mu \bar{v}(s) D(T - s) ds = -\nu \int_t^T \bar{\theta} C(T - s) ds - r B(T - t) - \theta C(T - t)$$
$$-v D(T - t) + R(t, T)(T - t), \ t \le T < \infty \tag{4.9}$$

which can further be written as

$$\mu \int_t^T \bar{v}(s) D(T - s) ds = M(t, T) \tag{4.10}$$

with $M(t, T)$ and $D(T - s)$ as known functions.

Performing Laplace transformation on both sides of the integral equation (4.10) yields

$$\mu \mathcal{L}(\bar{v}(\tau)) \mathcal{L}(D(\tau)) = \mathcal{L}(M(\tau)), \tag{4.11}$$

where operator $\mathcal{L}$ denotes Laplace transformation[1]. In (4.11) the convolution theorem of Laplace transformation has been used.[2] $\mathcal{L}(\bar{v}(\tau))$ can be solved from (4.11) and then be inverted to find $\bar{v}(s)$.

$$\bar{v}(s) = \frac{1}{2\pi i} \int_B e^{s\tau} \frac{\mathcal{L}(M(\tau))}{\mathcal{L}(D(\tau))} d\tau, \tag{4.12}$$

---

[1] $\mathcal{L}\{f(t)\} = \int_0^\infty e^{-st} f(t) dt.$

[2] The Convolution theorem says that if $F(s) = \mathcal{L}\{f(t)\}$ and $G(s) = \mathcal{L}\{g(t)\}$, then $F(s)G(s) = \mathcal{L}\{h(t)\}$, where

$$h(t) = \int_0^\infty f(t - u) g(u) du = \int_0^\infty f(u) g(t - u) du.$$

where B is the usual Bromwich contour which is conventionally defined from $\gamma - i\infty$ to $\gamma + i\infty$ with γ chosen to ensure that all the singularities of the integrand are to the left of the contour[3].

Once $\bar{v}(s)$ is found, substituting it into equation (4.7) to determine $A(t, T)$,

$$A(t, T) = A(0, T)e^{-\int_t^T \nu\bar{\theta}C(s,T)ds - \int_t^T \mu\bar{v}(s)D(s,T)ds}.$$

The price of any bond is thus given by

$$A(t, T)e^{-rB(t,T) - \theta C(t,T) - v(t,T)}.$$

---

[3]Because of the complexity of integrand involved here, it is difficult to obtain the inverse Laplace transformation analytically. Numerical algorithms should be employed.

Chapter 5

A Discrete-Time Version of the Model

5.1   Introduction

This chapter presents a discrete-time version of the model presented in Chapter 1 and, as such, makes contributions beyond that contained in Chapter 1. As a discrete time approximation to the continuous-time model, it provides a computational tool useful for numerical investigation of our continuous-time three-factor model of interest rates. In particular, it is an essential tool for computing values for derivatives with early exercise provisions like callable Treasury bonds and American options on Treasury futures.

General methods of constructing a numerical lattice (Nelson and Ramaswamy (1990), Hull and White (1990), and Tian (1993)) are employed in this chapter to convert the continuous-time version of our three-factor model of interest rates into a discrete-time version. The basic principle of the numerical lattice consists of the discrete approximation of a stochastic process and the transformation at each node of the lattice to obtain a corresponding variable value for the process being modeled. After this, suitable probabilities have to be specified to match the instantaneous drift and the volatility function.

As our model of interest rates involves three stochastic processes, the corresponding lattice extends in four dimensions: one in time and the other three in the state space. Given the specification of our model, the short mean and volatility follow independent processes and both processes affect the process of the short rate. Therefore, at each point in time, the construction of the four dimensional lattice consists of two steps. First, the lattices for the short mean and volatility are expanded one step further to determine the values of these two factors and the associated probabilities. Given these values as inputs, the next step is to accordingly extend the lattice for the short rate process. The method of constructing the tree for our model to be presented in this chapter is only one of several possible methods. Other methods, such as the one proposed in a recent paper of Hull and White (1994), of transforming the relevant stochastic processes to make them mutually independent of each other, are also feasible methods.

A procedure is outlined at the end of this chapter to fit our model to any given

initial term structure. With this procedure, therefore, the gap between the equilibrium approach and the no-arbitrage approach to the term structure modeling has
been filled.

The rest of this chapter is organized as follows. In the next section, the methodology for constructing the four-dimensional lattice is presented. A brief discussion
of applications of the lattice in valuing interest rate derivatives is given in the third
section. Section four is devoted to the procedure of fitting our model to a given
initial yield curve.

5.2   Construction of the Four-Dimensional Lattice

Multinomial Lattice

Consider a general diffusion process,

$$dx(t) \quad = \quad \mu_x dt + \sigma_x dB,$$

or in a risk-neutral world, an adjustment to the drift rate is required in the above
process:

$$dx(t) \quad = \quad (\mu_x - \lambda_x \sigma_x)dt + \sigma_x dB \equiv \mu(x,t)dt + \sigma(x,t)dB,$$

where λ_x is the market price of risk. To construct a multinomial lattice for this
process, a small time interval, Δt, and small change in x are chosen. A grid is then
constructed so that time is equal to

$$t_0, t_0 + \Delta t, ..., T; \quad \Delta t = \frac{T - t_0}{n},$$

where t_0 is the current date and T is the terminal date which is usually the maturity
of the derivative being considered. The evolution of x in the period $(t_i, t_{i+1}]$ is
assumed as follows: at the beginning of the period, x has a value $x(t_i)$. In the
interval (t_i, t_{i+1}), x remains this value till time t_{i+1} when it may jump to several
positions:

$$\begin{aligned} x_{i+1} \quad &= \quad x_i + \mu(x_i, t_i)\Delta t + \sigma(x_i, t_i)\sqrt{\Delta t}z_j(t_i) \\ &= \quad x_i + [\mu(x_i, t_i)\sqrt{\Delta t} + \sigma(x_i, t_i)z_j(t_i)]\sqrt{\Delta t}, \end{aligned} \quad (5.1)$$

where $z_j(t_i)$ is a discrete random variable with m possible outcomes defined as

$$prob\{z_j(t_i) = z_j\} = q_j, j = 1, 2, ..., m$$

such that

$$\sum_{j=1}^{m} q_j = 1, q_j \geq 0, E[z_j(t_i)] = 0, Var[z_j(t_i)] = 1.$$

These conditions ensure that the discrete process has correct drift and volatility which is crucial for its convergence to the continuous time model. Letting $m = 3$, it is easy to show that the three probabilities are given by

$$q_1 \equiv q_{j,j+1} = \frac{(\mu_x - \lambda\sigma_x)x_j\Delta t}{2\Delta x} + \frac{x_j^2\sigma_x^2\Delta t}{2\Delta x^2},$$

$$q_2 \equiv q_{j,j} = 1 - \frac{x_j^2\sigma_x^2\Delta t}{\Delta x^2},$$

$$q_3 \equiv q_{j,j-1} = -\frac{(\mu_x - \lambda\sigma_x)x_j\Delta t}{2\Delta x} + \frac{x_j^2\sigma^2\Delta t}{2\Delta x^2}.$$

The probabilities computed are exactly the weights one obtains when solving the PDE using the finite differencing method.

Transformation of the Feller Process

In our model, the short mean and volatility are independent and follow a Feller (square root) process. Conditional on the short mean and the volatility at a given time, the short rate also follows a square root process. To construct the numerical lattice for our three-factor model of interest rates, therefore, the first step is to construct the basic element of it, the lattice for the square root process.

The general form of a square root process is

$$dy(t) = \mu(\bar{y} - y(t))dt + \sigma\sqrt{y(t)}dB(t), \tag{5.2}$$

where parameters μ and σ are positive and real constants; the stochastic process $B = \{B(t), t \in [0,T]\}$ is standard Brownian Motion. The initial value of $y(0)$ is known.

Following the process (5.2), $y(x)$ will never become negative. The axis $y = 0$ serves as a reflecting barrier in the sense that whenever y becomes 0, it bounces up instantaneously into the positive region. Furthermore, if $2\mu\bar{y} - \sigma \geq 0$, the upward drift is sufficiently large to make $y = 0$ inaccessible. Thus the reflecting barrier at $y = 0$ may be reached only if $2\mu\bar{y} - \sigma < 0$.

In a risk neutral world, this process becomes

$$dy(t) = (\mu\bar{y} - \lambda'y(t))dt + \sigma\sqrt{y(t)}dB(t), \tag{5.3}$$

where $\lambda' = \mu + \lambda\sigma$ and $\lambda\sqrt{\bar{y}}$ is the market price of risk (see Cox-Ingersoll-Ross (1985)).

If the conventional method as introduced in the last section is applied to the stochastic process(5.3), the numerical lattice is not path-independent as the volatility function explicitly depends on $y(t)$. To avoid this path-dependency, the original process must be transformed such that its instantaneous standard deviation is equal to a constant. The transformation used to obtain a stochastic process with a constant volatility function is standard now [1]:

$$x(y,t) = \int^{y(t)} \frac{du}{\sigma\sqrt{u}}$$

yielding

$$x(y,t) = \frac{2\sqrt{y(t)}}{\sigma}.$$

The inverse transformation is

$$y(x) = \begin{cases} \frac{\sigma^2 x^2}{4} & \text{if} \quad x \geq 0 \\ 0 & \text{otherwise} \end{cases}$$

The resulting stochastic differential equation for the transformed process x is

$$dx(t) = \left(\frac{\alpha_1}{\alpha_2 + \alpha_3 x(t)} + \alpha_4 x(t) + \alpha_5 \right) dt + dB(t) \equiv \mu_x dt + dB(t), \quad (5.4)$$

where

$$\begin{aligned} \alpha_1 &= 4\mu\bar{y} - \sigma^2, \\ \alpha_2 &= 4\sigma\sqrt{y(0)}, \\ \alpha_3 &= 2\sigma^2, \\ \alpha_4 &= -\frac{\mu}{2}, \\ \alpha_5 &= -\frac{\mu}{\sigma}\sqrt{y(0)}. \end{aligned}$$

Trinomial Lattice for the Transformed Process

The transformed stochastic process (5.4), denoted in a general form

$$dx = \mu(x,t)dt + dB(t)$$

can be approximated by a path-independent trinomial lattice consisting of n steps.

Divide the time interval $[t_0, T]$ into n subintervals $[t_i, t_{i+1}]$ of equal length, where $t_{i+1} - t_i = \Delta t = T/n, i = \{0, ..., n\}$. The value of x on the lattice at time zero is the current value of the factor x_0; the values of x at other nodes have the form $x_j = x_0 + j\Delta x, j = -i, ..., i;$ [2] $i = 0, ..., n$, for some Δx. The relationship between Δx and Δt is

$$\Delta x = \omega\sqrt{\Delta t}$$

---

[1] See Hull and White (1990) and Nelson and Ramaswamy (1990).
[2] The number of x values is reduced because of the combining of the tree.

and ω is a positive constant. The partition of (x, t) space forms a grid. Each node of the grid is denoted (ij), representing $x_j = x_0 + j\Delta x$ and $t_i = t_0 + i\Delta t$ at this node. The construction of a lattice on the grid requires the specification of a branching process which describes the movement of the discrete process in a single period of length Δt. Considering a trinomial lattice, given any node of the lattice (ij), the lattice chain can reach nodes $(i + 1, j + 1), (i + 1, j)$, and $(i + 1, j - 1)$ at time t_{i+1} with the (risk-neutral) probabilities $q_{j,j+1}(t_i), q_{j,j}(t_i)$, and $q_{j,j-1}(t_i)$ respectively. These probabilities are chosen to match the instantaneous drift term and the volatility function exactly:

$$\sum_{l=-1}^{1} q_{j,j+l} x_{i+l} = x_j + \mu_x \Delta t,$$

$$\sum_{l=-1}^{1} q_{j,j+l} x_{i+l}^2 = (x_j + \mu_x \Delta t)^2 + \Delta t. \tag{5.5}$$

Thus the construction of the lattice is now equivalent to a search for a feasible solution to (5.5). It can be shown that the following is a set of solutions (Hull and White 1991),

$$\begin{aligned}
q_{j,j+1}(t_i) &= \frac{\mu_x(x_j, t_i)\Delta t}{2\Delta x} + \frac{\Delta t}{2\Delta x^2} + \frac{(\mu_x(x_j, t_i)\Delta t)^2}{2\Delta x^2}, \\
q_{j,j}(t_i) &= 1 - \frac{\Delta t}{\Delta x^2} - \frac{(\mu_x(x_j, t_i)\Delta t)^2}{\Delta x^2}, \\
q_{j,j-1}(t_i) &= -\frac{\mu_x(x_j, t_i)\Delta t}{2\Delta x} + \frac{\Delta t}{2\Delta x^2} + \frac{(\mu_x(x_j, t_i)\Delta t)^2}{2\Delta x^2},
\end{aligned} \tag{5.6}$$

where $j = \{-i, ..., 0, ..., i\}$ and $i = \{0, ..., n\}$.

It can be verified that given these probabilities the discrete-time process converges to the continuous-time process as $\Delta t \to 0$.

Figure 3.1 shows the building of block of a trinomial lattice:

The building block together with the transition probabilities (5.6) generate a trinomial model. In particular, the model is path-independent in the sense that starting at any node, the trinomial chain reaches the same state by following the different paths, as long as these paths have the same number of different movements: up, down, and no-change.

The probabilities (5.6) are positive if both

$$\begin{aligned}
1 &> \frac{\Delta t}{\Delta x^2} + \frac{(\mu_{ij}\Delta t)^2}{\Delta x^2}, \\
\frac{\mu_{ij}\Delta t}{\Delta x} &< \frac{\Delta t}{\Delta x^2} + \frac{(\mu_{ij}\Delta t)^2}{\Delta x^2}
\end{aligned} \tag{5.7}$$

are satisfied, where $\mu_{ij} \equiv \mu_x(x_j, t_i)$.

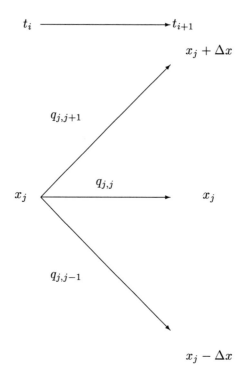

Figure 3.1: A Building Block of Trinomial Tree

The set of nodes for which these conditions hold is defined as

$$\Omega = \left\{(i,j)\Big|1 > \frac{\Delta t}{\Delta x^2} + \frac{(\mu_{ij}\Delta t)^2}{\Delta x^2}; \quad \frac{\mu_{ij}\Delta t}{\Delta x} < \frac{\Delta t}{\Delta x^2} + \frac{(\mu_{ij}\Delta t)^2}{\Delta x^2}\right\}.$$

From equation (5.7) it can be seen that when x gets large, some nodes of the lattice may not be elements of Ω. In this case a modification of the branching process in these particular nodes is needed to enable retention of positive probabilities and ensure convergence. In general, at some node (i, j) of the lattice, one wants to reach the following three different nodes: $(t_{i+1}, j + k + 1), (t_{i+1}, j + k)$, and $(t_{i+1}, j + k - 1)$ at time t_{i+1} with the probabilities $q_{j,j+k+1}(t_i), q_{j,j+k}(t_i)$, and $q_{j,j+k-1}(t_i)$ respectively. Matching of the first and second moments now yields

$$
\begin{aligned}
q_{j,j+k+1}(t_i) &= \frac{1}{2}\left((k^2 - k) + (1 - 2k)\frac{\mu_x \Delta t}{\Delta x} + \frac{\Delta t}{2\Delta x^2} + \frac{(\mu_x \Delta t)^2}{2\Delta x^2}\right), \\
q_{j,j+k}(t_i) &= 1 - k^2 + 2k\frac{\mu_x \Delta t}{\Delta x} - \frac{\Delta t}{\Delta x^2} - \frac{(\mu_x \Delta t)^2}{\Delta x^2},
\end{aligned}
\tag{5.8}
$$

$$q_{j,j+k-1}(t_i) = \frac{1}{2}((k^2 + k) - (1 + 2k)\frac{\mu_x \Delta t}{\Delta x} + \frac{\Delta t}{2\Delta x^2} + \frac{(\mu_x \Delta t)^2}{2\Delta x^2}).$$

If a node of the binomial lattice is not an interior point of Ω, the probabilities at the outside region of the lattice are modified to ensure that only elements of Ω can be reached. Practically this means, for the lower part of the lattice, identified as

$$x_{I^L(t_i)+1} \in \Omega \quad \text{and} \quad x_{I^L(t_i)} \notin \Omega$$

for $i = \{1, ..., n-1\}$, the number of extra upward jumps $K(I^L)$ at this node necessary to return to the trinomial tree is

$$K(I^L) = \begin{cases} \text{The smallest, positive integer } k \text{ such that} \\ \quad q_{I^L, I^L+k+1}(t_i) \geq 0 \\ \quad q_{I^L, I^L+k}(t_i) \geq 0 \qquad\qquad \text{If } x_{I^L+k-1}(t_{i+1}) \in \Omega \\ \quad q_{I^L, I^L+k-1}(t_i) \geq 0 \\ \qquad\qquad 1. \qquad\qquad\qquad\qquad \text{otherwise} \end{cases}$$

Similarly, for the upper part of the lattice, identified by

$$x_{I^U(t_i)-1} \in \Omega \quad \text{and} \quad x_{I^U(t_i)} \notin \Omega$$

for $i = \{1, ..., n-1\}$, the number of extra downward jumps $K(I^U)$ at this point necessary to return to the trinomial tree is

$$K(I^U) = \begin{cases} \text{The smallest, positive integer } k \text{ such that} \\ \quad q_{I^U, I^U+k+1}(t_i) \geq 0 \\ \quad q_{I^U, I^U+k}(t_i) \geq 0 \qquad\qquad \text{If } x_{I^U+k+1}(t_{i+1}) \in \Omega \\ \quad q_{I^U, I^U+k-1}(t_i) \geq 0 \\ \qquad\qquad 1. \qquad\qquad\qquad\qquad \text{otherwise} \end{cases}$$

If, at these nodes, one of the trinomial probabilities is still negative, these probabilities are censored by equating them to $\frac{1}{3}$.

To implement the modified method, consider the nodes at time $i\Delta t$ where $x = x_0 + j\Delta x$. One first calculates the expected value of x at time $(i + 1)\Delta t$ given that it starts at this node. The value of k is then chosen to make $x_0 + k\Delta x$ as close as possible to this expected value of x and draw the tree so that the three possible values of x that can be reached at time $(i + 1)\Delta t$ are $x_0 + (k - 1)\Delta x$, $x_0 + k\Delta x$, and $x_0 + (k + 1)\Delta x$.

Lattices of Short Mean and Volatility

The short mean follows the process

$$d\theta(t) = \nu(\overline{\theta} - \theta(t))dt + \zeta\sqrt{\theta(t)}dB_2(t), \ t \geq 0, \ \overline{\theta} > 0, \ \nu > 0. \qquad (5.9)$$

Following the procedures outlined in the previous section (i.e. making the process risk-neutral and transforming the process into a unit-variance process), the lattice of the short mean process can be constructed.[3] If a node (i, j) is in the set Ω defined in the previous section, the branching process is straightforward: Three different nodes $(i + 1, j + 1), (i + 1, j)$, and $(i + 1, j - 1)$ can be reached at time t_{i+1} with the probabilities

$$
\begin{aligned}
q^\theta_{j,j+1} &= \frac{\mu^\theta_{ij}\Delta t}{2\Delta\theta} + \frac{\Delta t}{2\Delta\theta^2} + \frac{(\mu^\theta_{ij}\Delta t)^2}{2\Delta\theta^2}, \\
q^\theta_{j,j} &= 1 - \frac{\Delta t}{\Delta\theta^2} - \frac{(\mu^\theta_{ij}\Delta t)^2}{\Delta\theta^2}, \\
q^\theta_{j,j-1} &= -\frac{\mu^\theta_{ij}\Delta t}{2\Delta\theta} + \frac{\Delta t}{2\Delta\theta^2} + \frac{(\mu^\theta_{ij}\Delta t)^2}{2\Delta\theta^2},
\end{aligned}
\tag{5.10}
$$

where

$$
\mu^\theta_{ij} \equiv \mu(\theta_j, t_i) = \frac{\alpha_6}{\alpha_7 + \alpha_8(\theta_0 + j\Delta\theta)} + \alpha_9(\theta_0 + j\Delta\theta) + \alpha_{10}
\tag{5.11}
$$

is the drift term of the transformed process. Parameters $\alpha_i, i = 6, 7, 8, 9, 10$ can be obtained from formula (5.4) with the appropriate transformations.

Since θ can take on any positive value, μ_{ij} is not bounded. It follows that the lattice constructed by the standard method may not converge; the modified method as described in the previous section should be used.

It is easy to see from equation (5.8) that $k = 0$ if

$$
-\frac{1}{2} \leq \left(\frac{\alpha_6}{\alpha_7 + \alpha_8\theta(t)} + \alpha_9\theta(t) + \alpha_{10} \right) \frac{\Delta t}{\Delta\theta} \leq \frac{1}{2}
$$

which is equivalent to

$$
0 \leq \theta_{\min} \leq \theta \leq \theta_{\max} \leq +\infty,
$$

where

$$
\begin{aligned}
\theta_{\min} &= \left| \frac{-b + \sqrt{b^2 + 4ac}}{2a} \right|, \\
\theta_{\max} &= \left| \frac{b + \sqrt{b^2 + 4ac}}{2a} \right|, \\
a &= \alpha_8\alpha_9, \\
b &= \alpha_7\alpha_8 + \alpha_8\alpha_{10} - \beta\alpha_8, \\
c &= \alpha_6 + \alpha_7\alpha_{10} - \beta\alpha_7, \\
\beta &= \frac{\Delta\theta}{2\Delta t}.
\end{aligned}
$$

---

[3] Here, for simplicity and easy identification, the same notation is used to represent both the original process and the transformed process.

The values of θ considered on the grid are now $\theta_0, \theta_1, ..., \theta_n$, where θ_0 is the largest multiple of $\Delta\theta$ less than $\theta_{\min}$, or formally,

$$\theta_0 = \sup_{m\Delta\theta < \theta_{\min}} \{m\Delta\theta\},$$

and similarly

$$\theta_n = \inf_{m\Delta\theta > \theta_{\max}} \{m\Delta\theta\}.$$

When the value θ_0 is reached, the lattice chain needs to jump up and the three possible values that might be obtained after Δt are θ_0, θ_1, and θ_2. The probabilities q_{00}, q_{01}, and q_{02} are calculated from equations (5.8) with $j = 0$ and $k = 1$. When the value θ_n is reached, the lattice chain needs to jump down and the three possible values that might be obtained after Δt are $\theta_{n-2}, \theta_{n-1}$, and θ_n. The probabilities $q_{n,n}, q_{n,n-1}$, and $q_{n,n-2}$ are calculated from equations (5.8) with $j = n$ and $k = -1$.

Finally, for later reference, a brief note on the volatility lattice is given in the following. Assume the transformed stochastic process for the volatility [4] has been approximated by a trinomial lattice. At a given node of the lattice (i, j), three different points $(i + 1, j + 1), (i + 1, j)$, and $(i + 1, j - 1)$ at time t_{j+1} can be reached with the probability $q^v_{j,j+1}(t_i), q^v_{j,j}(t_i)$, and $q^v_{j,j-1}(t_i)$, with

$$
\begin{aligned}
q^v_{j,j+1}(t_i) &= \frac{\mu^v_j \Delta t}{2\Delta v} + \frac{\Delta t}{\Delta v^2} + \frac{(\mu^v_j \Delta t)^2}{\Delta v^2}, \\
q^v_{j,j}(t_i) &= 1 - \frac{\Delta t}{\Delta v^2} - \frac{(\mu^v_j \Delta t)^2}{\Delta v^2}, \\
q^v_{j,j-1}(t_i) &= -\frac{\mu^v_j \Delta t}{2\Delta v} + \frac{\Delta t}{\Delta v^2} + \frac{(\mu^v_j \Delta t)^2}{\Delta v^2},
\end{aligned}
\tag{5.12}
$$

and

$$\mu^v_{ij} = \frac{\beta_1}{\beta_2 + \beta_3(v_0 + j\Delta v)} + \alpha_4(v_0 + j\Delta v) + \beta_5, \tag{5.13}$$

where $\beta_1, \beta_2, \beta_3, \beta_4, \beta_5$ can be obtained similarly from equation (5.4).

The Four-Dimensional Lattice

At each point in time, the lattice for the short rate is constructed after the lattice for the short mean and volatility have been constructed at this point and the values of the mean and volatility have been obtained.

Let $(ijkl)$ denote the node of the four dimensional grid where $t = t_0 + i\Delta t, r = r_0 + j\Delta r, \theta = \theta_0 + k\Delta\theta, v = v_0 + l\Delta v, i = 0, 1, ..., n$, and $j, k, l = -i, ..., i$. At any

---

[4] See footnote [3].

node $(ijkl)$, assuming that the lattices for the volatility and short mean have been constructed, the short rate can reach three possible values $r_0 + (j+1)\Delta r, r_0 + j\Delta r$, and $r_0 + (j-1)\Delta r$ at time $t_0 + (i+1)\Delta t.$[5] Let $q^r_{j,j+1}(t_i) \mid [\theta_k, v_l], q^r_{j,j}(t_i) \mid [\theta_k, v_l]$, and $q^r_{j,j-1}(t_i) \mid [\theta_k, v_l]$ denote the probabilities that the short rate transit from r_j, to r_{j+1}, r_j, r_{j-1} respectively, given the values of the short mean and volatility at time t_{i+1} θ_k and v_l [6]. It is easy to verify that these three probabilities are

$$q^r_{j,j+1} \mid [\theta_k, v_l] = \frac{[\mu_{ij} \mid \theta_k, v_l]\Delta t}{2\Delta r} + \frac{\Delta t}{2\Delta r^2} + \frac{([\mu_{ij} \mid \theta_k, v_l]\Delta t)^2}{2\Delta r^2},$$

$$q^r_{j,j} \mid [\theta_k, v_l] = 1 - \frac{\Delta t}{\Delta r^2} - \frac{([\mu_{ij} \mid \theta_k, v_l]\Delta t)^2}{\Delta r^2}, \qquad (5.14)$$

$$q^r_{j,j-1} \mid [\theta_k, v_l] = -\frac{[\mu_{ij} \mid \theta_k, v_l]\Delta t}{2\Delta r} + \frac{\Delta t}{2\Delta r^2} + \frac{([\mu_{ij} \mid \theta_k, v_l]\Delta t)^2}{2\Delta r^2},$$

where $[\mu_{ij} \mid \theta_k, v_l]$ is the drift term of the short rate given the values of the short mean and volatility at time t_{i+1}:

$$[\mu_{ij} \mid \theta_k, v_l] = \frac{\omega_1}{\omega_2 + \omega_3(r_0 + j\Delta r)} + \omega_4(r_0 + j\Delta r) + \omega_5 \qquad (5.15)$$

and

$$
\begin{aligned}
\omega_1 &= 4k(\theta_0 + k\Delta\theta) - (v_0 + l\Delta v), \\
\omega_2 &= 4(\sqrt{v_0 + l\Delta v})\sqrt{r(0)} \\
\omega_3 &= 2(v_0 + l\Delta v), \\
\omega_4 &= -\frac{k}{2}, \\
\omega_5 &= -\frac{k}{\sqrt{v_0 + l\Delta v}}\sqrt{r(0)}.
\end{aligned}
$$

With probabilities q^rs defined in this manner, the drift rate of the short rate is consistent with the value of the short mean obtained from the short mean lattice and the volatility of the short rate is equal to the value of volatility from the volatility lattice.

At any node of the lattice $(ijkl)$, there are three possible values for the short mean at the next time point, namely θ_{k+1}, θ_k, and θ_{k-1}, with the associated probabilities given by equation (5.10). And, similarly, there are also three possible values, v_{l+1}, v_l, and v_{l-1}, with probabilities given by (5.12).[7] So there are nine possible combinations of the short mean and the volatility, denoted by

$$(\theta_{k+h}, v_{l+m}) \qquad h = \{-1, 0, 1\}; m = \{-1, 0, 1\}.$$

---

[5] Here, to avoid redundancy in presentation, only the nodes that are not on the margin of the lattice are discussed. The marginal nodes can be treated by the same method.

[6] Here the assumption has been made that θ and v in the stochastic differential equation for the short rate can be treated as constant in each time period. A better treatment will involve a complex transformation of the SDE to make it have a constant variance.

[7] See footnote [5].

Given each combination (θ_{k+h}, v_{l+m}), the short rate takes three possible values, r_{j+1}, r_j, and r_{j-1} with probabilities given by (5.14). Thus, there are 27 possible combinations of θ, v, and r that can be reached at time t_{j+1} and 27 probabilities associated with each transition. The building block of the four-dimensional lattice is shown on the next page.

Given any node $(ijkl)$ of the four-dimensional lattice, the probability that the node $(i + 1, j + 1, k, l - 1)$ can be reached at time t_{j+1}, denote $p_{j,j+1;k;l,l-1}$, is

$$p_{i;j,j+1;k;l,l-1} \;\;=\;\; q^{\theta}_{k,k} q^{v}_{l,l-1} q^{r}_{j,j+1} \mid [\theta_k, v_{l-1}], \tag{5.16}$$

where $q^{\theta}_{k,k}, q^{v}_{l,l-1}$, and $q^{r}_{j,j+1}$ are given in equations (5.10), (5.12), and (5.14) respectively. Similar relations can be obtained for the other 26 probabilities. These probabilities may be used to evaluate interest rate derivatives.

Figure 3.2: A Building Block of the Four Dimensional Lattice

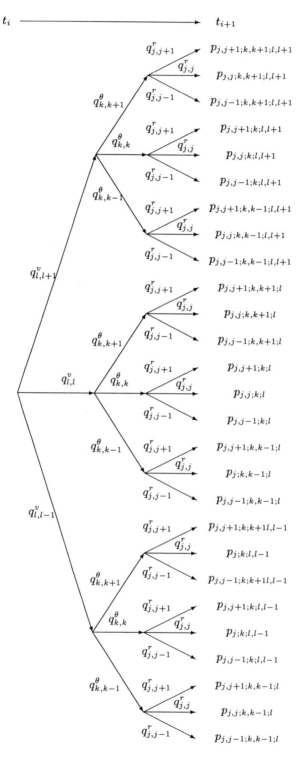

5.3 Applications

Valuation of Bonds

Assume that the four dimensional space (t, r, θ, v) has been partitioned into a grid where the time range expands from the current time t_0 to the maturity of bond T. Time takes value $t = t_0 + i\Delta t$, $i = 1, ..., n$. and three state variables take values $r = r_0 + j\Delta$, $\theta = \theta_0 + k\Delta\theta$, and $v = v_0 + l\Delta v$ respectively, with $j, k, l = -i, ..., i$. Assume that the lattice for the three factor model has been constructed following the procedures in the previous sections.

Let P_{ijkl} be the value of a zero-coupon bond at node $(ijkl) = (t_i, r_j, \theta_k, v_l)$. At maturity, the bond price is equal to its face value, so $P_{njkl} = 1$, for all $j, k, l = -n, ..., n$. The value of the bond prior to maturity can be calculated using the risk-neutral valuation. The arbitrage-free value of a security is equal to its discounted expectation with respect to the equivalent probability measure under which the relative value of a security is martingale. The probabilities obtained as the lattice is being constructed are risk-neutral by construction.

The attraction of the lattice model lies in the fact that once the one-period discount factor and probabilities are determined, securities are evaluated by backward induction, averaging and discounting at each node. Thus the price P_{ijkl} at node $(ijkl)$ of a zero-coupon bond is obtained from its prices at all the nodes in the next period by the backward equation. Formally,

$$
\begin{aligned}
P_{ijkl} &= \Big[p_{j;k;l-1} P_{i+1;j;k,l-1} + p_{j;k;l} P_{i+1;j;k,l} + p_{j;k;l+1} P_{i+1;j;k,l+1} + \\
&\quad p_{j-1;k;l-1} P_{i+1;j-1;k,l-1} + p_{j-1;k;l} P_{i+1;j-1;k,l} + \\
&\quad p_{j-1;k;l+1} P_{i+1;j-1;k,l+1} + p_{j+1;k;l-1} P_{i+1;j+1;k,l-1} + \\
&\quad p_{j+1;k;l} P_{i+1;j+1;k,l} + p_{j+1;k;l+1} P_{i+1;j+1;k,l+1} + \\
&\quad p_{j;k-1;l-1} P_{i+1;j;k-1,l-1} + p_{j;k-1;l} P_{i+1;j;k-1,l} + \\
&\quad p_{j;k-1;l+1} P_{i+1;j;k-1,l+1} + p_{j-1;k-1;l-1} P_{i+1;j-1;k-1,l-1} + \\
&\quad p_{j-1;k-1;l} P_{i+1;j-1;k-1,l} + p_{j-1;k-1;l+1} P_{i+1;j-1;k-1,l+1} + \\
&\quad p_{j+1;k-1;l-1} P_{i+1;j+1;k-1,l-1} + p_{j+1;k-1;l} P_{i+1;j+1;k-1,l} + \\
&\quad p_{j+1;k-1;l+1} P_{i+1;j+1;k-1,l+1} + p_{j;k+1;l-1} P_{i+1;j;k+1,l-1} + \\
&\quad p_{j;k+1;l} P_{i+1;j;k+1,l} + p_{j;k+1;l+1} P_{i+1;j;k+1,l+1} + \\
&\quad p_{j-1;k+1;l-1} P_{i+1;j-1;k+1,l-1} + p_{j-1;k+1;l} P_{i+1;j-1;k+1,l} + \\
&\quad p_{j-1;k+1;l+1} P_{i+1;j-1;k+1,l+1} + p_{j+1;k+1;l-1} P_{i+1;j+1;k+1,l-1} + \\
&\quad p_{j+1;k+1;l} P_{i+1;j+1;k+1,l} + p_{j+1;k+1;l+1} P_{i+1;j+1;k+1,l+1} \Big] e^{-r_j(t_i)\Delta t} \\
&= \left[\sum_{a,b,c=-1,0,-1} p_{j+a,k+b,l+c} P_{i+1,j+a,k+b,l+c} \right] e^{-r_j(t_i)\Delta t}. \qquad (5.17)
\end{aligned}
$$

The 27 probabilities $p_{j;k;l-1}, p_{j;k;l}, p_{j;k;l+1}, ...$ etc. are from (5.10), (5.12), and

(5.14).

For a coupon bond, the value of P_{ijkl} at any node must be augmented by any cash distribution that might occur at that node. In that case,

$$P_{ijkl} = \left[\sum_{a,b,c=-1,0,-1} p_{j+a,k+b,l+c} P_{i+1,j+a,k+b,l+c} + d_i \right] e^{-r_j(t_i)\Delta t}, \quad (5.18)$$

where d_i is the coupon paid at the end of period i. The iterations are conducted backward all the way to period zero, at which time the price of the bond is P_{0000}.

Valuation of American Options on Bonds

Let C_{ijkl} be the value of an American option at node $(ijkl)$ on the lattice. Suppose P is the unique solution of the bond price equation and P_{ijkl}, the bond price at $(ijkl), i = 1, .., n, j, k, l = -i, ..i$, has been determined following the procedures outlined in the previous section. If the option is retained, the risk-neutral valuation leads to

$$C_{ijkl} = \sum_{a=-1,0,-1} \sum_{b=-1,0,-1} \sum_{c=-1,0,-1} p_{j+a,k+b,l+c} C_{i+1,j+a,k+b,l+c} e^{-r_j(t_i)\Delta t}.$$

As it is an American option, this value must be compared with the option's intrinsic value at the node, therefore

$$C_{ijkl} = \max \left[K - P_{ijkl}, \sum_{a,b,c=-1,0,-1} p_{j+a,k+b,l+c} C_{i+1,j+a,k+b,l+c} e^{-r_j(t_i)\Delta t} \right]$$

$$(5.19)$$

Starting at the maturity date $T = n\Delta t$, the value of an American put at this date is known to be $\max[K - P(T), 0]$, so

$$C_{njkl} = \max[K - P_{njkl}, 0].$$

Using equation (5.19) to perform the iterations backward all the way to period zero, at which time the price of the American put option is read off as C_{0000}.

Computation of Hedge Ratios

Practitioners are interested not only in prices of derivatives but also in the hedge ratios and other parameters to evaluate and manage the risk of their derivatives books. Typically they need to know the sensitivities of derivative prices to changes in the underlying asset spot price, the volatility of the asset price, the time to maturity, etc. The sensitivities are first or second order derivatives of the derivatives price function with respect to relevant variables or parameters.

Sensitivities of interest rate derivatives can be readily extended to and conveniently computed in our framework. As in our model, there are three factors which can be considered as three underlying variables; the hedge ratios can therefore be defined correspondingly.

Let Π be the value of a derivative security or a portfolio of derivatives. The three delta's are naturally defined in the following:

$$\Delta_r = \frac{\partial \Pi}{\partial r}, \quad \Delta_\theta = \frac{\partial \Pi}{\partial \theta}, \quad \Delta_v = \frac{\partial \Pi}{\partial v}.$$

Taking an American put option as an example: in our four-dimensional tree model, the delta's can be calculated according to the following relation:

$$\Delta_r = \frac{C_{ijkl} - C_{i,j-1,kl}}{\Delta r}.$$

All other hedge ratios can be computed similarly. It is interesting to note that two conventional hedge ratios,

$$vega = \frac{\Delta \Pi}{\Delta r}, \quad \rho = \frac{\Delta \Pi}{\Delta v}$$

have been incorporated into our definition of deltas with respect to the short rate and the volatility.

In practice, practitioners are also interested in calculating the partial derivatives of a security price with respect to a number of different shifts in the term structure. They normally divide the yield curve or the forward curve into a number of sections and consider change in the yield curve due to a small shift in one section while holding other sections unchanged. Although practically useful, this approach is problematic since it is not based on an internally consistent model of the term structure of interest rates. The assumption that one section shifts and other sections remain unchanged may be inconsistent with the movements of the term struture. On the other hand, our model of the term structure allows for a variety of yield curve shifts which are impossible under one or two-factor models of the term structure. Changes in factors may change a part of the yield curve more significantly than the rest, the scenario that practitioners want to investigate. Furthermore, since the shifts of yield curves in this fashion are due to change in a few factors, it is much more tractable.

Fitting to the Initial Yield Curve

This section outlines a procedure to fit our discrete-time three factor model of interest rates to a given yield curve. Consistency with the initial yield curve requires that if the backward induction method, as discussed in the previous section, is applied to a single cash flow of unity at any period n, the price thus obtained must exactly equal the given price of the zero-coupon bond maturing at that time, P_n. It is generally impossible to do that if all the model parameters are constant. Therefore, a number of no-arbitrage models of interest rates manage to fit the given term structure by making some parameters time-varying. For example, in Ho and Lee (1986), the drift parameter of the short rate process is assumed to be time-varying; in Black-Derman-Toy (1990), both the drift and volatility parameters of the lognormal short rate process are assumed to be time-varying; in Longstaff and Schwartz (1993), which extends their two-factor equilibrium model of interest rates (Longstaff and Schwartz (1992)), the risk premium is assumed to be time-varying.

For easy presentation, to fit our model to the initial yield curve, the shift rate for the short interest rate is assumed time-varying. The continuous-time version of the short rate model to be fit is therefore

$$dr = [\alpha(t) + \mu(\theta - r)]dt + \sqrt{vr}dB,$$

after a few inverse transformations defined in the previous sections. To fit a given term structure to our model is to estimate the parameter α_i in every time step so that the bond price obtained from the tree equals the observed price of the discount bond, P_n. The method employed here is the discrete-time Green's function method. A similar method has been used by Hull and White (1990) and Jamshidian (1991) to fit a one-dimensional interest rate model into a given yield curve.

Let $G_{i,j,k,l;m,n,q,s}$ be the discrete Green's function or the value of an Arrow-Debreu security. More specifically, $G_{i,j,k,l;m,n,q,s}$ is the price, at node $[i, j, k, l]$ of the four-dimensional lattice of a security that pays off one unit if node $[m, n, q, s]$ is reached and zero elsewhere. The variables $[i, j, k, l]$ in the Green's function, $G_{i,j,k,l;m,n,q,s}$, are called backward variables, while $[m, n, q, s]$, with $m \geq i$, are forward variables. Formally, for fixed $[m, n, q, s]$, $G_{i,j,k,l;m,n,q,s}$, the price of an interest rate security, as the function of $[i, j, k, l]$, satisfies the backward equation given in the previous section:

$$
\begin{aligned}
G_{ijkl,mnqs} &\equiv G_{i,j,k,l;m,n,q,s} \\
&= \left[\sum_{a,b,c=-1,0,1} p_{j+a,k+b,l+c} G_{i+1,j+a,k+b,l+c;m,n,q,s} \right] d_{ijkl}.
\end{aligned}
$$

Here d_{ijkl} is the discount factor defined as the price at node $[i, j, k, l]$ of the zero-coupon bond maturing at period $i + 1$:

$$d_{ijkl} = e^{-(\alpha_i + r_j(t_i))\Delta t} = e^{-(\alpha_i + r_0 + j\Delta r)\Delta t}. \tag{5.20}$$

The Greens' function $G_{ijkl;mnqs}$[8] can also be treated as a function of the forward variables, $[m, n, q, s]$. It is easy to verify that

$$
\begin{aligned}
G_{ijkl;m+1,nqs} \;=\; & \left[\sum_{b,c=-1,0,1} p_{n+1,q+b,s+c} G_{ijkl;m,n+a,q+b,s+c} \right] d_{m,n+1,qs} \\
+\; & \left[\sum_{b,c=-1,0,1} p_{n,q+b,s+c} G_{ijkl;m,n+a,q+b,s+c} \right] d_{mnqs} \qquad (5.21)\\
+\; & \left[\sum_{b,c=-1,0,1} p_{n-1,q+b,s+c} G_{ijkl;m,n+a,q+b,s+c} \right] d_{m,n-1,qs}.
\end{aligned}
$$

The forward equation (5.21) will be used to fit the initial term structure to our model. The Green's function $G_{ijkl,mnqs}$ has the property that the value at $[0000]$ of all European-style derivatives with the terminal payoff g_{mnqs} at maturity $m\Delta t$ can be valued by [9]

$$
F_{0000} = \sum_n \sum_q \sum_s G_{0000,mnqs} g_{mnqs}.
$$

In particular, let P_{m+1} be the $m + 1$-maturity bond price, then

$$
P_{m+1} = \sum_n \sum_q \sum_s G_{0000,mnqs} d_{mnqs}. \qquad (5.22)
$$

With (5.20), (5.21), and (5.22), the procedure to estimate α_m can now be outlined. Given m, it is assumed that the Green's function $G_{0000,inqs}$ has been estimated up to $i \le m$ and the parameter α_i has been estimated up to time $i \le m - 1$ so that they are consistent with the given bond price data up to P_m. The following two steps will expand the estimation one step further.

Substituting $G_{0,0,0,0;m,n,q,s}$ and $d_{m,n,q,s}$ into the equation (5.22),

$$
\begin{aligned}
P_{m+1} \;=\; & \sum_n \sum_q \sum_s G_{0000,mnqs} d_{mnqs} \\
=\; & \sum_n \sum_q \sum_s G_{0000,mnqs} e^{-(\alpha_m + r_0 + n\Delta r)\Delta t}
\end{aligned}
$$

yields

$$
\alpha_m = \frac{\ln \sum_n \sum_q \sum_s G_{0000,mnqs} e^{-(r_0 + n\Delta r)\Delta t} - \ln P_{m+1}}{\Delta t}.
$$

---

[8] $G_{ijkl;mnqs}, G_{i,j,k,l;m,n,q,s}, G_{ijkl;m,n,q,s}$ etc. are the same and will be used interchangeably.
[9] This is the discrete-time version of the following relation:

$$
F(x, t, T) = \int G(y, T, x, t) g(y, T) dy.
$$

With α_m and $G_{0000,mnqs}$, using equation (5.21) and setting $i,j,k,l = 0$, to compute $G_{0000,m+1,nqs}$,

$$
\begin{aligned}
G_{0000;m+1,nqs} \\
= \Big[\sum_{b=-1,0,1} \sum_{c=-1,0,1} p_{n+1,q+b,s+c} G_{0000;m,n+a,q+b,s+c} \Big] d_{m,n+1,qs} + \\
\Big[\sum_{b=-1,0,1} \sum_{c=-1,0,1} p_{n,q+b,s+c} G_{0000;m,n+a,q+b,s+c} \Big] d_{mnqs} + \\
\Big[\sum_{b=-1,0,1} \sum_{c=-1,0,1} p_{n-1,q+b,s+c} G_{0000;m,n+a,q+b,s+c} \Big] d_{m,n-1,qs}
\end{aligned}
$$

for all n, q, s. Continue these steps inductively forward until all the given bond price data are used.

As the goal of this section is to fit our model into a given initial yield curve, only one parameter needs to be time-varying. By making more parameters time-varying the model can fit other data as well.

Chapter 6

Estimation of the Model

6.1 Introduction

This chapter outlines three methods to estimate our three factor model of the term structure. The first one is the Kalman filter method. The second is the maximum likelihood method. The third is the method of moments. A procedure to estimate the general interest rate dynamics by the simulated method of moments is also discussed. All these methods have been extensively used in empirical studies of the term structure models (Brown and Bybvig (1986), Chan et al (1992), Gibbons and Ramaswamy (1993), Chen and Scott (1993), Das (1993), Lund (1994), Pearson and Sun (1994)).

6.2 Kalman Filter

Consider yields on discount bonds of different maturities $\tau_i, i = 1, ..., n$, under the special interest rate dynamics:

$$
\begin{aligned}
R(r, \theta, v, t; \tau_i) &= -\frac{1}{\tau_i}[\ln A(\tau_i) - B(\tau_i)r(t) - C(\tau_i)\theta(t) - D(\tau_i)v(t)] \\
&= a(\tau_i) + b(\tau_i)r(t) + c(\tau_i)\theta(t) + d(\tau_i)v(t)] \\
&\equiv R(t, \tau_i), \quad i = 1, ..., n.
\end{aligned}
$$

Let

$$
Y(t) = \begin{pmatrix} R(t, \tau_1) \\ R(t, \tau_2) \\ \vdots \\ R(t, \tau_n) \end{pmatrix}.
$$

Let

$$
S(t) = \begin{pmatrix} r(t) \\ \theta(t) \\ v(t) \end{pmatrix}
$$

be the state vector.

The measurement equation relating the observable vector $Y(t)$ to the state vector is given by

$$Y(t) = A(\Phi) + C(\Phi)S(t), \tag{6.1}$$

where

$$C(\Phi) = \begin{pmatrix} b(\tau_1) & c(\tau_1) & d(\tau_1) \\ \vdots & \vdots & \vdots \\ b(\tau_n) & c(\tau_n) & d(\tau_n) \end{pmatrix},$$

$$A(\Phi) = \begin{pmatrix} a(\tau_1) \\ a(\tau_2) \\ \vdots \\ a(\tau_n) \end{pmatrix},$$

and

$$\Phi = \begin{pmatrix} k & \nu & \zeta & \bar{\theta} & \mu & \eta & \bar{v} & \lambda_r & \lambda_\theta & \lambda_v \end{pmatrix}.$$

The transition equation of the state variables is given by the following system of stochastic differential equations:

$$\begin{aligned} dr(t) &= k(\theta(t) - r(t))dt + \sqrt{v(t)}dz_1(t), \\ d\theta(t) &= \nu(\bar{\theta} - \theta(t))dt + \zeta\sqrt{\theta(t)}dz_2(t), \\ dv(t) &= \mu(\bar{v} - v(t))dt + \eta\sqrt{v(t)}dz_3(t), \end{aligned}$$

which can be written as

$$dS(t) = [H(\Phi)S(t) + J]dt + V(S(t), \Phi)dZ(t), \tag{6.2}$$

where

$$dZ(t) = \begin{pmatrix} dZ_1 \\ dZ_2 \\ dZ_3 \end{pmatrix}, \quad J = \begin{pmatrix} 0 \\ \nu\bar{\theta} \\ \mu\bar{v} \end{pmatrix},$$

$$H(\Phi) = \begin{pmatrix} -k & k & 0 \\ 0 & -\nu & 0 \\ 0 & 0 & -\mu \end{pmatrix},$$

$$V(S(t), \Phi) = \begin{pmatrix} \sqrt{v} & 0 & 0 \\ 0 & \zeta\sqrt{\theta} & 0 \\ 0 & 0 & \eta\sqrt{v} \end{pmatrix}.$$

Divide the time interval $T - t$ into κ sub-intervals $\tau_1, \tau_2, ..., \tau_\kappa$ and denote $\tau_k = t_k - t_{k-1}$, $k = 1, 2, ...\kappa$, $t_0 = t, t_\kappa = T$. Approximate the variance vector

$V(S(t), \Phi)$ over a sub-interval by its value at the beginning of the sub-interval. So that the transition equation (6.2) can be approximated by

$$dS(t) = (HS_k + J)dt + V_k dZ(t), \qquad (6.3)$$

$$S_k = S(t_k), V_k = V(S(t_k), \Phi).$$

The linear SDE (6.3) can be integrated to yield

$$S_{k+1} = e^{H\tau_k} S_k + \int_0^{\tau_k} e^{H(\tau_k - u)} J du + \int_0^{\tau_k} e^{H(\tau_k - u)} V_k dZ(u). \qquad (6.4)$$

Let $\tilde{S}_k$ denote the optimal estimator of S_k based on the observations up to and including Y_k. Let P_k denote the covariance matrix of the estimation error:

$$P_k = E[(S_k - \tilde{S}_k)(S_k - \tilde{S}_k)^\top].$$

Given $\tilde{S}_k$, the optimal forecast of S_{k+1} and the covariance matrix of the estimation error, $P_{k+1|k}$, are

$$\tilde{S}_{k+1|k} = e^{H\tau_k} \tilde{S}_k + \int_0^{\tau_k} e^{H(\tau_k - u)} J du, \qquad (6.5)$$

$$P_{k+1|k} = e^{H\tau_k} P_k (e^{H^\top \tau_k}) + Q_{k+1}, \qquad (6.6)$$

where

$$Q_{k+1} = Cov[S_{k+1}] = \int_0^{\tau_k} e^{Hu} V_k V_k^\top (e^{H^\top u}) du.$$

Equations (6.5) and (6.6) are prediction equations. Once the new observation Y_{k+1} becomes available, the estimator $\tilde{S}_{k|k-1}$ can be updated. The updating equations are

$$\tilde{S}_{k+1} = \tilde{S}_{k+1|k} + K_{k+1}(Y_{k+1} - C_{k+1}\tilde{S}_{k+1|k} - A_{k+1}), \qquad (6.7)$$

$$P_{k+1} = P_{k+1|k} - P_{k+1|k} C_{k+1}^\top F_k^{-1} C_{k+1} P_{k+1|k}, \qquad (6.8)$$

where the Kalman gain matrix is

$$K_{k+1} = P_{k+1|k} C_{k+1}^\top F_{k+1}^{-1} \qquad (6.9)$$

with

$$F_{k+1} = C_{k+1} P_{k+1|k} C_{k+1}^\top.$$

Conditional on $Y_1, ..Y_{k-1}$, S_k is normally distributed with a mean of $\tilde{S}_{k|k-1}$ and the covariance matrix $P_{k|k-1}$. If the measurement equation is written as

$$Y_k = C_k \tilde{S}_{k|k-1} + C_k(S_k - \tilde{S}_{k|k-1}) + A_k,$$

it can be seen that the conditional distribution of Y_k is normal with the mean

$$\tilde{Y}_{k+1|k} = C_{k+1}\tilde{S}_{k+1|k} + A_{k+1}$$

and a covariance of

$$F_{k+1} = C_{k+1}P_{k+1|k}C_{k+1}^\top.$$

Apart from a constant, the log-likelihood function is given by

$$\log L(\Phi \mid Y_1, ..., Y_T) = -\frac{1}{2}\sum_{k=1}^T \log \mid F_k \mid -\frac{1}{2}\sum_{k=1}^T \nu_k^\top F_k^{-1}\nu_k, \tag{6.10}$$

where

$$\nu_k = Y_k - \tilde{Y}_{k|k-1}.$$

The estimates of the parameters can be obtained by using the appropriate algorithm to maximize the likelihood (6.10) with respect to Φ. It can be shown that such estimation yields consistent and asymptotically efficient estimators $\hat{\Phi}$:

$$p\lim_{n\to\infty}\hat{\Phi} = \Phi \quad \sqrt{n}(\hat{\Phi} - \Phi)N(0, \Sigma^{-1}(\Phi)),$$

where the asymptotic covariance matrix $\Sigma^{-1}(\Phi)$ is the inverse of the information matrix $\Sigma(\Phi)$ given by

$$\Sigma(\Phi) = \lim_{n\to\infty}\frac{1}{n}\sum E\left(\frac{\partial^2 \ln L}{\partial\Phi\partial\Phi'}\right).$$

Before employing numerical optimization procedures to maximize the likelihood function (6.10), the matrix integrals in (6.5) and (6.6) need to be evaluated. The well-known computationally efficient method developed by van Loan (1978) is often used for this purpose. The idea is to calculate the following matrix exponential:

$$\exp\left(\begin{pmatrix} H & VV^\top \\ 0 & -H^\top \end{pmatrix}\tau\right) \equiv \begin{pmatrix} F_{11}(\tau) & F_{12}(\tau) \\ 0 & F_{22}(\tau) \end{pmatrix}. \tag{6.11}$$

It can be shown that the sub-matrix $F_{11}(\tau)$, $F_{12}(\tau)$, and $F_{22}(\tau)$ are given by

$$F_{11}(\tau) = e^{H\tau}; \quad F_{22}(\tau) = e^{-H^\top\tau}; \quad F_{12}(\tau) = \int_0^{\tau_k} e^{H(\tau-u)}V_kV_k^\top(e^{-H^\top u})du,$$

and

$$F_{12}(\tau)F_{11}(\tau)^\top = \int_0^{\tau_k} e^{Hu}V_kV_k^\top(e^{H^\top u})du,$$

which is the desired integral (6.6). The matrix integral in (6.5) can be computed in a similar way. First calculate the matrix exponential

$$\exp\left(\begin{pmatrix} H & J \\ 0 & 0 \end{pmatrix}\tau\right) \equiv \begin{pmatrix} G_{11}(\tau) & G_{12}(\tau) \\ 0 & G_{22}(\tau) \end{pmatrix} \tag{6.12}$$

so that

$$G_{12}(\tau) = \int_0^{\tau_k} e^{H(\tau_k - u)} J du.$$

6.3 Maximum Likelihood

The joint density for $r(s), \theta(s), v(s)$ conditional on $r(t), \theta(t), v(t)$ for $s > t$ is

$$f(r(s), \theta(s), v(s) \mid r(t), \theta(t), v(t)) = f_r(r(s) \mid r(t), \theta(t), v(t)) \times \\ f_\theta(\theta(s) \mid \theta(t)) f_v(v(s) \mid v(t)) \quad (6.13)$$

where

$$f_r(r(s) \mid r(t), \theta(t), v(t)) = \frac{e^{-ks}}{2\pi} \int_{-\infty}^{\infty} e^{i\xi(r(t)e^k - r(s)e^{ks})} \\ \times e^{A(s,\xi)v(t) + B(s,\xi) + A'(s,\xi)\theta(t) + B'(s,\xi)} d\xi,$$

$$f_\theta(\theta(s) \mid \theta(t)) = ce^{-u-w} \left(\frac{w}{u}\right)^{q/2} I_q(2\sqrt{uw}),$$

$$f_v(v(s) \mid v(t)) = c'e^{-u'-w'} \left(\frac{w'}{u'}\right)^{q'/2} I_{q'}(2\sqrt{u'w'}),$$

where

$$A(s,\xi), B(s,\xi), A'(s,\xi), B'(s,\xi), c, u, w, q, c', u', w', q'$$

are given in section 1.7.

Assume that the state variables are not observable and that observable variables are yields on discount bonds of different maturities. As the yields are related to the state variables by the closed form expressions, the likelihood function for a sample of observations on yields can be obtained by the change of variable technique.

Given the yields on discount bonds of three different maturities

$$R(s,\tau_i) = -\frac{1}{\tau}[\ln A(\tau_i) - B(\tau_i)r(s) - C(\tau_i)\theta(s) - D(\tau_i)v(s)], i = 1, 2, 3$$

the values at time s of the three factors, $r(s), \theta(s)$, and $v(s)$, can be solved as

$$r(s) = \frac{\begin{vmatrix} M(s,\tau_1) & C(\tau_1) & D(\tau_1) \\ M(s,\tau_2) & C(\tau_2) & D(\tau_2) \\ M(s,\tau_3) & C(\tau_3) & D(\tau_3) \end{vmatrix}}{\begin{vmatrix} B(\tau_1) & C(\tau_1) & D(\tau_1) \\ B(\tau_2) & C(\tau_2) & D(\tau_2) \\ B(\tau_3) & C(\tau_3) & D(\tau_3) \end{vmatrix}}, \quad \theta(s) = \frac{\begin{vmatrix} B(\tau_1) & M(s,\tau_1) & D(\tau_1) \\ B(\tau_2) & M(s,\tau_2) & D(\tau_2) \\ B(\tau_3) & M(s,\tau_3) & D(\tau_3) \end{vmatrix}}{\begin{vmatrix} B(\tau_1) & C(\tau_1) & D(\tau_1) \\ B(\tau_2) & C(\tau_2) & D(\tau_2) \\ B(\tau_3) & C(\tau_3) & D(\tau_3) \end{vmatrix}},$$

$$v(s) = \frac{\begin{vmatrix} B(\tau_1) & C(\tau_1) & M(s,\tau_1) \\ B(\tau_2) & C(\tau_2) & M(s,\tau_2) \\ B(\tau_3) & C(\tau_3) & M(s,\tau_3) \end{vmatrix}}{\begin{vmatrix} B(\tau_1) & C(\tau_1) & D(\tau_1) \\ B(\tau_2) & C(\tau_2) & D(\tau_2) \\ B(\tau_3) & C(\tau_3) & D(\tau_3) \end{vmatrix}},$$

where

$$M(s,\tau_i) = \ln A(\tau_i) + \tau_i R(s,\tau_i) \ , i = 1,2,3.$$

The Jacobian of the transformation is

$$J = \frac{\partial(r(s),\theta(s),v(s))}{\partial(R(s,\tau_1),R(s,\tau_2),R(s,\tau_3))}$$

$$\equiv \begin{vmatrix} \frac{\partial r(s)}{\partial R(s,\tau_1)} & \frac{\partial r(s)}{\partial R(s,\tau_2)} & \frac{\partial r(s)}{\partial R(s,\tau_3)} \\ \frac{\partial \theta(s)}{\partial R(s,\tau_1)} & \frac{\partial \theta(s)}{\partial R(s,\tau_2)} & \frac{\partial \theta(s)}{\partial R(s,\tau_3)} \\ \frac{\partial v(s)}{\partial R(s,\tau_1)} & \frac{\partial v(s)}{\partial R(s,\tau_2)} & \frac{\partial v(s)}{\partial R(s,\tau_3)} \end{vmatrix}$$

$$= \begin{vmatrix} \frac{\partial R(s,\tau_1)}{\partial r(s)} & \frac{\partial R(s,\tau_2)}{\partial r(s)} & \frac{\partial R(s,\tau_3)}{\partial r(s)} \\ \frac{\partial R(s,\tau_1)}{\partial \theta(s)} & \frac{\partial R(s,\tau_2)}{\partial \theta(s)} & \frac{\partial R(s,\tau_3)}{\partial \theta(s)} \\ \frac{\partial R(s,\tau_1)}{\partial v(s)} & \frac{\partial R(s,\tau_2)}{\partial v(s)} & \frac{\partial R(s,\tau_3)}{\partial v(s)} \end{vmatrix}^{-1}$$

$$= \begin{vmatrix} \frac{B(\tau_1)}{\tau_1} & \frac{B(\tau_2)}{\tau_2} & \frac{B(\tau_3)}{\tau_3} \\ \frac{C(\tau_1)}{\tau_1} & \frac{C(\tau_2)}{\tau_2} & \frac{C(\tau_3)}{\tau_3} \\ \frac{D(\tau_1)}{\tau_1} & \frac{D(\tau_2)}{\tau_2} & \frac{D(\tau_3)}{\tau_3} \end{vmatrix}^{-1} . \tag{6.14}$$

The joint density for $R(s,\tau_1), R(s,\tau_2), R(s,\tau_3)$ conditional on $R(t,\tau_1), R(t,\tau_2),$ $R(t,\tau_3)$ is thus

$$\begin{aligned} &f(R(s,\tau_1), R(s,\tau_2), R(s,\tau_3) \mid R(t,\tau_1), R(t,\tau_2), R(t,\tau_3)) \\ &= f(r(s),\theta(s),v(s) \mid r(t),\theta(t),v(t)) \mid J \mid \\ &= f_r(r(s) \mid r(t),\theta(t),v(t)) f_\theta(\theta(s) \mid \theta(t)) f_v(v(s) \mid v(t)) \mid J \mid . \tag{6.15} \end{aligned}$$

The undesirable property of the method outlined above is that only yields of three maturities can be used. To be able to extract more cross-sectional information in the term structure, the method can be modified to include yields of more three maturities by assuming that yields are observed with errors. This method is suggested by and used in Chen and Scott (1993).

Suppose that there are observed yields on discount bonds of m different maturities and assume that they are related to our yield formula by the following

$$R(s,\tau_i) = -\frac{1}{\tau}[\ln A(\tau_i) - B(\tau_i)r(s) - C(\tau_i)\theta(s) - D(\tau_i)v(s)], \ i = 1,2,3 \tag{6.16}$$

$$R(s,\tau_i) = -\frac{1}{\tau}[\ln A(\tau_i) - B(\tau_i)r(s) - C(\tau_i)\theta(s) - D(\tau_i)v(s)] + u_{is}, i = 3,4,...,m$$

where $u_i, i = 3, 4, \ldots m$, are measurement errors, which are assumed to have a joint normal distribution and are also assumed to be serially correlated as

$$u_{is} = \rho_j u_{i,s-1} + \epsilon_{js}.$$

Measurement errors in the observed bond prices reflect noise arising from, for example, averaging of bid and ask quotes or possible quotations errors.

With this setup, it is then a simple matter to apply the maximum likelihood method to estimate the model parameters.

6.4 Method of Moments

To use the method of moments, or generalized method of moments, one needs to find proxies for the unobservable variable θ and v.

Given the pricing formulas of three discount bonds of different maturities

$$\begin{aligned}
R(s, \tau_1) &= -\frac{1}{\tau_1}\left(\ln A(\tau_1) - B(\tau_1)r - C(\tau_1)\theta - D(\tau_1)v\right), \\
R(s, \tau_2) &= -\frac{1}{\tau_2}\left(\ln A(\tau_2) - B(\tau_2)r - C(\tau_2)\theta - D(\tau_2)v\right), \quad (6.17) \\
R(s, \tau_3) &= -\frac{1}{\tau_3}\left(\ln A(\tau_3) - B(\tau_3)r - C(\tau_3)\theta - D(\tau_3)v\right).
\end{aligned}$$

Introducing

$$R_i = R(s, \tau_i), A_i = A(\tau_i), B_i = B(\tau_i), C_i = C(\tau_i), D_i = D(\tau_i),$$

and eliminating r and v from (6.17) yields

$$\begin{aligned}
\theta &= H_0(\cdot) + H_1(\cdot)\Big[\tau_1 R_1(B_2 D_3 - B_3 D_2) + \tau_2 R_2(B_1 D_3 - B_3 D_1) \\
&\quad + \tau_3 R_3(B_1 D_2 - B_2 D_1)\Big], \quad (6.18)
\end{aligned}$$

where $H_0(\cdot)$ and $H_1(\cdot)$ are known functions with maturities τ_1, τ_2 and τ_3 as argumets. Equation (6.18) justifies the proxy or first-order approximation for θ which will be used in the empirical analysis. The proxy, denoted by $\hat{\theta}$, is given in the following:

$$\hat{\theta} = a_0 + a_1[\tau_1 R_1(B_2 D_3 - B_3 D_2) + \tau_2 R_2(B_1 D_3 - B_3 D_1) + \tau_3 R_3(B_1 D_2 - B_2 D_1)].$$

Similarly, the proxy for v can be given as

$$\hat{v} = b_0 + b_1[\tau_1 R_1(B_2 C_3 - B_3 C_2) + \tau_2 R_2(B_1 C_3 - B_3 C_1) + \tau_3 R_3(B_1 C_2 - B_2 C_1)].$$

The following moments equations can be employed in the method of moments estimation:

$$
\begin{aligned}
0 &= E[\epsilon_t] = E[r_{t+1} - r_t - k(\theta_t - r_t)\Delta t], & (6.19)\\
0 &= E[\epsilon_t^2 - v_t \Delta t], & (6.20)\\
\theta_t &= a_0 + a_1[\tau_1 R_1(B_2 D_3 - B_3 D_2) + \tau_2 R_2(B_1 D_3 - B_3 D_1)\\
&\quad + \tau_3 R_3(B_1 D_2 - B_2 D_1)], & (6.21)\\
v_t &= b_0 + b_1[\tau_1 R_1(B_2 C_3 - B_3 C_2) + \tau_2 R_2(B_1 C_3 - B_3 C_1)\\
&\quad + \tau_3 R_3(B_1 C_2 - B_2 C_1)]. & (6.22)
\end{aligned}
$$

6.5   Simulated Moments

Under the general interest rate dynamics, the prices of discount bonds can be shown to evolve as a first-order Markov process

$$ P_{t+1} = M(P_t, \epsilon_{t+1}, \Phi_0), $$

where Φ_0 denotes the true unknown parameter vector lying in a compact parameters space Γ.

The times series of prices can be simulated according to (1.24) in chapter 1 for any given admissible parameter vector $\Phi \in \Gamma$,

$$ P_{t+1}(\Phi) = M(P_t(\Phi), \epsilon_{t+1}, \Phi). $$

Choose moment conditions for the observed data

$$ h_t^* = h(P_t, ..., P_{t-j}) \equiv h(P_t, \Phi_0), $$

and the simulated data

$$ h_t(\Phi) = h(P_t(\Phi), ..., P_{t-j}(\Phi)). $$

Let T be the actual data size and T' be the simulated data size, where $T'(T) \to \infty$ and $T \to \infty$. Define

$$ H_T = \frac{1}{T} \sum_{t=1}^{T} h_t^*, $$

and

$$ H_{T'}(\Phi) = \frac{1}{T'} \sum_{t=1}^{T'} h_t(\Phi). $$

For any trial parameter vector Φ, choose Φ to minimize a criterion function, for example,

$$J_T(\Phi) = [H_T - H_{T'}(\Phi)]'\Omega_T(\Phi)[H_T - H_{T'}(\Phi)], \qquad (6.23)$$

where $\Omega_T(\Phi)$, a weighting matrix, is the asymptotic covariance matrix of the vector of sample moments conditions. A Φ that minimizes $J_T(\Phi)$ is called a simulated moments estimator:

$$\tilde{\Phi}_T = \arg\min_{\Phi \in \Gamma} J_T(\Phi).$$

Duffie and Singleton (1989) have proven the consistency and asymptotic normality of the simulated moments estimator under an α-matrix condition.

Minimizing $J_T(\Phi)$ with respect to Φ is equivalent to solving the homogeneous system of equations

$$D'(\Phi)\Omega_T(\Phi)[H_T - H_{T'}(\Phi)] = 0,$$

where $D(\Phi)$ is the Jacobian matrix of $H_T - H_{T'}(\Phi)$ with respect to Φ.

Chapter 7

Managing Interest Rate Risk

7.1 Introduction

The managing of interest rate risk is concerned with selecting which risk to be exposed to and which risk to be immunized against, assessing the risks of different securities, and constructing the portfolio with the specified risk return characteristics. Better managing of interest rate risk requires a better understanding of interest rate risk.

Interest rate risk is usually considered to consist of market risk and yield curve risk.[1] The market risk is caused by changes in the overall level of interest rates on straight, default free securities. It is associated with a uniform increase in all default-free interest rates. In our framework, this risk results from changes in the stochastic short rate. The yield curve risk can be further decomposed into the shape risk and the volatility risk. The shape risk is associated with changes in the stochastic short mean. As shown in Chapter 1, a change in the short mean changes the slope of the yield curve. Finally, the volatility risk is largely caused by changes in the curvature of the yield curve which, in our framework, is due to changes in the stochastic interest rate volatility.

Many financial instruments can be used as vehicles for managing interest rate risk. Some fixed-income products are especially created to have the specified risk return characteristics. For example, interest rate futures and forwards, floating rate notes, and inverse floaters are targeted at isolating the market risk. Interest rate swaps can be thought of as shape instruments since their returns depend on changes in the shape of the yield curve. Options are well known to be volatility products. Our model of interest rates, being able to explicitly deal with the effects of stochastic mean and stochastic volatility, is potentially useful for analyzing risk \ return profiles of interest rate derivatives, helping to design risk management schemes more effectively. However, these topics are beyond the scope of this chapter which is intended to focus on the managing of interest rate risk with bond portfolios.

---

[1]Technical terms used in the area of risk management are sometimes inconsistent. To be sure, in this chapter, yield curve risk represents risk associated with non-parallel shifts in yield curves, which are sometimes called reshaping shifts, e.g. twisting, pivoting, steepening, and flattening.

Until recently, the managing of interest rate risk with bond portfolios has been largely limited to the use of conventional duration. Conventional duration measures an asset's sensitivity to interest rate change under the assumption of infinitesimal parallel shifts in the term structure. Many years of using the conventional duration method for managing risk have enabled most financial institutions to eliminate market risk successfully. As a result of this, other risks have gained prominence, such as yield curve risk which is significant in portfolios containing options, mortgage derivatives, and exotic securities as well as bonds.

There is a significant body of literature focusing on developing better measures of the interest rate risk associated with non-parallel yield curve shifts. For example, Kaufman, Bierwag, and Toevs (1980) propose different duration measures for additive, multiplicative, logarithmic, and exponential shifts in the term structure, as well as various combinations of these shifting patterns; Gultekin and Rogalski (1984), Elton, Gruber, and Nabar (1988), and Elton, Gruber and Michaely (1990) develop general multi-factor duration measures based on empirical studies; Leibowitz, Krasker, and Nozari (1988) and Klaffky, Ma and Nozari (1992) invent "functional duration"; Waldman (1992) introduces "partial duration"; Ho (1992) proposes "key rate duration". The major problem with all these measures is that they are not based on a sound model of the term structure of interest rates. The term structure and general functional forms of yield curve shifts are arbitrarily pre-specified. Such pre-specified yield curve shifts may be internally inconsistent with the interest rate dynamics and in violation of the no-arbitrage principle.

Our model, being a three-factor model of the term structure of interest rates, naturally provides a unified framework to develop the concept of multi-factor duration in dealing with yield curve shifts, parallel or non-parallel. The risk management methods based on our model would add values in almost all situations where the conventional duration is used, including hedging, immunization, dedication, indexation, scenario analysis, etc. Although not discussed in this chapter, our method is expected to be especially valuable in the management of portfolios that include options and exotic options because of our method's ability to deal with interest rate volatility explicitly.

The rest of this chapter consists of two parts. In the first part, the concepts of duration and convexity are extended to our model of interest rates to be measures of interest rate risk with respect to stochastic factors. Second, the immunization method is generalized to a multi-factor case where the sensitivity of the term structure to changes in factors is not unity for all maturities.

7.2 Generalized Duration and Convexity

Interest rate risk is measured by considering price sensitivity, that is, the change in the value of an asset or liability cash flow in response to a change in the yield. In our three-factor model, besides the short rate, the short mean and volatility affect yield as well. Changes in these two factors, as shown in Chapter 1, result in a variety of changes in yield curves, including twisting, steepening, pivoting etc. Our model provides a theoretical background upon which a method of managing those risks which are associated with non-parallel yield curve shifts can be developed. To do so, one first needs to develop a more complete riskiness measure.

Factor Duration

The price at time t of a default-free discount bond promising \$1 at maturity T is a function of factors r, θ, v:

$$P(r, \theta, v, t; T) \equiv P(t, T) = \exp\left[-(T - t)Y(r, \theta, v, t, T)\right], \tag{7.1}$$

where $Y(t, T; r, \theta, v)$ is the yield to maturity. Using Ito's lemma, the local change in bond price can be written as

$$
\begin{aligned}
dP(t, T) \quad = \quad & \mu_P(\cdot)dt - (T - t)P(t, T)\{\frac{\partial Y(t, T)}{\partial r}\sqrt{v}dB_1 + \\
& \frac{\partial Y(t, T)}{\partial \theta}\zeta\sqrt{\theta}dB_2 + \frac{\partial Y(t, T)}{\partial v}\eta\sqrt{v}dB_3\}.
\end{aligned}
\tag{7.2}
$$

In equation (7.2) the drift component of price change $\mu_P(\cdot)$ involves the drift rates of three factor processes and the second-order terms. As our purpose is to construct an immunizing portfolio, the full functional form of the $\mu_P(\cdot)$ may be suppressed.

A coupon bond making n payments c_j, at times $t_j, j = 1, ..., n$, is simply a portfolio of discount bonds, with price at time t:

$$\mathcal{P}(r, \theta, v, t; T) \equiv \mathcal{P}(t, T) = \sum_{j=1}^{n} c_j P(r, t; t_j).$$

Using equation (7.2), it follows immediately that

$$
\begin{aligned}
d\mathcal{P} \quad = \quad & \sum_{j=1}^{n} c_j \mu_P(\cdot)dt - \sum_{j=1}^{n} c_j(t_j - t)P(t, t_j)\frac{\partial Y(t, t_j)}{\partial r}\sqrt{v}dB_1 - \\
& \sum_{j=1}^{n} c_j(t_j - t)P(t, t_j)\frac{\partial Y(t, t_j)}{\partial \theta}\zeta\sqrt{\theta}dB_2
\end{aligned}
$$

$$-\sum_{j=1}^{n} c_j(t_j - t)P(t, t_j)\frac{\partial Y(t, t_j)}{\partial v}\eta\sqrt{v}dB_3. \qquad (7.3)$$

The equation (7.3) may further be written as

$$\frac{dP}{P} = \frac{1}{P}\mu_P(\cdot)dt + \rho_r\sqrt{v}dB_1 + \rho_\theta\zeta\sqrt{\theta}dB_2 + \rho_v\eta\sqrt{v}dB_3,$$

where

$$\mu_P(\cdot) = \sum_{j=1}^{n} c_j\mu_P(\cdot),$$

$$\rho_r = -\frac{1}{P}\sum_{j=1}^{n} c_j(t_j - t)P(t, t_j)\frac{\partial Y(t, t_j)}{\partial r},$$

$$\rho_\theta = -\frac{1}{P}\sum_{j=1}^{n} c_j(t_j - t)P(t, t_j)\frac{\partial Y(t, t_j)}{\partial \theta},$$

$$\rho_v = -\frac{1}{P}\sum_{j=1}^{n} c_j(t_j - t)P(t, t_j)\frac{\partial Y(t, t_j)}{\partial v}.$$

The parameters ρ_k, ρ_θ, and ρ_v which measure the sensitivity of the bond's return to factors, represent the extended duration. This extended duration is different from the conventional duration in two important aspects. First there are three durations, one for each factor, rather than just one. Second, there is an extra term,

$$\frac{\partial Y(t, t_j)}{\partial x} \qquad x = r, \theta, v; j = 1, ..., n,$$

which measures the sensitivity of the yield to maturity to each factor.

Definition (Factor Duration). *The durations ρ_r, ρ_θ, and ρ_v of a bond paying coupon c_j at time t_j with $j = 1, .., n$, with respect to the three factors r, θ, and v are defined as*

$$\rho_r = -\frac{1}{P}\sum_{j=1}^{n} c_j(t_j - t)P(t, t_j)\frac{\partial Y(t, t_j)}{\partial r},$$

$$\rho_\theta = -\frac{1}{P}\sum_{j=1}^{n} c_j(t_j - t)P(t, t_j)\frac{\partial Y(t, t_j)}{\partial \theta}, \qquad (7.4)$$

$$\rho_v = -\frac{1}{P}\sum_{j=1}^{n} c_j(t_j - t)P(t, t_j)\frac{\partial Y(t, t_j)}{\partial v},$$

where $P(t; t_j)$ is the zero-coupon bond pricing formula.

For a discount bond $\mathcal{P} = P$ and $c_j = 1$ so the durations ρ_r, ρ_θ, and ρ_v of a zero-coupon bond with respect to the three factor r, θ, and v become

$$
\begin{aligned}
\rho_r &= -T\frac{\partial Y(t;T)}{\partial r} \\
&= \frac{1}{P(t;T)}\frac{\partial P(t;T)}{\partial r} = B(t,T)
\end{aligned}
\tag{7.5}
$$

and similarly

$$
\begin{aligned}
\rho_\theta &= -T\frac{\partial Y(t;T)}{\partial \theta} \\
&= \frac{1}{P(t;T)}\frac{\partial P(t;T)}{\partial \theta} = C(t,T),
\end{aligned}
\tag{7.6}
$$

$$
\rho_v = \frac{1}{P(t;T)}\frac{\partial P(t;T)}{\partial v} = D(t,T),
$$

where functions $B(t;T), C(t;T)$, and $D(t;T)$ are given in chapter 1. This definition is consistent with our intuition that $B(t,T), C(t,T)$, and $D(t,T)$ are measures of risk exposure.

These extended durations can better quantify the yield curve risk of a portfolio. The measure ρ_θ, the duration with respect to the short mean, assesses the sensitivity of a portfolio to changes in the shape of the yield curve resulting from a change in the short mean which has more impact on the short end of the yield curve. The measure ρ_v, the duration with respect to volatility, assesses the sensitivity of a portfolio to changes in the yield curve resulting from changes in volatility which, as shown in Chapter 1, may increase the yield of certain maturities and decrease the yield for other maturities. Therefore, by dealing with these extended durations one is able to deal with the interest rate risk associated with non-parallel yield curve shifts. These extended durations have generalized so-called "functional duration", "partial duration", and "key rate duration" in the recent literature (Leibowitz, Krasker, and Nozari (1988), Klaffky, Ma and Nozari (1992), Ho (1992), Waldman (1992)) which were invented to deal with non-parallel yield curve shifts.

By quantifying the exposure of a portfolio to yield curve shifts, the extended durations can play a key role in portfolio management. Investors who want to immunize their portfolios against yield curve shifts will structure a portfolio that has the same three durations as their benchmark.

Factor Convexity

Duration is not constant, but changes as a result of changes in three factors and because of the passage of time. Convexity measures the rate at which duration itself will change when each factor moves. Convexity is therefore a second-order effect; its influence on the value of a portfolio is small compared to that of duration. However, for large movements in market rates, for highly leveraged positions, and where option-like features are embedded, convexity can be important. Convexity can be similarly defined as follows.

Definition (Factor Convexity).*The convexity δ_r, δ_θ, and δ_v of a bond paying coupon a_j at time t_j, $j = 1, ..., n$, with respect to the three factors r, θ, and v are defined as*

$$
\begin{aligned}
\delta_r &= -\frac{1}{P}\sum_{j=1}^{n} a_j(t_j - t)P(t, t_j)\frac{\partial^2 Y(t, t_j)}{\partial r^2}, \\
\delta_\theta &= -\frac{1}{P}\sum_{j=1}^{n} a_j(t_j - t)P(t, t_j)\frac{\partial^2 Y(t, t_j)}{\partial \theta^2}, \qquad (7.7) \\
\delta_v &= -\frac{1}{P}\sum_{j=1}^{n} a_j(t_j - t)P(t, t_j)\frac{\partial^2 Y(t, t_j)}{\partial v^2},
\end{aligned}
$$

where $P(t; t_j)$ is the zero-coupon bond pricing formula.

The convexities δ_r, δ_θ, and δ_v of a zero-coupon bond with respect to the three factors r, θ, and v are given by

$$
\delta_r = \frac{1}{P}\frac{\partial^2 P}{\partial r^2} = B^2(t; T), \quad \delta_\theta = \frac{1}{P}\frac{\partial^2 P}{\partial \theta^2} = C^2(t; T),
$$

$$
\delta_v = \frac{1}{P}\frac{\partial^2 P}{\partial v^2} = D^2(t; T).
$$

7.3   Hedging Ratios

Based on our model of the term structure of interest rates, it is possible to develop more comprehensive measures of sensitivities of derivatives with respect to various factors and to formulate more sophisticated hedging schemes accordingly. For example, within our model of varying volatility, one is able to examine how conventional hedge ratios are affected by a change in volatility.

Given the bond option pricing formula from section 2.2,

$$
C(r, \theta, v, t, T; s, K) = P(t; s)\Psi(\alpha; \beta; \gamma) - P(t; T)K\Psi(\alpha'; \beta'; \gamma), \qquad (7.8)
$$

with

$$
\Psi(\eta_0, \eta_1, \eta_2, \eta_3; \xi_0, \xi_1, \xi_2, \xi_3; \gamma_0, \gamma_1, \gamma_2, \gamma_3)
$$

$$= \frac{1}{(2\pi)^{3/2}} \int_{-\infty}^{\infty} \int_{-\infty}^{\infty} \int_{-\infty}^{\infty} I(\xi_0(\phi,\psi,\varphi,\tau), \xi_1(\phi,\psi,\varphi,\tau), \xi_2(\phi,\psi,\varphi,\tau),$$

$$\xi_3(\phi,\psi,\varphi,\tau); \gamma_0, \gamma_1, \gamma_2, \gamma_3)\eta_0(\phi,\psi,\varphi,\tau)$$

$$\times e^{-\eta_1(\phi,\psi,\varphi,\tau)r - \eta_2(\phi,\psi,\varphi,\tau)\theta - \eta_3(\phi,\psi,\varphi,\tau)v} d\phi d\psi d\varphi \qquad (7.9)$$

and

$$I(\xi_0, \xi_1, \xi_2, \xi_3; \gamma_0, \gamma_1, \gamma_2, \gamma_3) \equiv \int \xi_0 e^{-ix_1\xi_1 - ix_2\xi_2 - ix_3\xi_3}$$

$$1_{\{\gamma_1 x_1 + \gamma_2 x_2 + \gamma_3 x_3 \le \gamma_0\}} dx_1 dx_2 dx_3, (7.10)$$

it is a simple matter to derive the following proposition.

Proposition 20: *Under the three factor model of the term structure of interest rates, the comparative statics for the European call option price on the discount bond are given by*

$$\Delta = \frac{\partial C(\cdot)}{\partial P(t,s)} = \Psi(\alpha,\beta,\gamma) + P(t,s)\Psi_{P(t,s)}(\alpha,\beta,\gamma)$$

$$+ \left[\frac{B(t,T)P(t,T)}{B(t,s)P(t,s)} + \frac{C(t,T)P(t,T)}{C(t,s)P(t,s)} + \frac{D(t,T)P(t,T)}{D(t,s)P(t,s)} \right] K\Psi(\alpha',\beta',\gamma)$$

$$- P(t,T)K\Psi_{P(t,s)}(\alpha',\beta',\gamma),$$

$$\Gamma = \frac{\partial^2 C(\cdot)}{\partial P(t,s)^2} = 2\Psi_{P(t,s)}(\alpha,\beta,\gamma) + P(t,s)\Psi_{P(t,s)^2}(\alpha,\beta,\gamma)$$

$$- \frac{P(t,T)}{P^2(t,s)} \left[\frac{B(t,T)}{B(t,s)} + \frac{C(t,T)}{C(t,s)} + \frac{D(t,T)}{D(t,s)} \right] K\Psi(\alpha',\beta',\gamma)$$

$$+ \frac{P(t,T)}{P^2(t,s)} \left[\frac{B(t,T)}{B(t,s)} + \frac{C(t,T)}{C(t,s)} + \frac{D(t,T)}{D(t,s)} \right]^2 K\Psi(\alpha',\beta',\gamma)$$

$$- \frac{2P(t,T)}{P(t,s)} \left[\frac{B(t,T)}{B(t,s)} + \frac{C(t,T)}{C(t,s)} + \frac{D(t,T)}{D(t,s)} \right] K\Psi(\alpha',\beta',\gamma)$$

$$- KP(t,T)\Psi_{P(t,s)^2}(\alpha',\beta',\gamma),$$

$$\rho = \frac{\partial C(\cdot)}{\partial r} = -B(t,s)P(t,s)\Psi(\alpha,\beta,\gamma) + P(t,s)\Psi_r(\alpha,\beta,\gamma)$$

$$+ B(t,T)P(t,T)K\Psi(\alpha',\beta',\gamma) - P(t,T)K\Psi_r(\alpha',\beta',\gamma),$$

$$\frac{\partial C(\cdot)}{\partial \theta} = -C(t,s)P(t,s)\Psi(\alpha,\beta,\gamma) + P(t,s)\Psi_\theta(\alpha,\beta,\gamma)$$

$$+ C(t,T)P(t,T)K\Psi(\alpha',\beta',\gamma) - P(t,T)K\Psi_\theta(\alpha',\beta',\gamma),$$

$$\frac{\partial C(\cdot)}{\partial v} = -D(t,s)P(t,s)\Psi(\alpha,\beta,\gamma) + P(t,s)\Psi_v(\alpha,\beta,\gamma)$$

$$+ D(t,T)P(t,T)K\Psi(\alpha',\beta',\gamma) - P(t,T)K\Psi_v(\alpha',\beta',\gamma),$$

$$\frac{\partial C(\cdot)}{\partial \tau} = P(t,s)\Psi_\tau(\alpha,\beta,\gamma) - P(t,T)K\Psi_\tau(\alpha',\beta',\gamma) - [A'(\tau)/A(\tau)]$$

$$-B'(\tau)r - C'(\tau)\theta - D'(\tau)v]P(t,T)K\Psi(\alpha',\beta',\gamma)$$

where

$$
\begin{aligned}
\Psi_r(\eta_0,\eta_1,\eta_2,\eta_3;\xi;\gamma) &= \Psi(-\eta_0\eta_1,\eta_1,\eta_2,\eta_3;\xi;\gamma), \\
\Psi_\theta(\eta_0,\eta_1,\eta_2,\eta_3;\xi;\gamma) &= \Psi(-\eta_0\eta_2,\eta_1,\eta_2,\eta_3;\xi;\gamma), \\
\Psi_v(\eta_0,\eta_1,\eta_2,\eta_3;\xi;\gamma) &= \Psi(-\eta_0\eta_3,\eta_1,\eta_2,\eta_3;\xi;\gamma), \\
\Psi_{P(t,s)}(\eta_0,\eta_1,\eta_2,\eta_3;\xi;\gamma) &= \frac{\Psi(-\eta_0\eta_1,\eta_1,\eta_2,\eta_3;\xi;\gamma)}{B(t,s)P(t,s)} \\
&\quad + \frac{\Psi(-\eta_0\eta_2,\eta_1,\eta_2,\eta_3;\xi;\gamma)}{C(t,s)P(t,s)} \\
&\quad + \frac{\Psi(-\eta_0\eta_3,\eta_1,\eta_2,\eta_3;\xi)}{D(t,s)P(t,s)}, \\
\Psi_T(\eta_0,\eta_1,\eta_2,\eta_3;\xi;\gamma) &= \Psi(\eta_0 T,\eta_1,\eta_2,\eta_3;\xi;\gamma) \\
&\quad + \Psi(-\eta_0\eta_1 T,\eta_1,\eta_2,\eta_3;\xi;\gamma) \\
&\quad + \Psi(-\eta_0\eta_2 T,\eta_1,\eta_2,\eta_3;\xi;\gamma) \\
&\quad + \Psi(-\eta_0\eta_3 T,\eta_1,\eta_2,\eta_3;\xi;\gamma).
\end{aligned}
$$

Other partial derivatives can be similarly given.

7.4   Hedging: General Approach

To see how the extended duration can be used in risk management, let us consider the problem of constructing a trading strategy involving certain securities to replicate the value of a target security. Once the replicating strategy is constructed, hedging the risk of the target security can be achieved by selling the replicating strategy.

Let the price process V for the security to be hedged be given by $V = F(r,\theta,v,t)$, which is the solution to the fundamental valuation PDE with appropriate boundary conditions under technical regularity conditions.

Assume that there are three other traded securities with market values at t given by $U_1 = \Phi_1(r,\theta,v,t), U_2 = \Phi_2(r,\theta,v,t), U_3 = \Phi_3(r,\theta,v,t)$. Assume that $F(r,\theta,v,t)$ and $\Phi_i(r,\theta,v,t), i = 1,2,3$, are at least once differentiable with respect to r, θ and v respectively. Further assume that

$$
\begin{vmatrix}
\Phi_{1r} & \Phi_{2r} & \Phi_{3r} \\
\Phi_{1\theta} & \Phi_{2\theta} & \Phi_{3\theta} \\
\Phi_{1v} & \Phi_{2v} & \Phi_{3v}
\end{vmatrix} \neq 0
$$

where subscripts denote partial derivatives.

Consider a hedged position consisting of one share of security V and n_i share of each security $U_i, i = 1,2,3$. The market value at time t of this hedged position is

$$M(r, \theta, v, t) = F(r, \theta, v, t) + n_1 \Phi_1(r, \theta, v, t) + n_2 \Phi_2(r, \theta, v, t) + n_3 \Phi_3(r, \theta, v, t).$$

By Ito's lemma,

$$dF(\cdot) = \sum_{i=1}^{3} \frac{\partial F}{\partial y_i}(dy_i - E(dy_i)] + E[dF]$$

and

$$d\Phi_i(\cdot) = \sum_{i=1}^{3} \frac{\partial \Phi_i}{\partial y_i}(dy_i - E(dy_i)] + E[d\Phi_i], \quad i = 1, 2, 3$$

where $(y_1, y_2, y_3) = (r, \theta, v)$. Letting

$$dM - E[dM] = 0$$

yields

$$\frac{\partial M(r, \theta, v, t)}{\partial r} = \frac{\partial M(r, \theta, v, t)}{\partial \theta} = \frac{\partial M(r, \theta, v, t)}{\partial v} = 0$$

and solving for $n_i, i = 1, 2, 3$, yields

$$n_1 = \frac{\begin{vmatrix} F_r & \Phi_{2r} & \Phi_{3r} \\ F_\theta & \Phi_{2\theta} & \Phi_{3\theta} \\ F_v & \Phi_{2v} & \Phi_{3v} \end{vmatrix}}{\begin{vmatrix} \Phi_{1r} & \Phi_{2r} & \Phi_{3r} \\ \Phi_{1\theta} & \Phi_{2\theta} & \Phi_{3\theta} \\ \Phi_{1v} & \Phi_{2v} & \Phi_{3v} \end{vmatrix}}, \quad n_2 = \frac{\begin{vmatrix} \Phi_{1r} & F_r & \Phi_{3r} \\ \Phi_{1\theta} & F_\theta & \Phi_{3\theta} \\ \Phi_{1v} & F_v & \Phi_{3v} \end{vmatrix}}{\begin{vmatrix} \Phi_{1r} & \Phi_{2r} & \Phi_{3r} \\ \Phi_{1\theta} & \Phi_{2\theta} & \Phi_{3\theta} \\ \Phi_{1v} & \Phi_{2v} & \Phi_{3v} \end{vmatrix}},$$

$$n_3 = \frac{\begin{vmatrix} \Phi_{1r} & \Phi_{2r} & F_r \\ \Phi_{1\theta} & \Phi_{2\theta} & F_\theta \\ \Phi_{1v} & \Phi_{2v} & F_v \end{vmatrix}}{\begin{vmatrix} \Phi_{1r} & \Phi_{2r} & \Phi_{3r} \\ \Phi_{1\theta} & \Phi_{2\theta} & \Phi_{3\theta} \\ \Phi_{1v} & \Phi_{2v} & \Phi_{3v} \end{vmatrix}},$$

where F_r, F_θ, F_v, and $\Phi_{ir}, \Phi_{i\theta}, \Phi_{iv}, i = 1, 2, 3$ are the extended durations of the securities with respect to three factors.

7.5 Hedging Yield Curve Risk

This section discusses the issue of hedging interest rate risks using the concepts of extended durations developed in the previous section. To begin with, let us first note that a number of portfolio management problems such as indexation, asset/liability management, portfolio immunization etc. can be treated in a unified framework because they all aim at protecting value relative to some benchmark. For indexation, the benchmark is an index of securities; for asset/liability management, the benchmark is liabilities; and for portfolio immunization, the benchmark is a targeted return. Because of this, this section addresses the issue of hedging interest rate risk in an asset/liability management context.

Consider an investor with a known liability L to meet at some future time m. Assume that the investor's wealth is equal to the present value of L, calculated according to the current term structure of interest rates. The investor seeks a bond portfolio to invest this amount of wealth. Similar problems have been studied under different settings by Granito (1984), Kaufman, Bierwag, and Toevs (1980), Prisman and Tian (1994), among others.

Let x_i be the holding of ith bond, $i = 1, 2..., n$, in the portfolio, where n is the number of bonds available in the market. Let P_i be the price of the ith bond. Let the principal amount of the bond be 1. Let $Y(0,t) \equiv Y(r_0, \theta_0, v_0, 0, t)$ be the current term structure of interest rates. A default-free coupon bond can be characterized by the coupon flow $c_i(t)$ and the maturity T_i, $i = 1, ..., n$.

The value at m of the bond i is

$$V_i(r_0, \theta_0, v_0) = \int_0^{T_i} c_i(t)e^{-Y(m,t)(t-m)}dt + e^{-Y(m,T_i)(T_i-m)} \qquad (7.11)$$

where

$$Y(t, m)(m - t) = Y(0, m)m - Y(0, t)t.$$

The value at m of the portfolio consisting of x_i units of ith bond, $i = 1, ...n$, is

$$V_p(r_0, \theta_0, v_0) = \sum_{i=1}^{n} x_i \int_0^{T_i} c_i(t)e^{-Y(m,t)(t-m)}dt + \sum_{i=1}^{n} x_i e^{-Y(m,T_i)(T_i-m)}. \qquad (7.12)$$

The present value of the liability L is $e^{-Y(0,m)m}L$, which is assumed to be 1 so that $L = e^{Y(0,m)m}$.

The value of the portfolio at future time m may be different from (7.12) if the yield curve shifts during the time interval, $[0, m]$. Without losing generality, it is assumed that the yield curve changes instantaneously after the bond portfolio is constructed at time 0. The new term structure is denoted $Y^*(0, t) \equiv Y(r, \theta, v; 0, t)$ indicating that a change in the term structure resulted from changing the three factors from r_0, θ_0, v_0 to r, θ, v.

The value at m of the bond i under the new yield curve is

$$V_i(r, \theta, v) = \int_0^{T_i} c_i(t) e^{-Y^*(m,t)(t-m)} dt + e^{-Y^*(m,T_i)(T_i-m)}$$

and the bond portfolio's value is

$$V_p(r, \theta, v) = \sum_{i=1}^n x_i V_i(r, \theta, v) = \sum_{i=1}^n x_i \int_0^{T_i} c_i(t) e^{-Y^*(m,t)(t-m)} dt$$
$$+ \sum_{i=1}^n x_i e^{-Y^*(m,T_i)(T_i-m)}.$$

The goal of hedging is to make sure that the lowest future value of the portfolio, as a function of r, θ, and v is L. The immunized portfolio, denoted $x^* = (x_1^*, ...x_n^*)$, must therefore make the optimal value of

$$\min_{r,\theta,v} \sum_{i=1}^n x_i^* V_i(r, \theta, v)$$

$$s.t. \quad \sum_{i=1}^n x_i^* P_i = 1$$

equal to L.

Here the constraint is that the present value of this portfolio is equal to the present value of the liability which is set to be 1.

So the optimal immunized portfolio x^* is the solution to the following problem:

$$\max_{x \geq 0} \quad \{\min_{r,\theta,v} \sum_{i=1}^n x_i V_i(r, \theta, v)\} \tag{7.13}$$

$$s.t. \quad \sum_{i=1}^n x_i P_i = 1, \tag{7.14}$$

That is, an immunization strategy is a maximin strategy. The term structure of interest rates in our model is

$$Y(r, \theta, v; m, t) = \alpha_0(t - m) + \alpha_1(t - m)r + \alpha_2(t - m)\theta + \alpha_3(t - m)v,$$

where $\alpha_1(t), \alpha_2(t)$, and $\alpha_3(t)$ are related to the extended durations as follows:

$$\alpha_0(t) = -\frac{1}{t} \ln A(t), \quad \alpha_1(t) = \frac{B(t)}{t}, \quad \alpha_2(t) = \frac{C(t)}{t}, \quad \alpha_3(t) = \frac{D(t)}{t}. \tag{7.15}$$

Substituting the term structure into the problem (4.10) yields

$$\max_{x \geq 0} \quad \min_{r,\theta,v} V_p(r, \theta, v)$$

$$= \sum_{i=1}^{n} x_i \int_{0}^{T_i} c_i(t) e^{-[\alpha_0(t-m)+\alpha_1(t-m)r+\alpha_2(t-m)\theta+\alpha_3(t-m)v](t-m)} dt$$

$$+ \sum_{i-1}^{n} x_i e^{-[\alpha_0(T_i-m)+\alpha_1(T_i-m)r+\alpha_2(T_i-m)\theta+\alpha_3(T_i-m)v](T_i-m)} \qquad (7.16)$$

$$s.t. \quad \sum_{i=1}^{n} x_i P_i = 1.$$

The optimal solution of the problem (4.12) can be given by the method of Kuhn-Tucker[2]

$$x_i^* \ge 0, \quad \text{if} \quad \frac{1}{P_i} V_i(r, \theta, v) = \max_{j=1,..,n} \frac{1}{P_j} V_j(r, \theta, v),$$

$$x_i^* = 0, \quad \text{if} \quad \frac{1}{P_i} V_i(r, \theta, v) < \max_{j=1,..,n} \frac{1}{P_j} V_j(r, \theta, v),$$

and

$$\frac{\partial V_r(r, \theta, v)}{\partial r} \Big|_{r_0, \theta_0, v_0} = m - D_r = 0,$$

$$\frac{\partial V_\theta(r, \theta, v)}{\partial \theta} \Big|_{r_0, \theta_0, v_0} = m - D_\theta = 0,$$

$$\frac{\partial V_v(r, \theta, v)}{\partial v} \Big|_{r_0, \theta_0, v_0} = m - D_v = 0,$$

where

$$D_r = \frac{1}{V_r} \Big[\sum_{i=1}^{n} x_i \int_{0}^{T_i} c_i(t) e^{-(\alpha_0(t-m)+\alpha_1(t-m)r_0+\alpha_2(t-m)\theta_0+\alpha_3(t-m)v_0)t} $$
$$\times \alpha_i(t-m)t dt + \qquad (7.17)$$
$$\sum_{i=1}^{n} x_i e^{-(\alpha_0(T_i-m)+\alpha_1(T_i-m)r_0+\alpha_2(T_i-m)\theta_0+\alpha_3(T_i-m)v_0)t} \alpha_i(T_i-m)T_i \Big]$$

---

[2] Generally, for the general nonlinear programming problem:

$$\max_{\mathbf{x}} F(\mathbf{x})$$

$$s.t. \quad g(\mathbf{x}) \le \mathbf{b}, \mathbf{x} \ge 0,$$

The Kuhn-Tucker conditions are:

$$\frac{\partial L}{\partial \mathbf{x}}(\mathbf{x}^*, \mathbf{y}^*) \le 0, \quad \frac{\partial L}{\partial \mathbf{y}}(\mathbf{x}^*, \mathbf{y}^*) \ge 0,$$

$$\frac{\partial L}{\partial \mathbf{x}}(\mathbf{x}^*, \mathbf{y}^*)\mathbf{x}^* = 0, \quad \mathbf{y}^* \frac{\partial L}{\partial \mathbf{y}}(\mathbf{x}^*, \mathbf{y}^*) = 0,$$

$$\mathbf{x}^* \ge 0, \qquad \mathbf{y}^* \ge 0,$$

where

$$L(\mathbf{x}, \mathbf{y}) = F(\mathbf{x}) + \mathbf{y}(\mathbf{b} - g(\mathbf{x})).$$

and

$$
\begin{aligned}
V_r &= \sum_{i=1}^{n} x_i \int_0^{T_i} c_i(t) e^{-(\alpha_0(t-m)+\alpha_1(t-m)r_0+\alpha_2(t-m)\theta_0+\alpha_3(t-m)v_0)t} \\
&\quad \times \alpha_i(t-m)dt + \\
&\quad \sum_{i=1}^{n} x_i e^{-(\alpha_0(T_i-m)+\alpha_1(T_i-m)r_0+\alpha_2(T_i-m)\theta_0+\alpha_3(T_i-m)v_0)t} \alpha_i(T_i-m)
\end{aligned} \tag{7.18}
$$

and similarly for D_θ and D_v.

Perfect immunization would be achieved if it were possible to manage the asset portfolio in such a way that at every instant, its value was precisely equal to that of the liabilities. Under the condition of continuous trading, diffusion processes, and frictionless markets, perfect immunization is feasible.

Chapter 8

Extensions of the Model

8.1 Introduction

Taking a brief look at any interest rate time series such as Treasury Bill rates, one feature is significant: the time series appears to exhibit diffusion behaviors, punctuated by unanticipated jumps.

There are compelling arguments to show that the mean, or central tendency of the short rate tends to move in a discreet fashion: that is, it jumps up and down. Central banks in many countries, such as the U.S. Federal Reserve System, normally enforce monetary policy by managing interest rates. After the central bank makes its announcement of changing the interest rate, most financial institutions follow the move to change their relevant interest rates. The shifts in the mean rate level are therefore frequently changed. All the changes jump up or down a significant percentage. This basic observation provides the rationale for incorporating a jumping rate into the interest rate model.

This chapter will add more realism to the model presented in Chapter 1 so that the short rate is a jump-diffusion process while volatility remains a stochastic diffusion process.

Recently, a few studies have attempted to develop a jump-diffusion model of interest rates, such as (Das (1994), Babbs and Webber (1994), Balduzzi and Bertola (1994), Balduzzi, Das, and Foresi (1995)). None of the models incorporate stochastic volatility. This is undesirable as it implies that all the interest rate volatility is caused by jumps corresponding to changes in the central bank's target rate. As a matter of fact, many others, such as political, economic and business factors can also cause volatility movements in the domestic and international debt markets.

The model presented in this paper intends to remedy this shortcoming of the existing jump-diffusion models of interest rates by adding another factor, volatility, which is assumed to follow a stochastic process.

8.2 Extension I: Jumping Mean and Diffusing Volatility

The dynamics of the short rate $r(t)$ and its volatility $v(t)$ are assumed in the following:

Assumption 1. *The dynamics of the short rate is given by the following stochastic differential equation:*

$$dr(t) = k(\theta - r(t))dt + \sqrt{v(t)}dB_1(t) + J(\alpha, \gamma^2)d\pi(h), \ t \geq 0, \ k > 0, \quad (8.1)$$

where θ is the short-term mean of the short rate, $v(t)$ is the instantaneous variance (volatility) of the short rate, J is the jump in the short rate characterized by α and γ^2, and π is the Poisson arrival probability with parameter h.

Assumption 2. *The development of the volatility of the short rate is given by the following stochastic differential equation:*

$$dv(t) = \mu(\bar{v} - v(t))dt + \eta\sqrt{v(t)}dB_2(t), \ t \geq 0, \ \mu > 0, \ \bar{v} > 0, \quad (8.2)$$

where $\bar{v}$ is the long-term mean of the volatility and η is the volatility parameter.

In addition, for analytical tractability, three processes $B_1(t), B_2(t)$, and $\pi(h)$ are assumed to be uncorrelated:

$$dB_1(t)dB_2(t) = dB_1(t)d\pi(h) = dB_2(t)d\pi(h) = 0.$$

By Ito's lemma, the stochastic differential equation that determines the bond price $P(r, v, t; T) \equiv P(r, v; \tau)$ is given by

$$
\begin{aligned}
dP(r, v; \tau) = & \ [k(\theta - r)P_r + \mu(\bar{v} - v)P_v + P_t + \frac{1}{2}vP_{rr} + \frac{1}{2}\eta^2 vP_{vv}]dt \\
& + \sqrt{v}P_r dB_1 + \eta\sqrt{v}P_v dB_2 + [P(r + J, v, \tau) - P(r, v, \tau)|J]d\pi.
\end{aligned}
$$

The risk premium is assumed to be:

$$\lambda_r v\frac{P_r}{P} + \lambda_v \eta^2 v\frac{P_v}{P} + \frac{\lambda_v}{P}Var[(P(r + J, v, t) - P(r, v, t))d\pi].$$

By the arbitrage argument,

$$E(\frac{dP}{P}) = r + \lambda_r v\frac{P_r}{P} + \lambda_v \eta^2 v\frac{P_v}{P} + \frac{\lambda_v}{P}Var[(P(r + J, v, t) - P(r, v, t))d\pi].$$

Therefore, the equilibrium bond price is determined by the following partial differential equation:

$$\frac{1}{2}vP_{rr} + \frac{1}{2}\eta^2 vP_{vv} + [k(\theta - r) + \lambda_r v]P_r + [\mu\bar{v} - \acute{\mu}v]P_v$$
$$+hE[P(r + J, v; \tau) - P(r, v; \tau)]$$
$$-\lambda_v h Var[(P(r + J, v; \tau) - P(r, v; \tau)]d\pi - \dot{P} - rP = 0, \quad (8.3)$$

with the initial condition

$$P(r, v, T; T) = 1,$$

$\dot{P}$ in (8.3) denotes the derivative with respect to $\tau = T - t$.

Substituting the trial solution of the form:

$$P(r, v; \tau) = A(\tau)e^{-rB(\tau) - vC(\tau)}$$

into (8.3) and utilizing Taylor expansions,

$$E[e^{-JB} - 1] \simeq -\alpha B + 1/2(\alpha^2 + \gamma^2)B^2,$$

$$V[e^{-JB} - 1] \simeq \gamma^2 B^2,$$

PDE (8.3) becomes

$$r[kB + \dot{B} - 1] + v[-\lambda_r B + \dot{C} + \frac{1}{2}B^2 + \frac{1}{2}\eta C^2 + \acute{\mu}C] + k\theta(-B)$$
$$-\frac{\dot{A}}{A} - \mu\bar{v}C + h[-\alpha B + \frac{1}{2}(\alpha^2 + \gamma^2)B^2] - h\lambda_v \gamma^2 B^2 = 0 \quad (8.4)$$

with the initial condition

$$A(0) = 1, \quad B(0) = C(0) = 0.$$

Solving the three ODEs in (8.4) leads to the following proposition.

Proposition 21: *If the interest rate dynamics is specified by the stochastic differential equations (8.1) and (8.2), the the value at time t of a discount bond promising to pay one unit at time T, $P(r, v, t; T)$, is given by*

$$P(r, v; \tau) = A(\tau)e^{-B(\tau)r - C(\tau)v}, \quad (8.5)$$

where $\tau = T - t$, and

$$A(\tau) = e^{\Gamma} \left(\frac{X^\rho e^{-\phi X}[\Lambda U(Q, S, 2\phi X) + M(Q, S, 2\phi X)]}{\Lambda U(Q, S, 2\phi) + M(Q, S, 2\phi)} \right)^{-\frac{2\mu\bar{v}}{\eta^2}},$$

$$B(\tau) = \frac{1 - e^{-k\tau}}{k},$$

$$C(\tau) = \frac{2k}{\eta^2}\Bigg[-\rho + \phi X + \frac{2X\Lambda Q\phi U(Q+1, S+1, 2\phi X)}{\Lambda U(Q, S, 2\phi X) + M(Q, S, 2\phi X)}$$
$$- \frac{2X\phi\frac{Q}{S}M(Q+1, S+1, 2\phi X)}{\Lambda U(Q, S, 2\phi X) + M(Q, S, 2\phi X)}\Bigg],$$

with

$$
\begin{aligned}
X &= e^{-k\tau}, \\
\Gamma &= -\frac{2G + \tau(2kG + H)}{2k^2} - \frac{3H + HX^2 - (kG + H)X}{4k^3} \\
\Lambda &= -\frac{(\rho - \phi)M(Q, S; 2\phi) - 2\phi\frac{Q}{S}M(Q+1, S+1; 2\phi)}{(\rho - \phi)U(Q, S; 2\phi) + 2\phi Q U(Q+1, S+1; 2\phi)}, \\
G &= -k\theta - h\alpha, \\
H &= (\alpha^2 + \gamma^2) - 2\lambda_v \alpha\gamma^2 \\
Q &= -\frac{\chi}{2\phi} + \frac{S}{2}, \\
S &= 1 + \sqrt{1 - 4\omega - 2K + K^2}, \\
\rho &= \frac{1 - K + \sqrt{1 - 4\omega - 2K + K^2}}{2}, \\
\omega &= (1 - 2k\lambda_r)\frac{\eta^2}{4k^4}, \\
\chi &= (k\lambda_r - 1)\frac{\eta^2}{2k^4}, \\
\sigma &= \frac{\eta^2}{4k^4}, \\
K &= 1 - \frac{\mu'}{k}, \\
\phi &= \sqrt{-\sigma}.
\end{aligned}
$$

(8.6)

Following the methods used in chapter 1, the Green's function for the interest rate dynamics (8.1) and (8.2) can also be derived. With the Green's function the values of most European type derivatives and some exotic derivatives can be expressed in closed form and evaluated by numerical integrations.

8.3   Extension II: Jumping Mean and Jumping Volatility

Another meaningful extension to the interest rate dynamics presented in chapter 1 is to model the volatility process as a jump process rather than a Feller process. Besides empirical considerations, an advantage of such an extension is its analytical tractability. Solutions for a diffusion process normally involve messy special functions while solutions for a jump process are given in simple analytical forms.

The dynamics of the short rate $r(t)$, its short term mean $\theta(t)$, and its volatility $v(t)$ are assumed in the following.

Assumption 1. *The dynamics of the short rate is given by the following stochastic differential equation:*

$$dr(t) = k(\theta(t) - r(t))dt + \sqrt{v(t)}dB_1(t), \ t \geq 0, \ k > 0, \tag{8.7}$$

where $\theta(t)$ is the short-term mean of the short rate and $\sqrt{v(t)}$ is instantaneous variance (volatility) of the short rate.

Assumption 2. *The development of the short-term mean is given by the following stochastic differential equation:*

$$d\theta(t) = \nu(\bar{\theta} - \theta(t))dt + J_1(\alpha_1, \gamma_1^2)d\pi_1, \ t \geq 0, \ \bar{\theta} > 0, \ \nu > 0, \tag{8.8}$$

where $\bar{\theta}$ is the constant long-term mean of the short-term mean and J_1 is the jump in short mean which is normally distributed, $N(\alpha_1, \gamma_1^2)$, and π_1 is the Poisson arrival probability with intensity parameter h_1.

Assumption 3. *The development of the volatility of the short rate is given by*

$$dv(t) = \mu(\bar{v} - v(t))dt + J_2(\alpha_2, \gamma_2^2)d\pi_2, \ t \geq 0, \ \bar{v} > 0, \ \nu > 0, \tag{8.9}$$

where $\bar{v}$ is the constant long-term mean of volatility, J_2 is the jump in the short rate characterized by α_2 and γ_2^2, and π_2 is the Poisson arrival probability with parameter h_2.

In addition, the three processes B, π_1, π_2 are assumed to be instantaneously uncorrelated:

$$d\pi_1 d\pi_2 = d\pi_1 dB = d\pi_2 dB = 0.$$

Using Ito's lemma the stochastic differential equation that determines bond price, $P(r, v, t; T) \equiv P(r, v; \tau)$, is given by

$$
\begin{aligned}
dP(r, v; \tau) =\ & [k(\theta - r)P_r + \mu(\bar{v} - v)P_v + \nu(\bar{\theta} - \theta)P_\theta + P_t + \frac{1}{2}vP_{rr}]dt + \\
& \sqrt{v}P_r dB + [(P(r, \theta + J_1, v, \tau) - P(r, \theta, v, \tau))|J_1]d\pi_1 \\
& + [(P(r, \theta, v + J_2, \tau) - P(r, \theta, v, \tau))|J_2]d\pi_2.
\end{aligned} \tag{8.10}
$$

Assume that the risk premium for the three stochastic processes is proportional to their variances:

$$\lambda_r v \frac{P_r}{P} + \frac{\lambda_\theta}{P} Var[(P(r, \theta + J_1, v, t) - P(r, \theta, v, t))d\pi_1]$$

$$+\frac{\lambda_v}{P}Var[(P(r,\theta,v+J_2,t)-P(r,\theta,v,t))d\pi_2].$$

By the arbitrage argument the equilibrium bond price is determined by the following partial differential equation:

$$\frac{1}{2}vP_{rr}+[k(\theta-r)+\lambda_r v]P_r+\mu(\bar{v}-v)P_v+\nu(\bar{\theta}-\theta)P_\theta$$
$$+h_1E[P(r,\theta+J_1,v;\tau)-P(r,v;\tau)]$$
$$-\lambda_\theta h_1Var[(P(r,\theta+J_1,v;\tau)-P(r,v;\tau)]$$
$$+h_2E[P(r,\theta,v+J_2;\tau)-P(r,v;\tau)]$$
$$-\lambda_v h_2Var[(P(r,\theta,v+J_2;\tau)-P(r,v;\tau)]-\dot{P}-rP=0,\quad (8.11)$$

with initial condition

$$P(r,\theta,v,T;T)=1.$$

Substituting the trial solution of the form

$$P(r,v;\tau)=A(\tau)e^{-rB(\tau)-\theta C(\tau)-vD(\tau)}$$

into PDE (8.12) and utilizing the Taylor expansions

$$E[e^{-J_1C}-1]=-\alpha_1C+1/2(\alpha_1^2+\gamma_1^2)C^2,\quad V[e^{-J_1C}-1]=\gamma_1^2C^2$$

and similar expressions for $E[e^{-J_2D}-1]$ and $V[e^{-J_2D}-1]$ yields

$$\frac{1}{2}vB^2+[k(\theta-r)+\lambda_r v](-B)+\mu(\bar{v}-v)(-D)+\nu(\bar{\theta}-\theta)(-C)$$
$$+h_1[-\alpha_1C+\frac{1}{2}(\alpha_1^2+\gamma_1^2)C^2]-h_1\lambda_\theta\gamma_1^2C^2+h_2[-\alpha_2D+$$
$$\frac{1}{2}(\alpha_2^2+\gamma_2^2)D^2]-h_2\lambda_v\gamma_2^2D^2-\frac{\dot{A}}{A}+(r\dot{B}+\theta\dot{C}+v\dot{D})-r=0.(8.12)$$

The solution to (8.12) can be easily obtained.

Chapter 9

Concluding Remarks

A three-factor model of the term structure of interest rates has been presented. This model has incorporated the empirical realism that both the short mean and volatility of short interest rates are stochastic. Because of this, the model is able to generalize many empirical features of the term structure and provide additional insights and explanatory powers for the behavior of interest rates.

There are a few other multi-factor models of the term structure of interest rates in the literature (Langetieg (1980), Chen and Scott (1992)). They basically share the same modeling characteristic: assuming that the short rate is the sum of a few factors, say n,

$$r = x_1 + x_2 +, ..., + x_n,$$

and that each factor follows the same stochastic process, say Feller process,

$$x_i = \mu_i(\overline{x_i} - x_i)dt + \nu_i\sqrt{x_i}dB_i, \quad i = 1, ..., n.$$

Although these multi-factor models may be able to fit the data better with more parameters, the problem is that because the factors are unspecified and not related to any observable variables, these models provide little insight as to how observable variables affect the interest rate dynamics and derivative prices.

The appealing attributes of the model presented are not only its ability to fit data better but also its ability to explicitly relate the dynamics of the short mean and volatility to the movements of the term structure and the values of interest rate derivatives. It is this very property that makes the model useful in dealing with the practical day-to-day problems of pricing derivatives and managing risks of fixed income securities.

As the term structure of interest rates is of fundamental importance in finance, a new model of interest rates opens a new avenue for further research and lays new ground for applications. Our model, being more realistic and tractable, is expected to have an impact in many areas in finance. The examples presented in this book serve only as an introduction to the model's potential usefulness in derivatives pricing and risk management. Further research can be carried out at least along the following directions:

a) To test of the model's empirical implications, including the model's predictions of bond price, option price, futures price, and other interest rate derivatives prices.

b) To apply the methodology presented in this monograph to the pricing of non-interest rate derivatives under multi-factor models, such as equity derivatives with stochastic interest rates and derivatives on currencies, which normally involve a few stochastic processes.

c) To extend the model to an international or multi-currency model which incorporates both stochastic exchange rates and stochastic interest rates.

d) To model default risk in a consistent way given our framework while maintaining tractability.

e) To develop algorithms to compute the type of high-dimensional integrals involved in our derivative pricing formula to a high degree of accuracy in order to enhance the usefulness of the model for practical purposes.

Proof of Lemma 1

Let $F^j(r, \theta, v, t)$ denote the price of a derivative security the value of which depends on r, θ, v, t, $j=1,...,$ with

$$\frac{dF^j}{F^j} = \alpha^j dt + \sigma_1^j dz_1 + \sigma_2^j dz_2 + \sigma_3^j dz_3. \qquad (A.1)$$

By Ito's Lemma,

$$
\begin{aligned}
\alpha^j &\equiv \frac{1}{F^j}[\frac{1}{2}vF_{rr} + \frac{1}{2}\eta^2 vF_{vv} + \frac{1}{2}\zeta^2\theta F_{\theta\theta} + \kappa(\theta - r)F_r + \\
&\quad \nu(\bar\theta - \theta)F_\theta + \mu(\bar v - v)F_v + F_t], \\
\sigma_1^j &\equiv \frac{F_r^j \sqrt{v}}{F^j}, \\
\sigma_2^j &\equiv \frac{F_\theta^j \zeta\sqrt{\theta}}{F^j}, \\
\sigma_3^j &\equiv \frac{F_v^j \eta\sqrt{v}}{F^j}. \qquad (A.2)
\end{aligned}
$$

Let $V(t)$ denote the value of portfolio at time t that holds N_i units of security i with price F^i; N_j units of security j with price F^j; N_k units of security k with price F^k; N_l units of security l with price F^l; the balance of the portfolio, $V - N_i F^i - N_j F^j - N_k F^K - N_l F^l$, in the riskless security. The dynamics of $V(t)$ are given by

$$
\begin{aligned}
dV &= rV dt + N_i(dF^i - rF^i dt) + N_j(dF^j - rF^i dt) + N_k(dF^k - rF^k dt) \\
&\quad + N_l(dF^l - rF^l dt) \\
&= rV dt + [N_i F^i(\alpha^i - r) + N_j F^j(\alpha^j - r) \\
&\quad + N_k F^k(\alpha^k - r) + N_l F^l(\alpha^l - r)]dt \\
&\quad + [N_i F^i \sigma_1^i + N_j F^j \sigma_1^j + N_k F^k \sigma_1^k + N_l F^l \sigma_1^l]dz_1 \\
&\quad + [N_i F^i \sigma_2^i + N_j F^j \sigma_2^j + N_k F^k \sigma_2^k + N_l F^l \sigma_2^l]dz_2 \\
&\quad + [N_i F^i \sigma_3^i + N_j F^j \sigma_3^j + N_k F^k \sigma_3^k + N_l F^l \sigma_3^l]dz_3. \qquad (A.3)
\end{aligned}
$$

Consider the family of hedged portfolio strategies, (*)-strategies, in which $(N_i^*, N_j^*, N_k^*, N_l^*)$ are chosen so that the coefficients in the stochastic terms dz_1, dz_2, and dz_3 become zero:

$$N_i^* F^i \sigma_1^i + N_j^* F^j \sigma_1^j + N_k^* F^k \sigma_1^k + N_l^* F^l \sigma_1^l = 0,$$

$$N_i^* F^i \sigma_2^i + N_j^* F^j \sigma_2^j + N_k^* F^k \sigma_2^k + N_l^* F^l \sigma_2^l = 0,$$
$$N_i^* F^i \sigma_3^i + N_j^* F^j \sigma_3^j + N_k^* F^k \sigma_3^k + N_l^* F^l \sigma_3^l = 0.$$

Provided that securities i, j, and k are not just levered blow-ups of each other [i.e $\Delta \equiv \sigma_1^i \sigma_2^j \sigma_3^k + \sigma_1^k \sigma_2^i \sigma_3^j + \sigma_1^j \sigma_2^k \sigma_3^i - \sigma_1^k \sigma_2^j \sigma_3^i - \sigma_1^i \sigma_2^k \sigma_3^j - \sigma_1^j \sigma_2^i \sigma_3^k \neq 0]$, then the (*)-strategies are given by

$$
\begin{aligned}
N_i^* &= -\frac{N_l^* F^l}{F^i} \frac{\sigma_1^l \sigma_2^j \sigma_3^k + \sigma_1^k \sigma_2^l \sigma_3^j + \sigma_1^j \sigma_2^k \sigma_3^l - \sigma_1^k \sigma_2^j \sigma_3^l - \sigma_1^l \sigma_2^k \sigma_3^j - \sigma_1^j \sigma_2^l \sigma_3^k}{\sigma_1^i \sigma_2^j \sigma_3^k + \sigma_1^k \sigma_2^i \sigma_3^j + \sigma_1^j \sigma_2^k \sigma_3^i - \sigma_1^k \sigma_2^j \sigma_3^i - \sigma_1^i \sigma_2^k \sigma_3^j - \sigma_1^j \sigma_2^i \sigma_3^k} \\
&= -N_l^* [\frac{F_r^i F_\theta^j F_v^k}{\Delta} \frac{F_r^l}{F_r^i} - \frac{F_r^i F_\theta^k F_v^j}{\Delta} \frac{F_r^l}{F_r^i} - \frac{F_r^j F_\theta^i F_v^k}{\Delta} \frac{F_\theta^l}{F_\theta^i} \\
&\quad + \frac{F_r^j F_\theta^k F_v^i}{\Delta} \frac{F_v^l}{F_v^i} + \frac{F_r^k F_\theta^i F_v^j}{\Delta} \frac{F_\theta^l}{F_\theta^i} - \frac{F_r^k F_\theta^j F_v^i}{\Delta} \frac{F_v^l}{F_v^i}],
\end{aligned}
$$

$$
\begin{aligned}
N_j^* &= -N_l^* [\frac{F_r^j F_\theta^i F_v^k}{\Delta} \frac{F_r^l}{F_r^j} - \frac{F_r^j F_\theta^k F_v^i}{\Delta} \frac{F_r^l}{F_r^j} - \frac{F_r^i F_\theta^j F_v^k}{\Delta} \frac{F_\theta^l}{F_\theta^j} \\
&\quad + \frac{F_r^i F_\theta^k F_v^j}{\Delta} \frac{F_v^l}{F_v^j} + \frac{F_r^k F_\theta^j F_v^i}{\Delta} \frac{F_\theta^l}{F_\theta^j} - \frac{F_r^k F_\theta^i F_v^j}{\Delta} \frac{F_v^l}{F_v^j}],
\end{aligned}
$$

$$
\begin{aligned}
N_k^* &= -N_l^* [\frac{F_r^k F_\theta^j F_v^i}{\Delta} \frac{F_r^l}{F_r^k} - \frac{F_r^k F_\theta^i F_v^j}{\Delta} \frac{F_r^l}{F_r^k} - \frac{F_r^j F_\theta^k F_v^i}{\Delta} \frac{F_\theta^l}{F_\theta^k} \\
&\quad + \frac{F_r^j F_\theta^i F_v^k}{\Delta} \frac{F_v^l}{F_v^k} + \frac{F_r^i F_\theta^k F_v^j}{\Delta} \frac{F_\theta^l}{F_\theta^k} - \frac{F_r^i F_\theta^j F_v^k}{\Delta} \frac{F_v^l}{F_v^k}].
\end{aligned}
\tag{A.4}
$$

From (A.3) and (A.4)

$$
\begin{aligned}
dV^* &= rV^* dt + N_l^* F^l [\alpha^l - r] - \left[\eta_{jk}^i \frac{\sigma_1^l}{\sigma_1^i} + \zeta_{jk}^i \frac{\sigma_2^l}{\sigma_2^i} + \xi_{jk}^i \frac{\sigma_3^l}{\sigma_3^i} \right] (\alpha^i - r) \\
&\quad \left[\eta_{ik}^j \frac{\sigma_1^l}{\sigma_1^j} + \zeta_{ki}^j \frac{\sigma_2^l}{\sigma_2^j} + \xi_{ik}^j \frac{\sigma_3^l}{\sigma_3^j} \right] (\alpha^j - r) \\
&\quad - \left[\eta_{ij}^k \frac{\sigma_1^l}{\sigma_1^k} + \zeta_{ji}^k \frac{\sigma_2^l}{\sigma_2^k} + \xi_{ji}^k \frac{\sigma_3^l}{\sigma_3^k} \right] (\alpha^k - r)]
\end{aligned}
\tag{A.5}
$$

where

$$\eta_{jk}^i = \frac{F_r^i F_\theta^j F_v^k - F_r^i F_\theta^k F_v^j}{\Delta},$$

$$\zeta_{kj}^i = \frac{F_r^k F_\theta^i F_v^j - F_r^j F_\theta^i F_v^k}{\Delta},$$

$$\xi_{jk}^i = \frac{F_r^j F_\theta^k F_v^i - F_r^k F_\theta^j F_v^i}{\Delta}.$$

Since V^* is instantaneously riskless and since N_l^* can be chosen arbitrarily to avoid arbitrage, the second term in (A.5) vanishes for all securities (i, j, k, l) with dynamics that satisfy (A.1), so that:

$$\alpha^l - r = \sigma_1^l \left[\eta_{jk}^i \frac{\alpha^i - r}{\sigma_1^i} + \eta_{jk}^i \frac{\alpha^j - r}{\sigma_1^j} + \eta_{jk}^i \frac{\alpha^k - r}{\sigma_1^k} \right]$$

$$+\sigma_1^2 \left[\zeta_{ik}^j \frac{\alpha^i - r}{\sigma_2^i} + \zeta_{ik}^j \frac{\alpha^j - r}{\sigma_2^j} + \zeta_{ik}^j \frac{\alpha^k - r}{\sigma_2^k} \right]$$

$$+\sigma_3^l \left[\xi_{ji}^k \frac{\alpha^i - r}{\sigma_3^i} + \xi_{ji}^k \frac{\alpha^j - r}{\sigma_3^j} + \xi_{ji}^k \frac{\alpha^k - r}{\sigma_3^k} \right]. \tag{A.6}$$

To better interpret this equation, suppose that security i's return is uncorrelated with dz_2 and dz_3 and that security j's return is uncorrelated with dz_1 and dz_3 and security k's return is uncorrelated with dz_1 and dz_2. It follows that

$$F_\theta^i = F_v^i = 0 = \sigma_2^i = \sigma_3^i,$$

$$F_r^j = F_v^j = 0 = \sigma_1^j = \sigma_3^j,$$

$$F_\theta^k = F_r^k = 0 = \sigma_1^k = \sigma_3^k.$$

Therefore

$$\alpha^l - r = \sigma_1^l \left(\frac{\alpha^i - r}{\sigma^i} \right) + \sigma_2^l \left(\frac{\alpha^j - r}{\sigma^j} \right) + \sigma_3^l \left(\frac{\alpha^k - r}{\sigma^k} \right)$$

where the relations

$$\sigma^i = \sigma_1^i, \sigma^j = \sigma_2^j, \sigma^k = \sigma_3^k$$

have been made use of. The equation holds for all securities l with dynamics satisfying (A.1). Because the above relation must hold for such securities including ones that are either perfectly correlated with dz_1 or perfectly correlated with dz_1 and dz_3, it follows that

$$\frac{\alpha^i - r}{\sigma_1^i} = \rho^r(r, \theta, v, t),$$

$$\frac{\alpha^j - r}{\sigma_2^j} = \rho^\theta(r, \theta, v, t),$$

$$\frac{\alpha^k - r}{\sigma_3^k} = \rho^v(r, \theta, v, t),$$

where the function $\rho^r, \rho^\theta, \rho^v$ can depend only on r, v, t, θ and not on any characteristics specific to the terms of securities i, j or k.

From (A.6),

$$
\begin{aligned}
\alpha^l &= r + \sigma_1^l \rho^r(r, \theta, v, t) + \sigma_2^l \rho^\theta(r, \theta, v, t) + \sigma_1^3 \rho^v(r, \theta, v, t) \\
&= r + F_r^l \sqrt{v} \rho^r(r, \theta, v, t) + F_\theta^l \zeta \sqrt{\theta} \rho^\theta(r, \theta, v, t) + F_v^l \eta \sqrt{v} \rho^v(r, \theta, v, t) \\
&= r + F_r^l \psi^r(r, \theta, v, t) + F_\theta^l \psi^\theta(r, \theta, v, t) + F_v^l \psi^v(r, \theta, v, t) \tag{A.7}
\end{aligned}
$$

where the following relations

$$\psi^r = \sqrt{v} \rho^r(r, \theta, t),$$

$$\psi^\theta = \zeta\sqrt{\theta}\rho^\theta(r,\theta,t),$$

$$\psi^v = \eta\sqrt{v}\rho^v(r,\theta,t)$$

have been defined.

The equation (A.7) is the necessary condition to rule out arbitrage opportunities. It follows that to avoid arbitrage, F^k must satisfy the PDE,

$$\frac{1}{2}vF_{rr} + \frac{1}{2}\eta^2 vF_{vv} + \frac{1}{2}\zeta^2\theta F_{\theta\theta} + [\kappa(\theta - r) - \psi^r]F_r$$
$$+[\nu(\bar{\theta} - \theta) - \psi^\theta]F_\theta + [\mu(\bar{v} - v) - \psi^v]F_v + F_t - rF = 0, \quad (A.8)$$

where the superscript has been suppressed. The partial differential equation (A.8) is the fundamental valuation equation for interest rate contingent claims. If the risk premium function is assumed proportional to the variance:

$$\begin{aligned} \psi^v &= a^r v = -\lambda_r v, \\ \psi^\theta &= a^\theta \zeta^2\theta = -\lambda_\theta \theta, \\ \psi^v &= a^v \eta^2 v = -\lambda_v v. \end{aligned}$$

The PDE used as in the text is obtained:

$$\frac{1}{2}vF_{rr} + \frac{1}{2}\eta^2 vF_{vv} + \frac{1}{2}\zeta^2\theta F_{\theta\theta} + [\kappa(\theta - r) + \lambda_r v]F_r$$
$$+[\nu\bar{\theta} - \acute{\nu}\theta]F_\theta + [\mu\bar{v} - \acute{\mu}v]F_v + F_t - rF = 0. \quad (A.9)$$

As it stated in the text, these assumptions are internally consistent.

Appendix B

Proof of Proposition 2

Substituting the trial form of solution

$$P(\tau) = A(\tau)e^{-B(\tau)r - C(\tau)\theta - D(\theta)v}$$

into the fundamental valuation PDE,

$$\frac{1}{2}vP_{rr} + \frac{1}{2}\eta^2 vP_{vv} + \frac{1}{2}\zeta^2\theta P_{\theta\theta} + [\kappa(\theta - r) + \lambda_r v]P_r$$
$$+ [\nu\bar{\theta} - \nu'\theta]P_\theta + [\mu\bar{v} - \acute{\mu}v]P_v + P_t - rP = 0,$$

yields the system of ODEs

$$1 = kB + B' \tag{B.1}$$

$$0 = -kB + \frac{1}{2}\zeta^2 C^2 + \acute{\nu}C + C' \tag{B.2}$$

$$0 = \frac{1}{2}B^2 + \frac{1}{2}\eta^2 D^2 - \lambda_r B + \acute{\mu}D + D' \tag{B.3}$$

$$0 = \nu\bar{\theta}C + \mu\bar{v}D + \frac{A'}{A} \tag{B.4}$$

with initial conditions

$$A(0) = 1, B(0) = C(0) = D(0) = 0.$$

Equation (B.1) has the solution

$$B(\tau) = \frac{1 - e^{-k\tau}}{k}. \tag{B.5}$$

Equation (B.2) has Ricatti form

$$C' = 1 - e^{-k\tau} - \nu'C - \frac{\zeta^2 C^2}{2}.$$

The solution is

$$C(\tau) = \frac{2}{\zeta^2}\frac{u'}{u}, \tag{B.6}$$

where $u(\tau)$ satisfies

$$u'' + \nu'u' + \frac{\zeta^2}{2}(e^{-k\tau} - 1)u = 0. \tag{B.7}$$

Let $X = e^{-k\tau}$ and denote $u(\tau) = U(X)$. Then (B.7) becomes

$$X^2 U'' + (1 - L)XU' + \frac{H^2}{2}(X - 1)U = 0, \tag{B.8}$$

where

$$L = \nu'/k, H = \zeta/k$$

and the prime denotes differentiation with respect to X. Let

$$U(X) = X^{\frac{L}{2}} F(Z)$$

where

$$Z = \sqrt{2}HX^{1/2}.$$

Then, (B.8) becomes

$$Z^2 \frac{d^2 F}{dZ^2} + Z \frac{dF}{dZ} + (Z^2 - G^2)F = 0 \tag{B.9}$$

where

$$G^2 = 2H^2 + L^2.$$

(B.9) is the Bessel equation of order G with independent solutions $J_G(Z)$ and $Y_G(Z)$. So

$$u(x) = U(X) = X^{L/2} \left[A_1 J_G(H'X^{1/2}) + A_2 Y_G(H'X^{1/2}) \right], \tag{B.10}$$

where A_1, A_2 are constants, $H' = \sqrt{2}H$.

The initial condition $C(0) = 0$ is equivalent to $\frac{dU}{dX}\mid_{X=1} = 0$ which becomes the following after some calculations

$$L[A_1 J_G(H') + A_2 Y_G(H') + \frac{H'}{2}[A_1(J_{G-1}(H') - J_{G+1}(H'))]$$
$$+ A_2(Y_{G-1}(H') - Y_{G+1}(H')) = 0 \tag{B.11}$$

The ratio $\frac{A_1}{A_2}$ can be computed as

$$\frac{A_1}{A_2} = -\frac{\zeta\sqrt{2}Y_{G-1}(\sqrt{2}\zeta/k) + 2\nu'Y_G(\sqrt{2}\zeta/k) - \zeta\sqrt{2}Y_{G+1}(\sqrt{2}\zeta/k)}{\zeta\sqrt{2}J_{G-1}(\sqrt{2}\zeta/k) + 2\nu'J_G(\sqrt{2}\zeta/k) - \zeta\sqrt{2}J_{G+1}(\sqrt{2}\zeta/k)} \equiv \Gamma.$$

The solution to (B.3) is given by

$$D(\tau) = \frac{2}{\eta^2} \frac{\nu'}{\nu}, \tag{B.12}$$

where $\nu(\tau)$ satisfies

$$\nu'' + \mu'\nu' + \frac{\eta^2}{2} \left[\frac{\lambda_r}{k}(e^{-k\tau} - 1) + \frac{1}{2k^2}(e^{-k\tau} - 1)^2 \right] \nu = 0.$$

Let $X = e^{-k\tau}$ and $V(X) = v(\tau)$. The above equation becomes

$$X^2 \frac{d^2 V}{dX^2} + (1 - \frac{\mu'}{k})X\frac{dV}{dX} + \frac{\eta^2}{2k^2}\left[(\frac{1}{2k^2} - \frac{\lambda_r}{k}) + (\frac{\lambda_r}{k} - \frac{1}{k^2})X + \frac{X^2}{2k^2}\right]V = 0.$$
(B.13)

Introducing

$$\begin{aligned}
\kappa &= 1 - \frac{\mu'}{k}, \\
\gamma &= \frac{\eta^2}{4k^4}, \\
\alpha &= \gamma(1 - 2k\lambda_r), \\
\beta &= 2\gamma(k\lambda_r - 1),
\end{aligned}$$

equation (B.13) becomes

$$X^2 \frac{d^2 V}{dX^2} + KX\frac{dV}{dX} + (\alpha + \beta X + \gamma X^2)V = 0.$$
(B.14)

Equation (B.14) can be transformed to

$$Y^2 \frac{d^2 W}{dY^2} + (S - Y)\frac{dW}{dY} - QW = 0,$$
(B.15)

where

$$\begin{aligned}
Y &= -2\phi X, \\
V(X) &= e^{\phi X} X^\rho W(Y), \\
Q &= -\frac{\beta}{2\phi} + \frac{S}{2}, \\
S &= \frac{k + \sqrt{\mu'^2 - 4\alpha k^2}}{k}, \\
\rho &= \frac{\mu' + \sqrt{\mu'^2 - 4\alpha k^2}}{2k}, \\
\phi &= (-\gamma)^{1/2}.
\end{aligned}$$
(B.16)

The general solution of $W(Y)$ is

$$W(Y) = A_1 M(Q, S; Y) + A_2 U(Q, S; Y),$$
(B.17)

where A_1 and A_2 are constants to be determined by the initial condition.
Define

$$\Lambda \equiv \frac{A_1}{A_2}$$

which can be solved from the intial condition as

$$\Lambda = -\frac{(\rho - \phi)M(Q, S; 2\phi) - 2\phi\frac{Q}{S}M(Q + 1, S + 1; 2\phi)}{(\rho - \phi)U(Q, S; 2\phi) + 2\phi QU(Q + 1, S + 1; 2\phi)}.$$

From (B.6) and (B.12), each of the functions $C(s)$ and $D(s)$ has the form $\frac{w'(s)}{w(s)}$. Integrating (B.4) yields

$$\ln A(x) = -\frac{2\nu\bar{\theta}}{\zeta^2} \ln \frac{u(x)}{u(0)} - \frac{2\mu\bar{v}}{\eta^2} \ln \frac{v(x)}{v(0)}$$

or

$$A(x) = \left(\frac{u(x)}{u(0)}\right)^{\frac{-2\nu\bar{\theta}}{\zeta^2}} \left(\frac{v(x)}{v(0)}\right)^{\frac{-2\mu\bar{v}}{\eta^2}}.$$

Proof of Lemma 2

The Green's function for the general interest rate dynamics, $G(y_1, y_2, y_3, s, x_1, x_2, x_3, t)$, is the solution to the following PDE:

$$\frac{1}{2}x_3 G_{x_1 x_1} + \frac{1}{2}\eta^2 x_3 G_{x_3 x_3} + \frac{1}{2}\zeta^2 x_2 G_{x_2 x_2} + [k(x_2 - x_1) + \lambda_r x_3]G_{x_1} +$$
$$[\nu\bar{\theta} - \dot{\nu}x_2]G_{x_2} + [\mu\bar{\nu} - \dot{\mu}x_3]G_{x_3} + G_t - x_1 G = 0 \qquad \text{(C.1)}$$

with

$$G(y_1, y_2, y_3, s, x_1, x_2, x_3, s) = \delta(x_1 - y_1)\delta(x_2 - y_2)\delta(x_3 - y_3).$$

It is easy to see that the Fourier transformation of $G(y_1, y_2, y_3, s, x_1, x_2, x_3, t)$,

$$
\begin{aligned}
F(\phi, \psi, \varphi, s, x_1, x_2, x_3, t) &= \tilde{G}(\phi, \psi, \varphi, s, x_1, x_2, x_3, t) \\
&= \frac{1}{(2\pi)^{3/2}} \int_{-\infty}^{\infty} e^{iy_1\phi + iy_2\psi + iy_3\varphi} \times \\
&\quad G(y_1, y_2, y_3, s, x_1, x_2, x_3, t)dy_1 dy_2 dy_3,
\end{aligned}
$$

is the solution to the following PDE,

$$\frac{1}{2}x_3 F_{x_1 x_1} + \frac{1}{2}\eta^2 x_3 F_{x_3 x_3} + \frac{1}{2}\zeta^2 x_2 F_{x_2 x_2} + +[k(x_2 - x_1) + \lambda_r x_3]F_{x_1}$$
$$+[\nu\bar{\theta} - \dot{\nu}x_2]F_{x_2} + [\mu\bar{\nu} - \dot{\mu}x_3]F_{x_3} + F_t - x_1 F = 0 \qquad \text{(C.2)}$$

with the initial condition

$$F(x_1, x_2, x_3, s, \phi, \psi, \varphi, s) = e^{ix_1\phi + ix_2\psi + ix_3\varphi}. \qquad \text{(C.3)}$$

To use the method of the separation of variables, try the solution of the form

$$F(x_1, x_2, x_3, \phi, \psi, \varphi, \tau) = A(\tau, \phi, \psi, \varphi)e^{-B(\tau,\phi,\psi,\varphi)x_1 - C(\tau,\phi,\psi,\varphi)x_2 - D(\tau,\phi,\psi,\varphi)x_3}.$$

It can be shown that to solve PDE (C.2) with the initial condition (C.3) is equivalent to solving the following system of ODEs

$$1 = \kappa B(\tau, \cdot) + \dot{B}(\tau, \cdot),$$

$$0 = -\kappa B(\tau, \cdot) + \frac{1}{2}\varsigma^2 C^2(\tau, \cdot) + \acute{\nu} C(\tau, \cdot) + \dot{C}(\tau, \cdot),$$

$$0 = \frac{1}{2}B^2(\tau, \cdot) + \frac{1}{2}\eta^2 C^2(\tau, \cdot) - \lambda_r B(\tau, \cdot) + \acute{\mu} D(\tau, \cdot) + \dot{D}(\tau, \cdot),$$

$$0 = \nu\bar{\theta} C(\tau, \cdot) + \mu\bar{\upsilon} D(\tau, \cdot) + \dot{A}(\tau, \cdot)/A(\tau, \cdot)$$

with initial conditions,

$$B(\tau = 0, \cdot) = e^{ix_1\phi}, C(\tau = 0, \cdot) = e^{ix_2\psi}, D(\tau = 0, \cdot) = e^{ix_3\varphi}, A(\tau = 0, \cdot) = 1.$$

The above system of ODEs is similar to the one in the bond pricing section and can be solved similarly.

Appendix D

Proof of Proposition 8

Let $C(r, \theta, v, t, T; s, K)$ denote the value at time t with $r(t) = r, \theta(t) = \theta$, and $v(t) = v$, of a European call option on a zero-coupon bond maturing at date s, with option exercise price K and expiration date $T, (s \geq T \geq t)$. At the expiration date, $t = T$,

$$C(r, \theta, v, T, T; s, K) = [P(r, \theta, v, T, s) - K]^+,$$

where $P(r, \theta, v, T, s)$ is the bond price given by (1.12) in section 1.3.

The range of values of r, θ, and v over which the option is in the money at the expiration date T is denoted $\mathcal{B}$:

$$\mathcal{B} = \{(r, \theta, v) \mid B(T, s)r + C(T, s)\theta + D(T, s)v \leq K^* \equiv \ln \frac{A(T, s)}{K}\}.$$

The option value $C(r, \theta, v, t, T; s, K)$ can be written as

$$
\begin{aligned}
C&(r, \theta, v, t, T; s, K) \\
&= \int \int^{\mathcal{B}} \int [P(x_1, x_2, x_3, T, s) - K]G(x_1, x_2, x_3, T, r, \theta, v, t)dx_1 dx_2 dx_3 \\
&\equiv \int [P(x_1, x_2, x_3, T, s) - K]G(x_1, x_2, x_3, T, r, \theta, v, t) \\
&\quad \times 1_{\{(x_1, x_2, x_3) \in \mathcal{B}\}} dx_1 dx_2 dx_3
\end{aligned}
\tag{D.1}
$$

where $1_{\{(x_1, x_2, x_3) \in \mathcal{B}\}}$ is the indicator function and $G(r, \theta, v, t, x_1, x_2, x_3, T)$ is the Green's function.

The second integral in (D.1) can be simplified as follows:

$$
\begin{aligned}
\int &\int \int G(x_1, x_2, x_3, T, r, \theta, v, t)1_{\{(x_1, x_2, x_3) \in \mathcal{B}\}} dx_1 dx_2 dx_3 \\
&= \frac{1}{(2\pi)^{3/2}} \int \int \int \int_{-\infty}^{\infty} \int_{-\infty}^{\infty} \int_{-\infty}^{\infty} e^{-ix_1\phi - ix_2\psi - ix_3\varphi} \hat{G}(\phi, \psi, \varphi, r, \theta, v, \tau) \\
&\quad \times 1_{\{(x_1, x_2, x_3) \in \mathcal{B}\}} d\phi d\psi d\varphi dx_1 dx_2 dx_3 \\
&= \frac{1}{(2\pi)^{3/2}} \int_{-\infty}^{\infty} \int_{-\infty}^{\infty} \int_{-\infty}^{\infty} \hat{G}(\phi, \psi, \varphi, r, \theta, v, \tau) d\phi d\psi d\varphi \\
&\quad \times \left(\int e^{-ix_1\phi - ix_2\psi - ix_3\varphi} 1_{\{(x_1, x_2, x_3) \in \mathcal{B}\}} dx_1 dx_2 dx_3 \right).
\end{aligned}
\tag{D.2}
$$

Define

$$I(\alpha_0, \alpha_1, \alpha_2, \alpha_3, \gamma_0, \gamma_1, \gamma_2, \gamma_3) \equiv \int \alpha_0 e^{-ix_1\alpha_1 - ix_2\alpha_2 - ix_3\alpha_3}$$
$$1_{\{\gamma_1 x_1 + \gamma_2 x_2 + \gamma_3 x_3 \le \gamma_0\}} dx_1 dx_2 dx_3 \quad \text{(D.3)}$$

Define

$$\Psi(\beta_0, \beta_1, \beta_2, \beta_3, \alpha_0, \alpha_1, \alpha_2, \alpha_3, \gamma_0, \gamma_1, \gamma_2, \gamma_3)$$
$$= \frac{1}{(2\pi)^{3/2}} \int_{-\infty}^{\infty} \int_{-\infty}^{\infty} \int_{-\infty}^{\infty} I(\alpha_0, \alpha_1, \alpha_2, \alpha_3, \gamma_0, \gamma_1, \gamma_2, \gamma_3) \beta_0(\phi, \psi, \varphi, \tau)$$
$$\times e^{-\beta_1(\phi,\psi,\varphi,\tau)r - \beta_2(\phi,\psi,\varphi,\tau)\theta - \beta_3(\phi,\psi,\varphi,\tau)v} d\phi d\psi d\varphi. \quad \text{(D.4)}$$

Therefore, the integral (D.2) becomes

$$\int G(x_1, x_2, x_3, T, r, \theta, v, t) 1_{\{(x_1, x_2, x_3) \in B\}} dx_1 dx_2 dx_3$$
$$= P(r, \theta, v, t, T) \Psi \Big(\frac{A(\tau, \phi, \psi, \varphi)}{A(\tau)}, B(\tau, \phi, \psi, \varphi) - B(\tau),$$
$$C(\tau, \phi, \psi, \varphi) - C(\tau), D(\tau, \phi, \psi, \varphi) - D(\tau); 1, \phi, \psi, \varphi;$$
$$\ln \frac{A(T, s)}{K}, B(T, s), C(T, s), D(T, s) \Big). \quad \text{(D.5)}$$

Similarly the first integral in (D.1) can be written as

$$\int P(x_1, x_2, x_3, T, s) G(x_1, x_2, x_3, T, r, \theta, v, t) 1_{\{(x_1, x_2, x_3) \in B\}} dx_1 dx_2 dx_3$$
$$= P(r, \theta, v, t, s) \Psi \Big(\frac{A(\tau, \phi, \psi, \varphi)}{A(s - t)}, B(\tau, \phi, \psi, \varphi) - B(s - t),$$
$$C(\tau, \phi, \psi, \varphi) - C(s - t), D(\tau, \phi, \psi, \varphi) - D(s - t);$$
$$A(s - T), \phi - iB(s - T), \psi - iC(s - T), \varphi - iD(s - T);$$
$$\ln \frac{A(T, s)}{K}, B(T, s), C(T, s), D(T, s) \Big). \quad \text{(D.6)}$$

Combining (D.5) and (D.6) yields the bond option pricing formula presented in the text.

Finally, $I(\alpha_0, \alpha_1, \alpha_2, \alpha_3, \gamma_0, \gamma_1, \gamma_2, \gamma_3)$ can be computed analytically as the following:

$$I(\alpha_0, \alpha_1, \alpha_2, \alpha_3, \gamma_0, \gamma_1, \gamma_2, \gamma_3) \equiv \int \alpha_0 e^{-ix_1\alpha_1 - ix_2\alpha_2 - ix_3\alpha_3}$$
$$1_{\{\gamma_1 x_1 + \gamma_2 x_2 + \gamma_3 x_3 \le \gamma_0\}} dx_1 dx_2 dx_3 \quad \text{(D.7)}$$

Introducing

$$y_i = \frac{\gamma_i x_i}{\gamma_0}, \quad a_i = \frac{\gamma_0 \alpha_i}{\gamma_i}, \quad i = 1, 2, 3,$$

it is a simple matter to verify that [1]

$$
\begin{aligned}
& I(\alpha_0, \alpha_1, \alpha_2, \alpha_3, \gamma_0, \gamma_1, \gamma_2, \gamma_3) \\
& = \frac{\alpha_0 \gamma_0^3}{\gamma_1 \gamma_2 \gamma_3} \int_0^1 \int_0^{1-y_3} \int_{-\infty}^{1-y_2-y_3} e^{-iy_1 a_1 - iy_2 a_2 - iy_3 a_3} dy_1 dy_2 dy_3 \\
& = \frac{\alpha_0 \gamma_0^3}{\gamma_1 \gamma_2 \gamma_3} \left\{ \pi \delta(a_1) \left[\frac{e^{-ia_3} - e^{-ia_2}}{a_2(a_2 - a_3)} + \frac{e^{-ia_3} - 1}{a_2 a_3} \right] \right. \\
& \left. + \left[\frac{e^{-ia_3} - e^{-ia_2}}{ia_1(a_3 - a_2)(a_2 - a_1)} - \frac{e^{-ia_3} - e^{-ia_1}}{ia_1(a_2 - a_3)(a_3 - a_1)} \right] \right]
\end{aligned}
\tag{D.8}
$$

---

[1] To compute $I(\alpha_0, \alpha_1, \alpha_2, \alpha_3)$, the following relations should be made use of. The Fourier transformation of the sign function $\epsilon(t)$ take the form,

$$
\frac{1}{\sqrt{2\pi}} \int_{-\infty}^{\infty} \epsilon(t) e^{i\omega t} dt = \frac{1}{\sqrt{2\pi}} \frac{2i}{\omega}.
$$

Because

$$
\frac{i}{\pi} \int_{-\infty}^{\infty} \frac{e^{-i\omega t}}{\omega} = \frac{2}{\pi} \int_0^{\infty} \frac{\sin \omega t}{\omega} = \epsilon(t)
$$

since the second integral is the Dirichlet integral which is a well known representation of the sign function.

The Fourier transformation of the unit step function,

$$
\theta(t) = [1 + \epsilon(t)]/2
$$

can be obtained by using the result for the delta and sign function,

$$
\frac{1}{\sqrt{2\pi}} \int_{-\infty}^{\infty} \theta(t) e^{i\omega t} dt = \frac{1}{\sqrt{2\pi}} \left[\pi \delta(\omega) - \frac{1}{i\omega} \right].
$$

Integral Equation for Derivative Prices

As shown in section 1.4, under the general interest rate dynamics specified by stochastic differential equations (1.1), (1.2), and (1.3), the value at time t, $F(x_1, x_2, x_3, t; T) \equiv F(x_1, x_2, x_3, \tau)$, of an interest rate derivative with the terminal payoff $g(x_1, x_2, x_3, T), 0 \le t \le T, \tau = T - t$, is

$$
\begin{aligned}
F(x_1, x_2, x_3, t; T) \quad = \quad & \int G(y_1, y_2, y_3, T, x_1, x_2, x_3, t) g(y_1, y_2, y_3, T) dy_1 dy_2 dy_3 \\
& + \int G(y_1, y_2, y_3, s, x_1, x_2, x_3, t) \hat{V}(y_1, y_2, y_3, \partial_{y_1}, \partial_{y_2}, \partial_{y_3}) \\
& \times F(y_1, y_2, y_3, s; T) dy_1 dy_2 dy_3 ds.
\end{aligned}
$$

For notational simplicity, let $x = (x_1, x_2, x_3)$, $dx = dx_1 dx_2 dx_3$, etc. The above equation can be written as

$$
F(x, t) = \int G(y, x, t) g(y) dy + \int \int G(y, s, x, t) \hat{V}(y, \partial_y) F(y, s) dy ds. \quad \text{(E.1)}
$$

The term

$$
\int G(y, x, t) g(y) dy,
$$

is the price of a derivative under the benchmark interest rate dynamics and can always be derived in closed form solution. Let $P(x, t)$ denote the benchmark derivative price. The equation (E.1) can be rewritten as

$$
F(x, t) = P(x, t) + \int \int G(y, s, x, t) \hat{V}(y, \partial_y) F(y, s) dy ds.
$$

Performing Laplace transformation with respect to t, the above equation becomes

$$
f(x, \xi) = p(x, \xi) + \int g(y, x, \xi) \hat{V}(y, \partial_y) f(y, \xi) dy \quad \text{(E.2)}
$$

where the convolution theorem for Laplace transformation has been used. In the equation (E.2),

$$
f(x, \xi) = \int_0^\infty e^{-\xi t} F(x, t) dt
$$

and similarly for $g(y, x, \xi)$ and $p(x, \xi)$.

Equation (E.2) is a standard Fredholm equation of the second kind, which can be solved by the method of iterated kernel. Let

$$K(y, x) = g(y, x, \xi)\hat{V}(y, \partial_y)$$

and suppress ξ. The equation (E.2) becomes

$$f(x) = p(x) + \int K(y, x)f(y)dy.$$

Then the nth approximation for the solution is

$$f_n(x) = p(x) + \phi_1(x) + \phi_2(x) + ... + \phi_n(x) = \sum_{i=0}^{n} \phi_i(x) \qquad \text{(E.3)}$$

where

$$
\begin{aligned}
\phi_0 &= p(x), \\
\phi_1(x) &= \int K(x, y_1)p(y_1)dy_1, \\
\phi_2(x) &= \int\int K(x, y_1)K(y_1, y_2)p(y_2)dy_2dy_1, \\
\phi_n(x) &= \int\int ..\int K(x, y_1)K(y_1, y_2)...K(y_{n-1}, y_n)p(y_n)dy_n...dy_1 \quad \text{(E.4)}
\end{aligned}
$$

It is expected that the solution $f(x)$ will be

$$f(x) = \lim_{n\to\infty} f_n(x) = \lim_{n\to\infty} \sum_{i=0}^{n} \phi_i(x).$$

The series (E.3) converge for $| B | < 1$, where

$$B = \sqrt{\int\int K^2(x, y)dxdy}.$$

Once $f(x) \equiv f(x, \xi)$ is obtained, $F(x, t)$, the derivative price under the general interest rate dynamics, can be computed by inverse Laplace transformation

$$F(x, t) = \frac{1}{2\pi i}\int_B e^{\xi t}f(x, \xi)d\xi$$

where B is the usual Bromwich contour.

Bibliography

[1] Abramowitz, M. and I.A Stegun. 1972. *Handbook of Mathematical Functions with Formulas, Graphs and Mathematical Tables.* US Department of Commerce.

[2] Babbs, S. and N. Webber. 1994. A Theory of the Term Structure with an Official Short Rate. Working Paper: University of Warwick.

[3] Backus, D.K., S. Foresi, and S. E. Zin. 1994. Arbitrage Opportunities in Arbitrage-Free Models of Bond Pricing. New York University Salomon Center Working Paper.

[4] Balduzzi, P., G. Bertola and S. Foresi, 1994. A Model of Target Changes and the Term Structure of Interest Rates. Working Paper: New York University.

[5] Barone-Adesi, G. and R. E. Whaley. 1987. Efficient Analytic Approximation of American Option Values. *The Journal of Finance* 42: 301-320.

[6] Bierwag, G. O., G. G. Kaufman, and C, M, Latta. 1987. Bond Portfolio Immunization: Test of Maturity, One and Two Factor Duration Matching Strategies, *Financial Review* 22: 203-219.

[7] Bierwag, G. O., G. G. Kaufman, and A. Toevs. 1980. *Innovations in Bond Portfolio Management: Duration Analysis and Immunization.* Greenwich, Connecticut: JAI Press Inc.

[8] Black, F., E. Derman, and W. Toy. 1990. A One-Factor Model of Interest Rates and Its Application to Treasury Bond Options. *Financial Analyst Journal*: 33-39.

[9] Boyle, P. P. 1988. A Lattice Framework for Option Pricing with Two State Variables. *Journal of Financial and Quantitative Analysis* 23: 1-12.

[10] Boyle,P. P. and Y. K. Tse. 1990. An Algorithm for Computing Values of Options on the Maximum or Minimum of Several Assets. *Journal of Financial and Quantitative Analysis* 25: 215-227.

[11] Brennan, M. J. and E. S. Schwartz. 1979. A Continuous Time Approach to the Pricing of Bonds. *Journal of Banking and Finance* 3: 133-155.

[12] Brown, S. and P. H. Dybvig. 1986. The Empirical Implications of the Cox, Ingersoll , Ross Theory of the Term Structure of Interest Rates. *Journal of Finance* 41: 617-630.

[13] Campbell J. Y. 1995. Some Lessons from the Yield Curve. *Journal of Economic Perspectives* 9:12: 129-152.

[14] Carr, P. 1988. Treasury Bond Futures and the Quality Option. Tech Memo: Graduate School of Management, UCLA.

[15] Carr, P., R. Jarrow, and R. Myneni. 1992. Alternative Characterization of American Put Options. *Mathematical Finance* 2: 87-105.

[16] Chan, K. C., G. Andrew Karolyi, F. Longstaff, and A. B. Sanders. 1992. An Empirical Comparison of Alternative Models of the Short-Term Interest Rates. *Journal of Finance* 47: 1209-1228.

[17] Chen , R. and L. Scott. 1993. Maximum Likelihood Estimation for a Multi-Factor Equilibrium Model of the Term Structure of Interest Rates, *Journal of Fixed Income* 4: 14-31.

[18] Chen , R. and L. Scott. 1992. Pricing Interest Rate Options in a Two Factor Cox-Ingersoll-Ross Model of the Term Structure. *Review of Financial Studies* 5:613-636.

[19] Chesney, M., R. Elliot, and R. Gibson. 1993. Analytical Solutions for the Pricing of American Bond and Yield Options. em Mathematical Finance 3: 277-294.

[20] Constantinides, G. M. and J. E. Ingersoll Jr. 1984. Optimal Bond Trading with Personal Taxes. *Journal of Financial Economics* 13: 299-335.

[21] Courtadon, G. 1982. The Pricing of Options on Default-Free Bonds. *Journal of Financial and Quantitative Analysis* 17: 75-101.

[22] Cox, J. C., J.E. Ingersoll, Jr., and S. A. Ross. 1981. A Relation Between Forward Prices and Futures Prices. *Journal of Financial Economics* 9: 321-346.

[23] Cox, J. C., J.E. Ingersoll, Jr., and S. A. Ross. 1985. Theory of the Term Structure of Interest Rate. *Econometrica* 53: 363-384.

[24] Das, S. 1993. Mean Rate Shifts and Alternative Models of the Intersect Rates: Theory and Evidence. Working Paper: New York University.

[25] Dothan, L. U. 1978. On the Term Structure of Interest Rates. *Journal of Financial Economics* 6: 59-69.

[26] Driffill, J. 1982. Changes in Regime and the Term Structure. *Journal of Economic Dynamics and Control.*

[27] Duffie, D. 1988. *Security Markets: Stochastic Models.* Boston: Academic Press.

[28] Duffie, D. 1992. *Dynamic Asset Pricing Theory.* Princeton University Press.

[29] Duffie, D. and R. Kan. 1993. A Yield-Factor Model of Interest Rates. Unpublished manuscript, Stanford University.

[30] Duffie, D. and K. Singleton. 1993. Simulated Moments Estimation of Markov Models of Asset Prices. *Econometrica* 61: 929-952.

[31] Dybvig, P. 1989. Bond and Bond Option Pricing Based on the Current Term Structure. Unpublished manuscript, Washington University.

[32] Elton, E. J., M. J. Gruber, and P. G. Nadar. 1988. Bond Returns, Immunization and the Returning Generating Process. *Studies in Banking and Finance* 5: 125-154.

[33] Elton, E. J., M. J. Gruber, and R. Michaely. 1990. The Structure of Spot Rates and Immunization. *Journal of Finance* 45:2: 629-642.

[34] Feldman, D. 1993. Options on Bond Futures. *Journal of Financial and Quantitative Analysis.*

[35] Feller, W. 1951. Two Singular Difussion Problems. *Annals of Mathematics* 54: 173-182.

[36] Flesaker, B. 1993. Testing of the Heath-Jarrow-Morton/ Ho-Lee Model of Interest Rate Contingent Claims Pricing. *Journal of Financial and Quantitative Analysis* 38: 483-495.

[37] Friedman. A. 1975. *Stochastic Differential Equations and Applications.* Volume 1, New York: Academic Press.

[38] Gardiner, C. W. 1983. *Handbook of Stochastic Methods for Physics, Chemistry and the Natural Sciences.* Berlin: Springer-Verlag.

[39] Gay, G. D. and S. Manaster. 1984. The Quality Option Implicit in Futures Contracts. *Journal of Financial Economics* 13: 353-370.

[40] Gibbons, M. and K. Ramaswamy. 1993. A Test of the the Cox, Ingersoll , Ross Theory of the Term Structure, *Review of Financial Studies* 6: 619-658.

[41] Goldman, M., H. B. Sosin and M. A. Gatto. 1979. Path Dependent Options: "Buy at the Low, Sell at the High". *Journal of Finance* 34: 1111-1127.

[42] Gultekin, N. B. and R. J. Rogalski. 1984. The Alternative Duration Specifications and the Measurement of Basis Risk: Empirical Tests. *Journal Business* 57:2:241-264.

[43] Hamilton, J. D. 1988. Rational Expectations Econometric Analysis of Changes in Regime: An Investigation of the Term Structure of Interest Rates. *Journal of Economic Dynamic and Control* 12: 385-423.

[44] Harrison, M. and D. Kreps. 1979. Martingales and Arbitrage in Multiperiod Security Markets. *Journal of Economic Theory* 20: 381-408.

[45] He, H., W. Keirstead and J. Rebholz. 1994. Double Lookbacks. Unpublished Manuscript.

[46] Heath, D. , R. Jarrow, and A. Morton. 1992. Bond Pricing and the Term Structure of Interest Rates: A New Methodology for Contingent Claim Valuation. *Econometrica* 60: 77-105.

[47] Heston, S. L. 1993. Closed-Form Solution for Options with Stochastic Volatility. *Review of Financial Studies* 6:2: 327-343.

[48] Hemler, M. 1990. The Quality Delivery Option in Treasury Bond Futures Contract. *Journal of Finance* 45: 1565-1586.

[49] Ho,T. S. and S.-B. Lee. 1986. Term Structure Movements and Pricing Interest Rate Contingent Claims. *Journal of Finance* 41: 1011-29.

[50] Ho, T. S. 1992. Key Rate Durations: Measures of Interest Rate Risks. *Journal of Fixed Income.*

[51] Hull, J. and A. White. 1990. Pricing Interest Rate Derivative Securities. *Review of Financial Studies* 3: 573-592.

[52] Hull, J. and A. White. 1993. One-Factor Interest Rate Model and the Valuation of Interest Rate Derivative Securities. *Journal of Financial and Quantitative Analysis* 28:2:235-254.

[53] Ikeda, N. and S. Watanabe. 1981. *Stochastic Differential Equations and Diffusion Processes.* Amsterdam: North-Holland.

[54] Ingersoll, J. 1987. *Theory of Financial Decision Making*. Rowman and Little-field.

[55] Jamshidian, F. 1991. Forward Induction and Construction of Yield Curve Diffusion Models. *The Journal of Fixed Income:* 63-74.

[56] Klaffky, T. F. , Y. Y. Ma, and A. Nozari. 1992. Managing Yield Curve Exposure. of Fixed Income 2:3:39-45.

[57] Langetieg, T. 1980. A Multivariate Model of the Term Structure. of Finance 35: 71-79.

[58] Leibowitz, M. L. , W. Krasker and A. Nozari. 1988. Spread Duration: A New Tool for Bond Portfolio Management. Salomon Brothers Inc.

[59] Litterman, R., J. Scheinkman, and L. Weiss. 1991. Volatility and the Yield Curve. *The Journal of Fixed Income*: 49-53.

[60] Litterman, R. and J. Scheinkman. 1991. Common Factors Affecting Bond Returns. *The Journal of Fixed Income*: 54-61.

[61] Longstaff, F. 1990. The Valuation of Options on Yields. *Journal of Financial Economics* 26: 97-121..

[62] Longstaff, F. and E. Schwartz. 1992. Interest Rate Volatility and the Term Structure: A Two-Factor General Equilibrium Model. *Journal of Finance* 47: 1259-1282.

[63] Longstaff, F. and E. Schwartz. 1993. Implementation of the Longstaff-Schwartz Interest Rate Model *Journal of Fixed Income.*

[64] Lund, J. 1994. Econometric Analysis of Continuous-Times Arbitrage-Free Models of the Term Structure of Interest Rates. Unpublished paper: Aarbus School of Business.

[65] Merton, R. C. 1970. A Dynamic General Equilibrium Model of the Asset Markets and its Application to the Pricing of the Capital Structure of the Firm, Working Paper, Sloan School of Management, Massachusetts Institute of Technology.

[66] Merton, R. C. 1973. A Rational Theory of Option Pricing. *Bell Journal of Economics and Management Science* 4: 141-183.

[67] Nelson, D. B. and K. Ramaswamy. 1990. Simple Binomial Processes as Diffusion Approximation in Financial Models. *Review of Financial Studies* 3: 393-430.

[68] Pearson, N. D. and T. S. Sun. 1993. An Empirical Examination of the Cox, Ingersoll and Ross Model of The Term Structure of Interest Rates Using the Method of Maximum Likelihood. *Journal of Finance* 54: 929-959

[69] Protter, P. 1990. *Stochastic Integration and Differential Equations.* New York: Springer-Verlag.

[70] Ramaswamy, K. and M. Sundaresan. 1986. The Valuation of Floating-Rate Instruments, Theory and Evidence. *Journal of Financial Economics* 19: 251-272.

[71] Richard, S. 1978. An Arbitrage Model of the Term Structure of Interest Rates. *Journal of Financial Economics* 6: 33-57..

[72] Richard, S. and M. Sundaresan. 1981. A Continuous Model of Forward and Futures Prices in a Multigood Economy. *Journal of Financial Economics* 9: 347-372.

[73] Rogers, L.C. G. 1994. Which model for term structure of interest rates? *Mathematical Finance.* New York: Springer-Verlag .

[74] Schaefer, S. M. and E. S. Schwartz. 1984. A Two- factor Model of the Term Structure: An Approximate Analytic Solution. *Journal of Financial and Quantitative Analysis* 19: 413-424.

[75] Stambaugh, R. F. 1988. The Information in Forward Rates: Implications for Models of the Term Structure. *Journal of Financial Economics* 21: 44-69.

[76] Stein, E. M. and J. C. Stein. 1991. Stock Price Distribution with Stochastic Volatility: An Analytic Approach, *Review of Financial Studies* 4: 727-752..

[77] Stroock, D. and S. R. Varadhan. 1979 *Multidimensional Diffusion Processes.* New York: Springer-Verlag.

[78] Sundaresan, S. 1991. Valuation of Swaps, in *Recent Advances in International Banking and Finance.* Edited by Sarkis Khoury, North Holland Publishers.

[79] Tian, Y. 1993. A Modified Lattice Approach to Option Pricing. *Journal of Futures Markets* 13: 563-577.

[80] van Loan, C. 1978. Computing Integrals Involving the Matrix Exponential.*IEEE Transactions on Automatic Control* AC-23, 3:395-404.

[81] Vasicek, O. A. 1977. An Equilibrium Characterization of the Term Structure. *Journal of Political Economics* 5: 177-188.

[82] Waldman, M. 1992. Beyond Duration: Risk Dimensions of Mortgage Securities. *Journal of Fixed Income* 2:3:5-15.

[83] Wilmott, P., J. Dewynne and S. Howison. 1993. *Option Pricing*. Oxford Financial Press.